Palm Computing®
For Dummies®

Cheat Sheet

GW00722735

Graffiti Letter Guide

Here's how to make all the letter characters in Graffiti:

Character	Stroke	Character	Stroke
A	Λ	G	G
B	B	H	h
C	C	I	i
D	D	J	j
E	Ɛ	K	ʮ
F	Γ	L	L

(continued)

Alternative Graffiti Strokes

There are easier ways to write several Graffiti characters. Cut out this card and carry it with you along with the Graffiti card that comes with your Palm device.

Character	Stroke	Description
B	3	Draw the number 3 on the letter side of the Graffiti area
D	Ձ	Draw a reverse cursive *L*
F	Γ	Start from the bottom
G	6	Draw the number 6 on the letter side of the Graffiti area
K	α	This Graffiti character is the trickiest . Just draw the "legs" on the side of the *K*, joined by a little loop. Leave out the vertical bar. To me, this character looks like a fish swimming from right to left.

Palm Computing® For Dummies®

Graffiti Letter Guide (continued)

Character	Stroke	Character	Stroke
M	M	T	T
N	N	U	U
O	O	V	V
P	P	W	W
Q	Q	X	X
R	R	Y	Y
S	S	Z	Z

Alternative Graffiti Strokes (continued)

Character	Stroke	Description
V	V	Draw the V backward (that is, start from the top right)
X	X	A reversed Graffiti letter *K*
Y	Y	Just draw the lower loop of a cursive capital *Y*. It's just a loop, just like the letter *K* except that the fish is swimming downward.

When You're in a Bind

When all else fails, go here for help.

Tech support (U.S): 847-676-1441

Tech support (Canada): 905-305-6530

Web site: www.palm.com

E-mail: support@palm.com

IDG BOOKS WORLDWIDE

...For Dummies®: Bestselling Book Series for Beginners

TM

BESTSELLING BOOK SERIES

References for the Rest of Us! ®

Are you intimidated and confused by computers? Do you find that traditional manuals are overloaded with technical details you'll never use? Do your friends and family always call you to fix simple problems on their PCs? Then the *...For Dummies*® computer book series from IDG Books Worldwide is for you.

...For Dummies books are written for those frustrated computer users who know they aren't really dumb but find that PC hardware, software, and indeed the unique vocabulary of computing make them feel helpless. *...For Dummies* books use a lighthearted approach, a down-to-earth style, and even cartoons and humorous icons to dispel computer novices' fears and build their confidence. Lighthearted but not lightweight, these books are a perfect survival guide for anyone forced to use a computer.

> *"I like my copy so much I told friends; now they bought copies."*
>
> — Irene C., Orwell, Ohio

> *"Quick, concise, nontechnical, and humorous."*
>
> — Jay A., Elburn, Illinois

> *"Thanks, I needed this book. Now I can sleep at night."*
>
> — Robin F., British Columbia, Canada

Already, millions of satisfied readers agree. They have made *...For Dummies* books the #1 introductory level computer book series and have written asking for more. So, if you're looking for the most fun and easy way to learn about computers, look to *...For Dummies* books to give you a helping hand.

IDG BOOKS WORLDWIDE ®

1/99

PALM COMPUTING®

FOR

DUMMIES®

PALM COMPUTING® FOR DUMMIES®

by Bill Dyszel

IDG Books Worldwide, Inc.
An International Data Group Company

Foster City, CA ◆ Chicago, IL ◆ Indianapolis, IN ◆ New York, NY

Palm Computing® For Dummies®

Published by
IDG Books Worldwide, Inc.
An International Data Group Company
919 E. Hillsdale Blvd.
Suite 400
Foster City, CA 94404
www.idgbooks.com (IDG Books Worldwide Web site)
www.dummies.com (Dummies Press Web site)

Library of Congress Catalog Card No.: 99-64903

ISBN: 0-7645-0581-5

Printed in the United States of America

10 9 8 7 6 5 4 3 2 1

1B/RR/QY/ZZ/IN

Distributed in the United States by IDG Books Worldwide, Inc.

Distributed by CDG Books Canada Inc. for Canada; by Transworld Publishers Limited in the United Kingdom; by IDG Norge Books for Norway; by IDG Sweden Books for Sweden; by IDG Books Australia Publishing Corporation Pty. Ltd. for Australia and New Zealand; by TransQuest Publishers Pte Ltd. for Singapore, Malaysia, Thailand, Indonesia, and Hong Kong; by Gotop Information Inc. for Taiwan; by ICG Muse, Inc. for Japan; by Norma Comunicaciones S.A. for Colombia; by Intersoft for South Africa; by Eyrolles for France; by International Thomson Publishing for Germany, Austria and Switzerland; by Distribuidora Cuspide for Argentina; by LR International for Brazil; by Galileo Libros for Chile; by Ediciones ZETA S.C.R. Ltda. for Peru; by WS Computer Publishing Corporation, Inc., for the Philippines; by Contemporanea de Ediciones for Venezuela; by Express Computer Distributors for the Caribbean and West Indies; by Micronesia Media Distributor, Inc. for Micronesia; by Grupo Editorial Norma S.A. for Guatemala; by Chips Computadoras S.A. de C.V. for Mexico; by Editorial Norma de Panama S.A. for Panama; by American Bookshops for Finland. Authorized Sales Agent: Anthony Rudkin Associates for the Middle East and North Africa.

For general information on IDG Books Worldwide's books in the U.S., please call our Consumer Customer Service department at 800-762-2974. For reseller information, including discounts and premium sales, please call our Reseller Customer Service department at 800-434-3422.

For information on where to purchase IDG Books Worldwide's books outside the U.S., please contact our International Sales department at 317-596-5530 or fax 317-596-5692.

For consumer information on foreign language translations, please contact our Customer Service department at 1-800-434-3422, fax 317-596-5692, or e-mail rights@idgbooks.com.

For information on licensing foreign or domestic rights, please phone +1-650-655-3109.

For sales inquiries and special prices for bulk quantities, please contact our Sales department at 650-655-3200 or write to the address above.

For information on using IDG Books Worldwide's books in the classroom or for ordering examination copies, please contact our Educational Sales department at 800-434-2086 or fax 317-596-5499.

For press review copies, author interviews, or other publicity information, please contact our Public Relations department at 650-655-3000 or fax 650-655-3299.

For authorization to photocopy items for corporate, personal, or educational use, please contact Copyright Clearance Center, 222 Rosewood Drive, Danvers, MA 01923, or fax 978-750-4470.

About the Author

Bill Dyszel writes frequently for such leading publications as *Chief Executive* magazine, *Success* magazine, *PC* magazine, and *Computer Shopper* while also working as a consultant to many of New York City's leading firms in the securities, advertising, and publishing businesses. His list of current and former clients includes Salomon Brothers, First Boston, Goldman Sachs, Ogilvy & Mather, KMPG Peat Marwick, and many others. As a public speaker, he regularly entertains audiences across the United States in his programs about using technology to keep life simple. He is the author of *Microsoft Outlook 2000 For Dummies* and is now working on a book about wireless commerce. You can reach him at his e-mail address: bill@jiffylearn.com.

The world of high technology has led Bill to grapple with such subjects as multimedia (or how to make your $2,000 computer do the work of a $20 radio), personal information managers (how to make your $3,000 laptop computer do the work of a $3 date book), and graphics programs (how to make your $5,000 package of computers and peripheral devices do the work of a 50-cent box of crayons). All joking aside, he has found that after you've figured out the process, most of this stuff can be useful, helpful, and, yes, even cool.

Like many public figures with skeletons in their closets, this author has a secret past. Before entering the computer industry, Bill sang with the New York City Opera and worked regularly on the New York stage as a singer and an actor in numerous plays, musicals, and operas. He also wrote the opera spoof *99% ARTFREE!,* which won critical praise from *The New York Times,* the *New York Daily News,* and the Associated Press when he performed the show off-Broadway.

ABOUT IDG BOOKS WORLDWIDE

Welcome to the world of IDG Books Worldwide.

IDG Books Worldwide, Inc., is a subsidiary of International Data Group, the world's largest publisher of computer-related information and the leading global provider of information services on information technology. IDG was founded more than 30 years ago by Patrick J. McGovern and now employs more than 9,000 people worldwide. IDG publishes more than 290 computer publications in over 75 countries. More than 90 million people read one or more IDG publications each month.

Launched in 1990, IDG Books Worldwide is today the #1 publisher of best-selling computer books in the United States. We are proud to have received eight awards from the Computer Press Association in recognition of editorial excellence and three from Computer Currents' First Annual Readers' Choice Awards. Our best-selling ...For Dummies® series has more than 50 million copies in print with translations in 31 languages. IDG Books Worldwide, through a joint venture with IDG's Hi-Tech Beijing, became the first U.S. publisher to publish a computer book in the People's Republic of China. In record time, IDG Books Worldwide has become the first choice for millions of readers around the world who want to learn how to better manage their businesses.

Our mission is simple: Every one of our books is designed to bring extra value and skill-building instructions to the reader. Our books are written by experts who understand and care about our readers. The knowledge base of our editorial staff comes from years of experience in publishing, education, and journalism — experience we use to produce books to carry us into the new millennium. In short, we care about books, so we attract the best people. We devote special attention to details such as audience, interior design, use of icons, and illustrations. And because we use an efficient process of authoring, editing, and desktop publishing our books electronically, we can spend more time ensuring superior content and less time on the technicalities of making books.

You can count on our commitment to deliver high-quality books at competitive prices on topics you want to read about. At IDG Books Worldwide, we continue in the IDG tradition of delivering quality for more than 30 years. You'll find no better book on a subject than one from IDG Books Worldwide.

John Kilcullen
Chairman and CEO
IDG Books Worldwide, Inc.

Steven Berkowitz
President and Publisher
IDG Books Worldwide, Inc.

IDG is the world's leading IT media, research and exposition company. Founded in 1964, IDG had 1997 revenues of $2.05 billion and has more than 9,000 employees worldwide. IDG offers the widest range of media options that reach IT buyers in 75 countries representing 95% of worldwide IT spending. IDG's diverse product and services portfolio spans six key areas including print publishing, online publishing, expositions and conferences, market research, education and training, and global marketing services. More than 90 million people read one or more of IDG's 290 magazines and newspapers, including IDG's leading global brands — Computerworld, PC World, Network World, Macworld and the Channel World family of publications. IDG Books Worldwide is one of the fastest-growing computer book publishers in the world, with more than 700 titles in 36 languages. The "...For Dummies®" series alone has more than 50 million copies in print. IDG offers online users the largest network of technology-specific Web sites around the world through IDG.net (http://www.idg.net), which comprises more than 225 targeted Web sites in 55 countries worldwide. International Data Corporation (IDC) is the world's largest provider of information technology data, analysis and consulting, with research centers in over 41 countries and more than 400 research analysts worldwide. IDG World Expo is a leading producer of more than 168 globally branded conferences and expositions in 35 countries including E3 (Electronic Entertainment Expo), Macworld Expo, ComNet, Windows World Expo, ICE (Internet Commerce Expo), Agenda, DEMO, and Spotlight. IDG's training subsidiary, ExecuTrain, is the world's largest computer training company, with more than 230 locations worldwide and 785 training courses. IDG Marketing Services helps industry-leading IT companies build international brand recognition by developing global integrated marketing programs via IDG's print, online and exposition products worldwide. Further information about the company can be found at www.idg.com. 1/24/99

Acknowledgments

Thanks to the many people who have made this book possible — most of all, my wise and ingenious project editor, Rebecca Whitney, who kept this book moving along smartly, thank heavens! Thanks also to Sherri Morningstar, my acquisitions editor; technical reviewers Gayle Ehrenman and Shawn Morningstar; in addition to Mary Bednarek and everyone else at IDG Books and my agent, Gloria Norris. Special thanks to the good folks at A & R Partners, Inc., for lending Palm devices to IDG Books during the development and production of this book.

Publisher's Acknowledgments

We're proud of this book; please register your comments through our IDG Books Worldwide Online Registration Form located at http://my2cents.dummies.com.

Some of the people who helped bring this book to market include the following:

Acquisitions, Editorial, and Media Development

Project Editor: Rebecca Whitney

Acquisitions Editor: Sherri Morningstar

Technical Editor: Gayle Ehrenman

Media Development Editor: Joell Smith, Marita Ellixson

Associate Permissions Editor: Carmen Krikorian

Media Development Coordinator: Megan Roney

Editorial Manager: Mary C. Corder

Media Development Manager: Heather Heath Dismore

Production

Project Coordinator: E. Shawn Aylsworth

Layout and Graphics: Amy M. Adrian, Angela F. Hunckler, Dave McKelvey, Barry Offringa, Douglas L. Rollison, Brent Savage, Brian Torwelle, Dan Whetstine

Proofreaders: Rebecca Senninger, Susan Sims

Indexer: Sharon Duffy

Special Help
Shawn Morningstar

General and Administrative

IDG Books Worldwide, Inc.: John Kilcullen, CEO; Steven Berkowitz, President and Publisher

IDG Books Technology Publishing Group: Richard Swadley, Senior Vice President and Publisher; Walter Bruce III, Vice President and Associate Publisher; Steven Sayre, Associate Publisher; Joseph Wikert, Associate Publisher; Mary Bednarek, Branded Product Development Director; Mary Corder, Editorial Director

IDG Books Consumer Publishing Group: Roland Elgey, Senior Vice President and Publisher; Kathleen A. Welton, Vice President and Publisher; Kevin Thornton, Acquisitions Manager; Kristin A. Cocks, Editorial Director

IDG Books Internet Publishing Group: Brenda McLaughlin, Senior Vice President and Publisher; Diane Graves Steele, Vice President and Associate Publisher; Sofia Marchant, Online Marketing Manager

IDG Books Production for Dummies Press: Michael R. Britton, Vice President of Production; Debbie Stailey, Associate Director of Production; Cindy L. Phipps, Manager of Project Coordination, Production Proofreading, and Indexing; Shelley Lea, Supervisor of Graphics and Design; Debbie J. Gates, Production Systems Specialist; Robert Springer, Supervisor of Proofreading; Laura Carpenter, Production Control Manager; Tony Augsburger, Supervisor of Reprints and Bluelines

◆

The publisher would like to give special thanks to Patrick J. McGovern, without whom this book would not have been possible.

◆

Contents at a Glance

Cartoons at a Glance

By Rich Tennant

page 313

page 9

page 165

page 71

page 289

Fax: 978-546-7747 • E-mail: the5wave@tiac.net

Table of Contents

Part IV: Extending the Life of Your Palm Organizer 289

Introduction

●●●

*B*e warned: The Palm organizer is addictive! You may not believe that you can become so wrapped up in a little block of plastic, but the experiences of millions of crazed Palm users indicate otherwise. I know that you won't find anything nasty, like tar or nicotine, in a Palm device, but after you're hooked, you'll have a tough time living without it. After you've enjoyed the convenience of carrying a little computing power in your pocket or purse, you'll want more and more.

For me, the most subversive effect of using a Palm organizer is the way that it's spoiled me against the way other computers work. I just can't wait patiently anymore for a regular computer to "boot up"; I'm too accustomed to my Palm organizer turning on instantly. I also get a little annoyed waiting for a regular computer to find and open the last document I was working on because I'm used to having my Palm device jump right to the last item I worked on. And I certainly get peeved when my laptop runs out of juice after an hour or so because my Palm organizer runs for a month on a set of AAA batteries.

Sadly, I can't dispense with my regular computer just yet. The Palm organizer isn't meant to replace conventional computers; it's intended to give you a handy and portable window for accessing information, much of which you keep on your computer. Don't be fooled, though: A Palm organizer is a powerful little machine.

Who Should Buy This Book

The Palm organizer is the most successful new electronic product in history. In the first three years following the product's introduction, nearly 4 million units were sold. That's hot. No gadget has ever sold as quickly, including hit products like the VCR, the Sony Walkman, and the answering machine. In the past year, sales for handheld units using the Palm system were greater than the sales for handhelds using the once-popular Macintosh system. Chances are strong that if you don't have a Palm organizer, someone you know either has one or wants one. As you read this book, you'll find out how a Palm device works and what it can do for you. You'll also get a taste of what kinds of peripherals you can add to a Palm device to make it suit your needs a bit better. If you fit in any of the following categories, this book is meant for you:

✔ You're planning to buy a Palm organizer, and you want to know what you can do with it and what it can do for you.

✔ You already own a Palm device, and you want to get the most from it quickly.

✔ You're looking for a gift to give someone who already has a Palm organizer. Palm devices are very popular gifts. You can send me one at any time.

✔ You own one of those Windows CE machines and have realized the error of your ways (say it isn't so!).

Even if you're just curious about the Palm phenomenon, this book is aimed at showing you what all the excitement's about. Nearly anyone in any walk of life can receive some benefit from a Palm organizer, even if all that person wants is a little fun.

Pilot, PalmPilot, Palm Whatever — Make Up Your Mind

I find it exciting to be a Palm owner because improvements for the thing come along so quickly. The rapid pace can also be confusing, though, because some of the features that are available for the current Palm devices weren't available on PalmPilots that were sold only a few months ago. Also, I don't know which model you're using, so I have to qualify everything I write to avoid confusing people who have older PalmPilots (older than 12 to 18 months).

In this book, I try to cover the whole range of products based on the design from 3Com. When the first handheld units were produced, they were simply called Pilots. When the little Pilots became popular, the Palm people changed the name to PalmPilot to avoid confusion with the popular Pilot-brand pens. Then the Palm people decided to drop the Pilot thing altogether and call their product Palm III and name all future models after famous numbers. Nowadays, the official name is the Palm Connected Organizer for the Palm Computing Platform. Technically, it's not a PalmPilot anymore.

A guy named Alan Macy is leading a crusade to rename The Device Formerly Known as the PalmPilot. If you want to add your suggestions, you can check out his Web site, at www.responsivesoftware.com. My favorite suggestions so far are Palomino and Palmalamadingdong. For now, I have to refer to it as a Palm organizer, a Palm device, or just a thingamajig. I hope that you'll bear with me on this issue.

Just to keep things clear, I try to stay generic-sounding when I'm talking about features that appear on all Palm whatchamacallits. When I discuss a feature that appears on only a particular model of Palm device, such as the Palm V, I say so. (For general information about what each model does, see Chapter 1.)

You may also be using another product that's based on Palm Computing technology but has a different name, like the IBM WorkPad. (Sheesh! What a drab name! I wish that they'd call it the IBM FunPad!). The information in this book applies to the WorkPad, too. A cellular telephone named the Qualcomm PDQ phone is a phone with a Palm organizer built right in. The information in this book is generally accurate for the PDQ phone, although some differences occur in the placement of buttons. Other products based on the Palm Computing design are in the pipeline also, and the general principles in this book should work for those products, too.

How This Book Is Organized

To help you more easily find out how to do what you want to do, I've divided this book into parts. Each part covers a different aspect of using your Palm organizer. The first couple of parts focus on the Palm device itself — what you can do if you just have that thing. In later parts, I discuss add-ons for your Palm thingy, as well as the desktop computer program that comes with your Palm device. (Yes, your Palm organizer can talk to your desktop computer. If this possibility really floats your boat, jump right into Part III.)

Here's a quick-and-dirty outline of this book — just enough to whet your appetite and make you want to buy it!

Part I: Getting to Know Your Palm Organizer

"Getting to know you, getting to know all about you. . . ." Ahem, sorry — I can't resist a little show tune every now and then. Anyway, nothing about using a Palm organizer is difficult, although many features and options aren't exactly obvious. The first part of this book describes what you have to work with on your Palm device and how you work with what you have. I explain what all those funny-looking buttons and other doodads on the outside of your Palm organizer do, and I give you a lesson in Graffiti — and no, not so that you can join a gang and practice spray-can art. Graffiti is the special alphabet you can use for entering information into your Palm device. If you're in the secret-agent biz (or if you're just security-minded), you can find out how to keep confidential information on your Palm organizer safe from prying eyes.

Part II: Getting Down to Business

Yes, Virginia, a Palm device is a computer. It doesn't act grouchy and forbidding like other computers, but it can do many of the jobs typically performed by enormous desktop units (ironically called microcomputers, of all things). The Palm organizer comes with a set of preinstalled programs when you buy it. Those programs act as a personal information manager (PIM) to help you keep track of your schedule, address book, and to-do list. If you've ever used a computer for personal organizing, the methods of the Palm organizer may seem familiar. It also has a memo pad for jotting down random notes to yourself or others, and you can even copy your e-mail to your Palm organizer and read it while you're sitting by the pool. (Sorry, the pool isn't included.) Later-model Palm devices, starting with the Palm III, feature infrared beaming, a method for sending information between two Palm devices through the air by using an invisible beam of light. How cool is that?

Part III: Palm Organizers and the Outside World

No computer is an island, especially the tiny Palm device. If it were, you'd be in trouble at high tide. The Palm people always figured that folks would use their Palm devices in conjunction with some other computer, simply because there's no denying the physical limitations of a tiny computer when you're entering data and connecting to other resources, like the Internet or a CD-ROM. This part of the book tells you all you need to know about HotSyncing (the process through which your Palm device and your Windows PC or Macintosh talk to each other) and walks you through the steps for installing and operating the desktop programs that come with your Palm device. And when you're out and about and you want to use the PalmModem to HotSync to your computer . . . well, I show you how to do that, too. How's that for a bargain?

Part IV: Extending the Life of Your Palm Organizer

Like any appliance, the day may come when you need more from your Palm organizer and the Maytag repairman is nowhere in sight. Or perhaps you need to make your Palm device do something new. In this part, I show you some options for making your little Palm thingy do big things. I cover upgrading your Palm device and software add-ons that may impress your peers in your particular profession. Whether you're a doctor or a bartender, an add-on software is out there for you.

Part V: The Part of Tens

Why ten? Beats me! All the other ...*For Dummies* books get a Part of Tens, so I'll be darned if mine doesn't have one, too! In this part, you find out what your Palm device *can't* do and how to stylishly accessorize your organizer without having to call Calvin Klein for wardrobe advice.

Appendixes

Just like the famous (or is that infamous?) Ginzu knife, "That's not all!" In the appendixes, I provide a list of the best Palm resources on the World Wide Web, and I show you how to shoot down trouble whenever it strikes your Palm device. And did you happen to notice that the back cover of this book is a little stiffer than the front? That's because you also get a CD; Appendix C tells you all about the cool stuff you can find on it.

Conventions Used in This Book

You may be a diehard reader of ...*For Dummies* books, living in a beautiful black-and-yellow home filled with black-and-yellow books. You may be familiar with the approach — this book works much like all the other books in the series.

If you've never read a ...*For Dummies* book, welcome. Buying and reading this book proves that you're one smart cookie who doesn't want to deal with those overgrown paperweights that litter the shelves of your local bookstore's computer section. Instead, you want a clear, no-nonsense explanation of the things you really need to know, and nothing else. That's what you get here.

How much do you need to know?

I figure that you know how to push a button. This skill will get you far with a Palm organizer because it's so simple to use. And although you can use a Palm device without HotSyncing it with a desktop computer, I assume that you will use your Palm device with a desktop machine at some point and that you already know how to use it. If you're still a little iffy on using your desktop computer, I suggest picking up a copy of the ...*For Dummies* book that covers the system you use. A few helpful titles include *Macs For Dummies,* 6th Edition, by David Pogue; *PCs For Dummies,* 6th Edition, by Dan Gookin; *Windows 95 For Dummies,* 2nd Edition, and *Windows 98 For Dummies,* both by Andy Rathbone; and *Mac OS 8.5 For Dummies,* by Bob LeVitus (all published by IDG Books Worldwide, Inc.).

Some helpful terms

To lessen confusion as you read this book, here are a few tidbits and terms you need to understand:

- ✔ When I refer to a desktop computer, I mean a conventional computer running either Microsoft Windows or the Mac OS. If your main computer is a laptop, that's fine. Please forgive me if I always say "desktop"; they all look so big next to a Palm device.

- ✔ Because the Palm organizer is made to work as an extension of more than one type of computer system, the terms I use to describe what you should do on your desktop machine usually cover both the Windows and Macintosh platforms. The book also has a separate chapter about the Mac version of the Palm Desktop.

- ✔ *Tapping* means touching your Palm stylus to a named area on the Palm display.

- ✔ *Clicking* means pressing the left mouse button on an item if you're using a Windows computer or pressing the only mouse button if you're using a Mac.

- ✔ *Choosing* means to either tap a menu choice on your Palm screen or click a specific menu choice with your desktop computer's mouse.

- ✔ *Right-clicking* means to press the right mouse button if you're using a computer running Windows. The Mac has no right mouse button to click. Seems suspicious to me, but that's how it is.

- ✔ *Double-clicking* means quickly clicking the left mouse button (or the only mouse button) twice.

- ✔ *Dragging* (on the Palm screen) means touching an item with your stylus and sliding the point of the stylus from one spot on the display to another.

- ✔ *Dragging* (on a Windows PC or a Mac) means holding down the mouse button while moving the mouse.

- ✔ *Selecting* or *highlighting* means either tapping a choice on a list or sliding your stylus across a specific area of text, which prepares the Palm device for you to do something to that piece of text.

All the tasks I describe in the preceding list are much easier to do than they sound. You'll catch on in no time. Here are a few items I mention from time to time:

- ✔ *Dialog boxes* are rectangles that pop up on the screen and can include messages for you to read, buttons for you to tap or click, lists for you to choose from, blanks for you to fill in, and check boxes for you to tap. Don't worry: I tell you what to do with each dialog box as you encounter it.

✔ *Buttons* are real, physical buttons on the case of your Palm device. I normally call each button by the name of the application it runs. Your Palm organizer comes with two types of buttons: hard and soft. *Hard* buttons are those at the bottom of your Palm device, below the screen. *Soft* buttons are just above the hard buttons but are part of the screen. You can find more about all this button stuff in Chapter 1.

I normally simplify menu commands by saying something like Go⇨Cubs, which means "Choose Go from the menu bar and then choose Cubs." Also, whenever I describe text that's shown on the screen, it appears in a special typeface, like this.

Icons Used in This Book

Sometimes the fastest way to find information in a book is to look at the pictures. In this case, icons draw your attention to specific types of information that are useful to know. Here are the icons I use in this book:

This icon clues you in on what you can find on the CD that accompanies this book. For the full lowdown, see Appendix C.

This icon indicates information that is specific to only the later models of the Palm organizer, the models that began with the Palm III. If you own an earlier model or haven't upgraded your older PalmPilot to a Palm III, you can ignore these sections — unless you're curious about what you're missing, of course.

I use this icon for really important info you shouldn't forget.

As though the Palm organizer weren't easy enough to use, I've found even shorter ways of doing things. The Shortcut icon points out super-speedy methods for performing a task. Don't confuse this Shortcut icon with official Palm ShortCuts, though — I cover those in a section unto themselves in Chapter 3.

The Tip icon notes a hint or trick for saving time and effort or highlights text that makes the Palm organizer easier to understand.

The Warning icon alerts you to something you should be careful about in order to prevent problems.

Part I

Getting to Know Your Palm Organizer

"These are the handheld devices you recommended our employees use to communicate with?!"

In this part . . .

You can do lots with the Palm organizer's few tiny buttons and little plastic stylus. Although you may figure out a great deal by just fiddling around, this part's quick tour gives you a head start. I also show you how to customize your Palm device to your specific needs.

Chapter 1

What Can a Palm Device Do?

· ·

In This Chapter

▶ Introducing Palm Computing

▶ Understanding all the buttons

▶ Working with Graffiti

▶ Which model is which?

▶ Making sense of the standard applications

▶ HotSyncing

▶ Replacing batteries

· ·

Asking "What can I do with a Palm device?" is like asking, "Where can I go on a bicycle?" You can go nearly anywhere you want on a bicycle — you can take a ride in the park or cross the Rocky Mountains. Most normal people are better off crossing the Rockies by car or bus, but they can handle the ride in the park quite nicely on a bike. Likewise, your Palm device is just the right tool for jotting down a quick note, although you probably wouldn't use it to write the sequel to *Moby Dick*.

Your Palm device can do many of the things a desktop or laptop computer can do, although some things are easier to handle on a larger computer, such as surfing the World Wide Web, and others are perfect for the Palm device, such as looking up a phone number. If you ask people what they do most with their Palm devices, you get a wide variety of answers: Sometimes they need to find addresses or check their schedules, and often they play games or entertain themselves with an electronic book or read their e-mail.

Although the Palm device comes in a small, friendly package, it has plenty of power inside. Even though the unit is barely bigger than a couple of candy bars, it has enough computing power inside to do more than some of the early-1980s Macintosh machines that took up most of your desktop (and may still be taking up your desktop today). Every day, people are finding clever new things to do with their Palm devices, and you'll probably figure out a few things on your own.

Does my Palm device do Windows?

Don't make me WinCE! A Palm device doesn't run Windows, and for that you should be glad. (The Palm Desktop does connect your Palm device to the world of Windows quite nicely, although the Palm device itself isn't running the Windows operating system.) Several Palm imitators are out there. Most use the Microsoft operating system that's specially made for palm-size computers; it's Windows CE (usually pronounced "WinCE," a word that sounds like the face you make when you smell something bad). WinCE looks a tiny bit like the version of Windows 95 you may be running on your desktop, including a Start button and some of the old menus. WinCE also has a feature from the desktop that we could all do without — an hourglass that shows up regularly when the system is too slow to do any work for you. Palm devices don't make you wait like that; they get right to work.

On the whole, Windows CE isn't any more compatible with your desktop machine than your Palm device is. The two types of machines are equally compatible with the version of Windows you have on your desktop. You can't run your desktop Windows programs, such as Excel, on your WinCE palmtop. As a matter of fact, many WinCE programs don't run on more than one type of WinCE device; for example, some WinCE programs run on a Hewlett-Packard handheld but not on a Casio. Virtually all Palm software runs on all Palm devices. Also, more software is being written for Palm devices than is being written for those WinCE devices. At the time I wrote this chapter, you could find nearly 4,000 programs available for Palm devices, compared to a few hundred for Windows CE machines. What can I say? Figures don't lie.

One way or another, you'll probably want to synchronize your palm-size computer to a desktop or laptop computer, and a Palm device synchronizes every bit as well as a WinCE palmtop. My recommendation: Stick with Palm Computing. It's the real thing.

You can add an endless variety of functions to your Palm device by installing programs that don't come in the package with your Palm device. Throughout most of this book, I focus on things you can do with the stuff that comes in the box with your Palm device, and that's plenty. In addition, I do provide a selection of useful applications on the CD-ROM that accompanies this book. (See Chapter 12 for more info about installing Palm applications, and Appendix C for the lowdown on what's on the CD.)

What Is This Thing, Anyway?

A Palm device is a simple little contraption with almost no moving parts. Sometimes it's hard to believe that it's a computer at all. After all, computers are supposed to have zillions of buttons and lights and make scary sounds when they start up, right? Well, you don't have to think of your Palm device as a computer; think of it as your little electronic friend that helps you keep track of your real friends. If you have imaginary friends, your Palm device can help you keep track of them too, along with all those nice people in the white coats. (I can't get my publisher to let me write _Delusions For Dummies,_ so you're on your own for now.)

A Palm device really has only three elements: the buttons, the screen, and the stylus. No mouse, no cables, no disks — none of it. You'll probably want to use your Palm device along with a normal computer that has all those annoying gizmos, but as long as you're just using your Palm device, you can keep things simple. Figure 1-1 shows you what one of the latest versions — the Palm IIIx — looks like, and the following sections tell you what all those funny little doodads do.

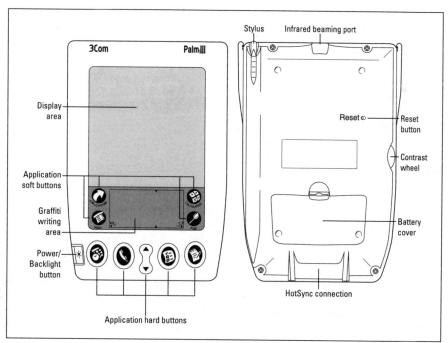

Figure 1-1:
The front
and back
of the
Palm IIIx.

What's on the Outside of Your Palm Device

The case of your Palm device has a bunch of little buttons on it that do all sorts of cool stuff. I explain in this section what those buttons do.

Application hard buttons

The *application hard buttons* are easy to use. I use the word *hard* to mean real, actual, physical buttons you can push with your finger to make something happen. Figure 1-2 shows you what those buttons look like.

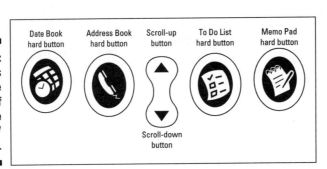

Figure 1-2:
The buttons at the bottom of the case are *hard* buttons.

Date Book hard button · Address Book hard button · Scroll-up button · To Do List hard button · Memo Pad hard button · Scroll-down button

The application buttons are the four round buttons at the bottom of the case on a Palm device. Push any of these buttons at any time, and the Palm device shows you the application (or program) assigned to that button. Applications are just jobs the Palm device is ready to do for you.

You can even push an application button when the Palm device is turned off. When you do, it automatically turns on and opens the application assigned to that button. A Palm device is a little like a microwave oven in that way: You don't have to turn on your microwave and then tell it to start cooking; just push the button and you're cooking. Unlike your microwave oven, your Palm device needs very little cleaning and it doesn't make your breakfast eggs explode.

Here's what those buttons do:

✔ **Date Book:** The leftmost application button; easy to identify by the little icon that looks like a clock on top of a bent-out-of-shape calendar. You don't need to get bent out of shape when you use the Date Book, which shows you dates and appointments. (See Chapter 8 for more info about the Date Book.)

Palm devices: Real computers

Don't be fooled — a Palm device is a real computer. Although it may look like those little electronic organizers that have been around for years, it contains the same Motorola computer chip that powered the first Macintosh. Yes, you can manage addresses and appointments on a Palm device, just like you can on those old organizers, and you can also run and load software, just like you can on a conventional computer.

The biggest difference between a Palm device and a regular computer is what computer geeks call the *user interface*. The Palm device has no keyboard; you write and tap on its touch-sensitive screen. Many types of programs people commonly use on conventional computers are being developed for Palm devices, including spreadsheets, database managers, and Web browsers. The software on the CD accompanying this book gives you a taste of how far you can go with the power of the Palm handheld computer.

✔ **Address Book:** The second button from the left, the one with the little telephone icon. That's the place you go to find names, addresses, and (naturally) phone numbers. (See Chapter 5 for more info about the Address Book.) The two applications on the right side of the Palm device are separated from the ones on the left by the scroll buttons, which I describe later in this chapter, in the section "Scroll buttons."

✔ **To Do List:** The third application button, second from the right side of the case and decorated with a little checklist. The To Do List button opens the application that tracks your tasks. (See Chapter 6 for more info about the To Do List.)

✔ **Memo Pad:** The rightmost button, the one with the picture of the tiny pen writing on an itty-bitty notebook. The Memo Pad is the place where you enter and store text. (See Chapter 7 for more info about the Memo Pad.)

You can assign different programs to the four application buttons than the ones that come installed on your Palm device. If you don't use the To Do List or the Memo Pad much, for example, and you want to reassign those buttons to other programs, see Chapter 3 to find out how it's done.

Scroll buttons

At the bottom-center of the case on a Palm device is a button (or a pair of buttons, on top of the pre–Palm III models) named *scroll buttons*. If you own a Palm III or later, the two scroll buttons have been merged into one button that rocks up and down. Scroll buttons work like the power window buttons in a car. If you want to move down through a screen to see what doesn't fit, use the bottom button. If you want to go back to the top of the screen, use the top button. Sometimes, the scroll buttons change the way they act in different applications. Sometimes, pressing a scroll button makes the information in the display area leap to the next screen rather than crawl gradually. Sometimes, the scroll buttons do nothing, especially when there's no next screen to see.

Power button

The green button with the little light bulb on at the left edge of the case is the *power* button.

The power button has a second job: It turns the backlight on and off. To turn the backlight on, hold the power button down for at least two seconds. (You can also customize your Palm device so that the backlight goes on with a certain stroke of your stylus. I discuss that subject in Chapter 3.) If you own an early Palm device (models 1000, 5000, or the PalmPilot Personal), you don't have a backlight. That's too bad. The backlight makes text on the screen of the PalmPilot Professional and the Palm III much easier to read when you're in a dark area and you can't read the screen or when you're in a bright area — outside, maybe — and lots of glare is reflecting off the screen. The Palm IIIx, Palm V, and Palm VII feature a reverse backlight that makes text much easier to read in complete darkness but helps only a little in dim light.

Although the backlight makes reading the screen on a Palm device easier in almost all conditions, the light itself drains the batteries like crazy. The best time to use your backlight is when you can't read text on-screen without it.

One nice thing about the way a Palm device works is a quality called a *persistent state*. No, that's not the feeling you get after you meet all the salesmen in Utah; it means that whatever is happening on the screen when you turn the power off will be happening when you turn the Palm device on again. It's like sleep mode on your desktop computer. That's a handy feature when you get interrupted in the middle of doing something and want to get right back to it, even if you get a call from a long-winded salesman from Utah.

Contrast wheel

The *contrast wheel* isn't really a button; it's a real moving part that looks like a little volume control on the left edge of the case. On most Palm devices, the contrast wheel is on the left edge of the back of the case. In certain kinds of light, you can see the text on the screen better if you adjust the contrast a little. If you own a Palm V, it has a contrast button on the top left side of the case. Pressing the Palm V contrast button makes the Adjust Contrast box appear on the screen. You can use your stylus to adjust the contrast by sliding the little button to the left or right.

Reset button

Sometimes you need to tell your Palm device to stop what it's doing and start all over again. That's called *resetting* your Palm device. Occasionally, a program you've installed on your Palm device misbehaves and makes it hang up or act crazy. That happens rarely, and resetting the Palm device usually fixes the problem.

You can reset your Palm device in two different ways: the hard way and the kinder, gentler, soft way. A *soft* reset just makes the everything stop and start again. You can perform a soft reset on your Palm device by pushing the end of a bent paper clip into the little hole labeled Reset on the back. The stylus that comes with the Palm III and later models includes a secret, built-in reset pin. Just unscrew the end of the stylus to find the reset pin.

A *hard* reset erases all your data and your username. Needless to say, you don't want to do a hard reset without a good reason. If you're selling your Palm device to someone else, you could do a hard reset to make the unit act like it did when it was brand-new. (I wish I could do that to myself now and then.) To perform a hard reset, hold down the power button and then press the end of a paper clip into the hole marked Reset on the back of your Palm device. When you do, a prompt appears on the screen, asking whether you really want to erase all your data. Think hard again whether you want to do that — then either press the scroll-up hard button if you do or the scroll-down button if you don't.

The Screen

You can't miss the most important part of a Palm device — the *screen,* which you can see in Figure 1-3. It shows you the information you've stored in your applications and lets you know what the applications are ready to do for you next.

An equally important function of the Palm organizer screen is to take information from you. Two parts of the screen, the display area and the Graffiti area, take information from you in different ways, and the soft buttons (not to be confused with the hard buttons described earlier in this chapter) let you do all sorts of other neat things.

The display area

The largest part of the Palm organizer screen is the main *display area,* as shown in Figure 1-4, which not only shows the text you're working with but also contains a number of active areas on which you can tap your stylus to make something happen, such as display the contents of a memo or mark a task as complete. You can also slide your stylus across the surface of the screen to select (or highlight) the text that's displayed in some applications.

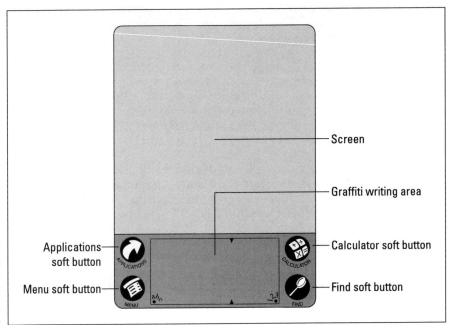

Figure 1-3:
The Palm organizer screen.

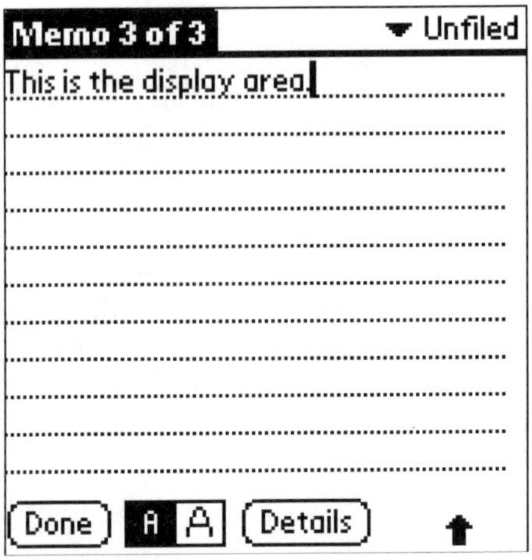

Screen

Graffiti writing area

Applications soft button

Calculator soft button

Menu soft button

Find soft button

Figure 1-4:
The display area.

Memo 3 of 3   ▾ Unfiled

This is the display area.

Done   A A   Details

Most standard Palm Computing applications organize the display area into areas that do pretty much the same job from one application to the next. The upper-left corner of the screen displays a tab that shows the name of the application you're using, such as Address List, To Do List, or Memo Pad. The upper-right corner usually tells you the category of the item you're viewing. The bottom of the display area usually contains buttons you can tap to create, find, or edit items in the application you're using. The main, central part of the display area is the part that shows the bulk of your information. Some applications offer a scroll bar on the right edge of the screen that enables you to scroll the display area to show information that's higher or lower on the list of items you're viewing. This scroll bar does the same thing as the scroll buttons at the bottom of your Palm device (refer to the section "Scroll buttons," earlier in this chapter).

I frequently use the words *sometimes* and *usually* when I'm describing the display area because every program works a little differently. Although not every element works the same way all the time, the preceding description is how most well-designed Palm Computing programs tend to work.

Soft buttons

Soft buttons aren't really soft, like a pillow; they're more like pictures of buttons painted on the screen of the Palm device. Unlike hard buttons, soft buttons have no moving parts, and they don't do anything until your Palm device is powered on. One advantage to soft buttons is that they're labeled with the name of the thing they do so that you don't have to guess. Figure 1-5 shows what the soft buttons look like.

Figure 1-5:
The soft buttons work only when the Palm device is powered on.

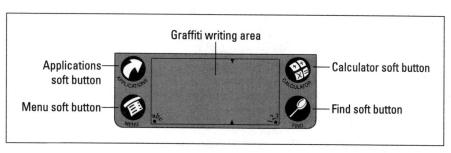

Graffiti writing area

Applications soft button

Calculator soft button

Menu soft button

Find soft button

To use one of the soft buttons, just tap it with your stylus. The four jobs assigned to the four soft buttons are Applications, Menu, Calculator, and Find. The following sections outline what each soft button does.

Applications

The *Applications* soft button calls up a list of all the applications on your Palm device, showing their icons. Figure 1-6 shows the icons you should see.

Several applications come already installed on your Palm device, including the following:

- ✔ **Expense:** Helps you keep track of what you spend.

- ✔ **Graffiti:** A little teaching program that helps you figure out the special Palm alphabet. (The Graffiti tutorial appears only on Palm IIIx and later. Earlier models feature a game named Giraffe.)

- ✔ **HotSync:** Makes your Palm device communicate with your desktop computer.

- ✔ **Mail:** Exchanges messages with the e-mail program on your desktop.

- ✔ **Memory:** Shows how much memory remains on your Palm device and how the memory you have is being used. (The Memory application appears only on models older than the Palm III.)

- ✔ **Preferences:** The application you use to configure your Palm device to suit your needs.

- ✔ **Security:** Sets up passwords and hides or shows private items.

Figure 1-6: Every program on your Palm device has an icon on the list of applications.

Any applications you install on your Palm device also show up on this list. I tell you later in this chapter more about the applications that come with your Palm device (see the section "What Do the Standard Applications Do?"), and in Chapter 12, I show you how to install other applications. You can start any application you see on the applications list by tapping the icon for that program. The little battery icon on the applications list tells you how much power is left in your batteries.

Menu

The *Menu* button activates the menus in any application you're running. Most Palm Computing programs have a set of menus that enable you to cut, copy, or paste text as well as create new items or delete old ones (these menus are similar to those you find in the applications for your desktop computer — except that these menus are not as involved). To use the menus in any application, start the application, and then tap the Menu button and tap the menu you want to use. Figure 1-7 shows a sample menu.

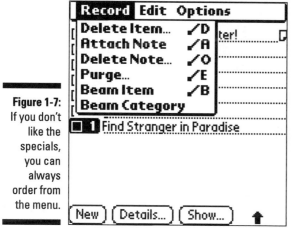

Figure 1-7:
If you don't like the specials, you can always order from the menu.

Calculator

The *Calculator* button contains no mysteries; it starts up the on-screen calculator, as shown in Figure 1-8. Tap the numbers just like you would on a handheld calculator. You can even press the on-screen calculator buttons with your finger. Naturally, it's not a good idea to put your fingers on the screen if you have gooey stuff like chocolate on your hands, because it leaves a mess on your screen, which makes your calculations hard to read. I don't know what happens if you try to lick chocolate off your Palm organizer screen (or worse, somebody else's Palm organizer screen). I wouldn't try it.

Find

The *Find* button starts up a little program that searches your entire Palm device for a certain string of text. If you want to find on your Palm device every item that contains the word *chocolate,* tap the Find button and enter the word **chocolate** by using either the on-screen keyboard or Graffiti (see Chapter 2 for more info about entering text), and then tap OK, as shown in Figure 1-9. The Find program then finds all the *chocolate* on your Palm device, which is faster and healthier than finding all the chocolate in your grocery store.

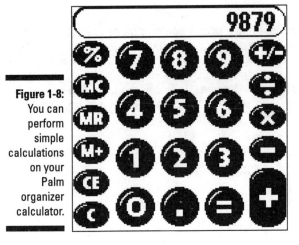

Figure 1-8:
You can perform simple calculations on your Palm organizer calculator.

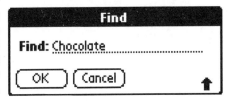

Figure 1-9:
Use Find to find a word that occurs in any Palm application.

I'll tell you one odd thing about the Find tool: If you enter only the first part of a word, it finds the word you're looking for; if you enter only the last part of the word, however, your word doesn't turn up. If you enter *choco,* you still find *chocolate,* but if you enter *late,* you come up with *late, later,* and *latest,* but not *chocolate.*

The Graffiti area

Most of the bottom part of the screen is occupied by a large box between the soft buttons called the *Graffiti area,* as shown in Figure 1-10. A pair of tiny triangles at the top and bottom of the Graffiti area separate the part for entering letters from the part for entering numbers. You can use the Palm organizer's stylus to write letters on the left side in the Palm Computing special alphabet, Graffiti. You can enter Graffiti-style numbers on the right side. Graffiti is much like the plain block printing you were taught to use in kindergarten, although a few letters are written a little differently. (For more info about using Graffiti to enter text, see Chapter 2.)

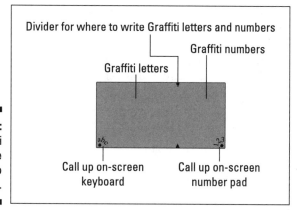

Divider for where to write Graffiti letters and numbers

Graffiti numbers

Graffiti letters

Call up on-screen keyboard

Call up on-screen number pad

Figure 1-10:
The Graffiti area is the place to enter text.

The letters *abc* appear in the lower-left corner of the Graffiti area, and the numbers *123* appear in the lower-right corner. As you may have guessed, tapping *abc* calls up an on-screen keyboard, and tapping *123* calls up a number pad. (For more information about entering text via the on-screen keyboard and number pad, see Chapter 2.)

"Which Palm Device Do I Have?"

This book covers the more recent models of the Palm devices — up through the Palm VII — but you may be using an earlier version. Users of earlier versions can find plenty of value here, too, not only because you can upgrade many early Palm devices but also because the Palm people tend not to make wholesale changes to basic applications, incorporating only slight changes and improvements with each new release. So newer versions should look familiar to you. (See Chapter 16 for more info about upgrading your Palm device.)

Because so many versions of the Palm organizer exist, you may appreciate this quick-and-dirty guide to all the Palm devices that are out there, somewhere:

- ✔ **PalmPilot 1000:** This little guy has only 128K of memory (barely ½₀ of the memory of a Palm III) and no backlight.

- ✔ **PalmPilot 5000:** This version kicks up the memory to 512K, but it still doesn't have a backlight.

- ✔ **PalmPilot Personal:** You get 512K of memory with this dude, and you finally get a backlight plus optional use of a modem to HotSync and better features in all the standard applications.

- ✔ **PalmPilot Professional:** This guy comes to you with 1MB of memory, a backlight, and an e-mail application.

- ✔ **Palm III:** This version gives you a whopping 2MB of memory and everything any earlier Palm device had plus infrared beaming — which enables you to beam items or whole programs to another Palm III user.

- ✔ **Palm IIIx**: A beefier, bulked-up version of the Palm III, the Palm IIIx has twice the memory, with 4MB, and a brighter screen than the Palm III.

- ✔ **Palm V**: This slim, trim version of the Palm III is for those who think that less is more. Only half as thick as any other Palm model, it has 2MB of memory and an attractive gold screen.

- ✔ **Palm VII**: The largest Palm, the Palm VII is as thick as the Palm IIIx and about ¾-inch longer to accommodate the transmitter that enables the Palm VII to connect you to the Internet at any time, wirelessly. Buck Rogers, eat your heart out.

- ✔ **IBM WorkPad:** This licensed version of the PalmPilot is sold by you-know-whom. The WorkPad is identical to the PalmPilot and has been upgraded right along with each new version of the PalmPilot.

If you bought your Palm device awhile back and you feel that you're missing all the fun that people are having with the new features, don't worry. You can upgrade early Palm devices and turn them into a Palm III. If you already have a Palm III or later, you can still make some improvements, but you can't turn a Palm III into a Palm IIIx, Palm V, or Palm VII. (I have more to say in Chapter 16 about upgrading your Palm device.)

What Do the Standard Applications Do?

Palm devices weren't designed to be just cool little computers, although they're definitely cool little computers. They were designed to do useful things for you as soon as you take them out of the box. I like nothing better than instant gratification, and that's what you get with a Palm device. (I do, anyway.)

The standard Palm Computing applications don't have to be installed, configured, or fussed with in any way; they're ready to use with one press of a button. You can configure the preferences for the applications, of course, to get them exactly the way you want them (for more info about preferences, see Chapter 3). To get started, just press the button assigned to that application or tap the Applications soft button for a list of your Palm Computing programs and pick the one you want to use.

The programs you can use as soon as you take your Palm device out of the box include the following:

✔ **Address Book:** This is your "little black book" of names, addresses, and phone numbers. You can keep a detailed description about everything you need to know about the people in your list by attaching a note to each record. You can also keep track of everyone's e-mail address and use the Address Book as your personal address book for e-mail you compose on your Palm device. (For more info about e-mail on a Palm device, see Chapter 10, and for more info about the Address Book, see Chapter 5.)

✔ **Calculator:** The calculator is a simple tool for punching in numbers and performing arithmetic. The PalmPilot calculator does one trick that a handheld calculator can't handle: It shows a list of recent calculations. After performing a series of calculations, tap Menu and then choose Options⇨Recent Calculations to see a recap of your last few calculations, as shown in Figure 1-11.

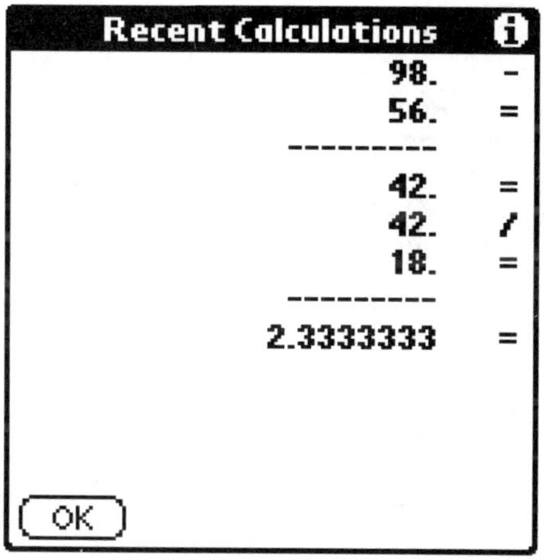

Figure 1-11:
You can see a series of calculations on your list of recent calculations.

Recent Calculations	ⓘ
98.	–
56.	=

42.	=
42.	/
18.	=

2.3333333	=

(OK)

✔ **Date Book:** Think of this program as your calendar of appointments and events. The Date Book, as shown in Figure 1-12, lets you set appointments and alarms to remind yourself of those appointments. You can also add notes to any appointment to keep details about each appointment handy. (For more info about the Date Book, see Chapter 8.)

✔ **Expense:** Here's a handy application for keeping track of what you spend. The Expense program, as shown in Figure 1-13, synchronizes to special Microsoft Excel spreadsheets on your desktop to enable you to collect expense figures on the road and then pull them together when you get home. (See Chapter 12 for more info about Expense.)

Figure 1-12:
Keep
up to date
with the
Date Book.

Figure 1-13:
You can
save in the
Expense
application
any data
about what
you've
spent.

✔ **Giraffe:** This program is actually a game, and it's also a great way to sharpen your skills in using Graffiti, which makes your Palm device that much more useful. Figure 1-14 shows a sample screen from the game. The Giraffe game comes preinstalled on the PalmPilot Professional and earlier models, although you have to add it from the CD that comes with the Palm III. Although the Palm IIIx, Palm V, and Palm VII don't have Giraffe, they do have the improved Graffiti tutorial.

✔ **HotSync:** This program links your Palm device to your desktop computer. The HotSync program has two parts: the part on the Palm device and the part on the desktop. Either a PC or a Mac can synchronize data with the same Palm device, although the PC and the Mac need different desktop software. (See Chapter 11 for more information about using HotSync.)

Figure 1-14:
The Giraffe
game
makes it fun
to find out
how to use
Graffiti.

✔ **Mail:** This simple e-mail program enables you to HotSync your e-mail with your desktop computer so that you can read e-mail, compose replies, and create messages to be sent through your desktop e-mail system. (This program is available only on PalmPilot Professional models and later.) (For more info about the Mail program, see Chapter 10.)

✔ **Memo Pad:** The Memo Pad is your collection of plain old text notes you can keep around for future reference. Figure 1-15 shows the memos that exist in your Palm device when you buy it. You can either create notes on your desktop computer and transfer them to your Palm device to keep critical information handy, or you can create memos on your Palm device for later transfer to desktop computer programs, such as your word processor. (For more info about the Memo Pad, see Chapter 7.)

Figure 1-15:
The Memo
List shows
your memos
whenever
you want to
read them.

✔ **Preferences:** This program lets you customize your Palm device by changing application button assignments, time and number formats, modem setup, and shortcuts. Figure 1-16 shows the General Preferences screen; for other preferences screens, choose from the pull-down menu in the upper-right corner. (For more info about setting preferences, see Chapter 3.)

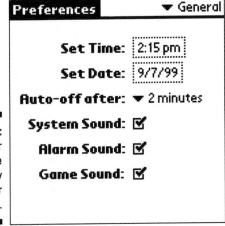

Figure 1-16:
Make your
Palm device
your own by
setting your
preferences.

✔ **Security:** This program lets you hide or show all the items you've marked as private on your Palm device. You can also set, remove, or change a password to protect your information. Figure 1-17 shows what to expect from the Security screen. (For more info about using the security features, see Chapter 3.)

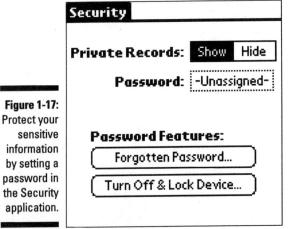

Figure 1-17:
Protect your
sensitive
information
by setting a
password in
the Security
application.

✔ **To Do List:** Here's a list of tasks you need to remember, sorted in order of priority or due date or by the name of the task. You can also keep track of tasks you've completed on the To Do List for reference. (For more info about the To Do List, see Chapter 6.)

The programs that come in the box with your Palm device are, of course, barely the beginning of what you can do. Thousands of software developers are busily writing new programs you can add to your Palm device to make it do things you may not even know that you want to do yet. Check out the CD-ROM that accompanies this book for a sampling of the best Palm Computing programs out there.

HotSyncing Is Definitely Hot Stuff

HotSyncing, put simply, is when you have your desktop computer and Palm device talk to each other — sort of like when you get together with a friend at happy hour. You compare your days, talk about what you did, and maybe exchange notes. HotSyncing does the same thing — only more efficiently.

During a HotSync, the two machines compare data and then match up that data exactly, keeping each other current on whom you know, what you've done, when you did it, and what you gotta do tomorrow. HotSyncing also enables you to install additional applications on your Palm device as well as back up (or *archive*) all your data on your desktop computer so that your data is safe. (Your Palm device does this automatically, so you don't even have to think about it.)

For more info about HotSyncing and using your Palm device with your desktop computer, see Chapters 11 through 13.

Getting Charged with Your Palm V

Although all the other PalmPilot models use regular, nonrechargeable AAA batteries, the Palm V is so thin that batteries wouldn't fit inside, so your Palm V has a built-in rechargeable battery. Because you can't change the battery in a Palm V, you have to be sure that you keep the unit charged up at all times.

When you take your brand-new Palm V out of the box, the battery has no charge. You have to plug the cradle into the AC adapter that comes in the box and plug the adapter into a wall socket. When the cradle is plugged in and you set the Palm V in the cradle, a light on the cradle comes on to show you that the Palm V is charging. You have to leave the Palm V in the cradle for three hours before using it the first time. You can plug the cradle into the back of your computer and set up your Palm V to work with the Palm Desktop software while charging up the unit.

I like to leave the Palm V in its cradle to charge whenever I'm not out and about. I also make it a point to HotSync my Palm V at least once a day, often two or three times, just to keep my data safe. Although a Palm V should run for several weeks on a charge, I still prefer to keep mine topped off.

When Batteries Are Included

If you don't have a Palm V, your Palm device doesn't plug into the wall. Although the cradle may look like it could recharge your Palm device, it doesn't do that for the Palm devices that use regular batteries. Instead, your Palm device runs on a pair of plain old AAA batteries, which should last nearly a month under normal use. If you use the backlight frequently, you drain the batteries faster.

When you change batteries, HotSyncing first is a good idea, just in case something goes wrong. When you take out a set of batteries, you have 30 seconds to insert a new set before the Palm device starts forgetting things.

If you press the Applications soft button, you can see on the applications screen how much power remains in your batteries. Palm III battery power is indicated by a silhouette of a battery at the top of the applications screen. When your batteries are at maximum power, the battery is completely black. As the batteries drain, the black part of the battery indicator gets smaller and smaller. Earlier Palm devices show just a bar graph labeled Battery at the bottom of the screen.

You can't change the batteries on a Palm V, of course. You can only recharge the built-in battery by leaving the Palm V in its cradle for a few hours. You can also buy a travel charger for your Palm V to keep the charge fresh when you're on the road.

Chapter 2

Going in Stylus

Although getting information from your Palm device is terribly easy, putting information into it is only sort of easy. If Palm devices had a built-in keyboard, I wouldn't have to explain how to enter data; you'd know how just by looking. If a Palm device *did* have a keyboard, you'd either be stuck with a set of teeny-weeny keys you could barely use or have a device the size of a laptop computer, in which case you'd be better off with a laptop computer.

The people who make the Palm devices recommend that you enter most of your data into it via the Palm Desktop program (described in Chapters 11, 12, and 13). Although that's the clearest way to deal with data entry, I think that being able to jot down a memo while riding on a train or sitting by a pool is half the fun of having a Palm device, so I like to use either Graffiti or the on-screen keyboard that's built into a Palm device. Although some programmers are creating products that offer interesting new ways to enter text into your Palm device, those products cost extra. I discuss them at the end of this chapter, in the section "Other Text-Entry Tricks."

Graffiti

Using words to explain Graffiti is like trying to describe a spiral staircase without using your hands. Even though a spiral staircase is tricky to describe, though, it's easy to use; the same goes for Graffiti. After you've used Graffiti for even a little while, you find that it comes naturally.

To write in Graffiti, you have to use a stylus. A *stylus* is a special pen with no ink. You can use the stylus that comes with your Palm device; the stylus is stored in a holder on the back or side of your Palm device (depending on which model you're using). Although you can also go out and buy a fancy, expensive stylus from people who also sell fancy, expensive writing pens, the cheap, plastic stylus that comes with your Palm device does the job just as well.

Although your Palm device will probably work perfectly for a long time with little or no trouble, if you accidentally scratch the screen, you'll start having problems. Don't use a sharp object as a stylus. Try to use a stylus that was designed to work with a Palm device, just to be safe.

You can use the stylus to tap on-screen buttons and select text; to write text in Graffiti, though, you have to write in the box at the bottom of the screen, cleverly named the Graffiti area, as shown in Figure 2-1.

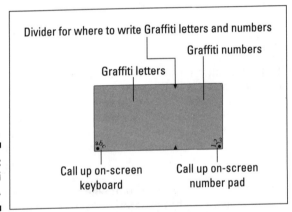

Figure 2-1:
The Graffiti
writing area.

The Graffiti tutorial

More recent versions of the Palm organizer — such as the Palm IIIx, Palm V, and Palm VII — include a Graffiti tutorial so that you can find out about the Palm Computing writing system whenever you're carrying your Palm device. I think that you'll get the hang of Graffiti after about 20 minutes of practice. The tutorial gives you step-by-step exercises for the characters you use most often. It also displays a trace of the actual characters you write as you write them so that you understand why your Palm device sometimes misunderstands the letters you enter. I'm often shocked at how well it interprets my hieroglyphics; half the time, I can't read the stuff myself. My Palm device makes me look good in spite of myself.

Graffiti letters and numbers

You can see the letters *abc* in the lower-left corner of the Graffiti area. That's to remind you that you have to write letters on the left side of the box. The numbers *123* are printed in the lower-right corner, to remind you that — you guessed it — you can write only numbers on the right side of the screen. Two tiny triangles separate the letter-writing area from the number-writing area.

Graffiti is a special alphabet you have to understand; it's not handwriting-recognition software that learns your handwriting style. Most of the letters and numbers in the Graffiti alphabet are the same as the plain block letters you were taught to use in the first grade, with one important adjustment: *Graffiti letters must be written with a single stroke of the stylus.* If you remember that one rule, Graffiti seems simple.

For example, Figure 2-2 shows the letter *A* in Graffiti.

Figure 2-2:
The letter *A*.

The Graffiti letter *A* looks just like a normal capital letter *A* without the crossbar. (That dot on the lower-left end of the A shows where you begin the stroke — it's the same place most people begin writing a capital *A.*) You don't write a crossbar because writing it requires a second stroke of the stylus. Picking up the stylus is the way you tell Graffiti that you've moved on to the next letter. For the letter *A,* just draw the upper, triangular part of the *A* and then move on to the next letter. (As I said, it takes much less time to do this than to read about doing it.)

Your Palm device comes with a little sticker that shows you the whole Graffiti alphabet. You can put the sticker on the back of your unit or on the inside cover of your Palm III so that you always have it as a reference.

Nearly all Graffiti charts display the alphabet as little squiggles with a dot at one end. The dot tells you where to begin drawing the Graffiti stroke. Think of it like those connect-the-dot games, except that you connect only one dot.

In case you've lost the little sticker, Figure 2-3 shows the whole Graffiti alphabet.

Figure 2-3:
The whole
Graffiti
alphabet.

As you can see, the Graffiti alphabet is easy to understand. The trick is remembering the tiny differences between regular printing and printing Graffiti.

If you need some help with Graffiti while using your Palm device, you can bring up a Graffiti cheat sheet right on the screen in most programs, like this:

1. **Tap the Menu soft button.**

   The menu bar appears.

2. **Choose Edit⇨Graffiti Help.**

   The Graffiti Help screen appears.

After you've found the Graffiti letter you want to use, tap the Done button to return to the program and write the letter.

The Graffiti Help screen appears only when it's possible for you to enter text. If you're looking at the To Do list, for example, the Graffiti Help screen doesn't appear because you have to select a To Do item or create a new to-do before you can enter text.

You may find that getting used to writing Graffiti takes a little time. Don't despair — that's normal. Like most computers, your Palm device can be finicky about what it accepts when it comes to individual things like human handwriting. Because my handwriting is pretty awful, I often have to write more slowly and carefully when I'm entering Graffiti characters than I do when I'm writing normal text on paper.

If you're a touch typist, you probably won't achieve the kind of speed when you're entering text in Graffiti as you do by typing. The point of Graffiti is not so much speed as convenience; you use Graffiti when dragging a keyboard around just isn't practical.

Moving the Graffiti cursor

When you're creating text in Graffiti, you always see a little blinking line in the display area, named the *insertion point* or the cursor, which shows you where the next letter you enter goes. Sometimes, you want to make the cursor move without entering a letter or you just want to enter a space between words or a line between paragraphs.

To create a space, draw the Graffiti space character in the Graffiti area, as shown in Figure 2-4. It's just a horizontal line drawn from left to right.

Figure 2-4:
The space
character.

If you make a mistake, you may want to backspace to erase the last letter you wrote. The backspace character works just like the Backspace key on a regular desktop computer. To backspace, draw the Graffiti backspace character in the Graffiti area, as shown in Figure 2-5. The character is just a horizontal line drawn from right to left, the opposite of the space character. Although some characters have to be entered either in the letters or numbers area of the Graffiti box, you can enter spaces and backspaces in either area.

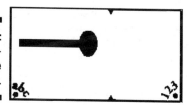

Figure 2-5:
The back-
space
character.

Whenever you want to delete a whole word or a larger block of text, it's quicker to select the text before drawing the backspace character to delete everything you've selected. To select text, draw an imaginary line through the text you want to select in the display area (not in the Graffiti area). You can see which text you've selected because it's highlighted. Backspacing after highlighting text erases that text. You can also just begin writing again after selecting text; the new text replaces the old.

If you're finished with the line you're writing and you want to begin entering text on a new line, use the Graffiti return character. It works a little like the Enter key on a regular desktop computer, although you use the return character much less on a Palm device than you do on a regular computer.

To insert a new line, draw the return character in the Graffiti area, as shown in Figure 2-6. It's a slanted line drawn from the upper-right to the lower-left part of the Graffiti area.

Figure 2-6:
The return
character.

Making capital letters without a shift key

When you type a capital letter on a regular keyboard, you hold the Shift key while typing the letter. Because you can't hold a key while entering a Graffiti letter, you have to enter the shift character before entering a letter you want capitalized.

The shift character is simply an upward, vertical stroke in the Graffiti text area, as shown in Figure 2-7. To enter a capital *A*, draw a vertical line upward in the Graffiti text area, followed by the letter **A.** After you draw the shift character, an upward-pointing arrow appears in the lower-right corner of the screen to show that your next letter will be capitalized.

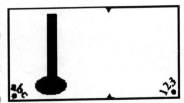

Figure 2-7:
The shift
character.

On a regular keyboard, if you want to capitalize a whole string of letters, you press the Caps Lock key and type away. After you finish typing capital letters, you press the Shift key to return to regular, lowercase text.

Entering two shift characters in a row in Graffiti, as shown in Figure 2-8, is the same as pressing the Caps Lock key. After you enter the shift character twice, you see an arrow with a dotted tail in the lower-right corner of the display area, which tells you that all the text you enter will be capitalized. You can cancel the Caps Lock by entering the shift command again.

Figure 2-8:
The Caps
Lock com-
mand.

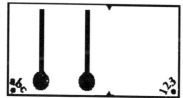

In quite a few cases, because Palm Computing applications assume that the first letter of a sentence or proper name should be capitalized, the shift arrow automatically shows up in the lower-right corner of the screen to indicate that the next letter will be capitalized. If you don't want to capitalize the beginning of a sentence, enter the shift character twice to return to lowercase text.

Graffiti has another type of shift character, the Extended Shift, which is entered as a downward, diagonal line starting from the top-left, as shown in Figure 2-9. The Extended Shift character offers a way to enter special characters, such as the copyright symbol (©) and the trademark symbol (™). You can also use Extended Shift to create certain punctuation characters, such as the upside-down question marks and exclamation points you need for entering text in Spanish in addition to some mathematical symbols, like plus signs. When you enter the Extended Shift stroke, a little, diagonal line appears in the lower-right corner of the screen.

Figure 2-9:
The
Extended
Shift stroke.

Another shift character you may use is Command Shift, an upward, diagonal line starting in the lower-left part of the Graffiti screen, as shown in Figure 2-10. You can perform quite a few common tasks in many Palm Computing programs by entering Command Shift followed by a letter. To delete a To Do item, for example, tap the item and then enter the Command Shift stroke followed by the letter *D*. That step opens the Delete dialog box, just as though you had chosen Record⇨Delete Item from the menu. You can see what Command Shift can do in any program by tapping the Menu soft button and looking at the list of commands on the right side of each menu.

Figure 2-10: The Command Shift stroke.

Punctuating your text

Although Graffiti letters and numbers look somewhat normal, Graffiti punctuation is strange. You may not want to punctuate when you're entering Graffiti text except for the occasional period and dash.

To enter punctuation characters (such as periods, dashes, and commas) you have to tap your stylus once in the Graffiti area before entering the character. Many punctuation characters have different meanings if you don't tap first before drawing them. When you tap once, a little dot appears in the lower-right corner of the display area to show that you've tapped.

The simplest punctuation character is the period. Tap twice in the Graffiti area to create a period. Figure 2-11 shows a dot where I'm making a period.

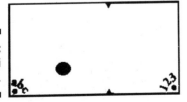

Figure 2-11: The Graffiti period.

The second simplest punctuation character is the dash. Tap once in the Graffiti area, and then draw a horizontal line from left to right. After you've used Graffiti for a while, you'll think of this as tapping and then drawing the space character.

If you need to enter e-mail addresses in the Address Book, you almost certainly need to be able to enter the @ sign, for e-mail addresses that look like somebody@something.com. The @ sign is simply a tap followed by the letter *O*.

Graffiti whiz secrets

I think that most people can get a good handle on Graffiti within a few hours, except for people under 15 years of age, who usually pick it up in about five minutes. I've heard stories of kids in junior high school who write notes to each other in Graffiti. That's clever. I hope that they don't write naughty words on walls in Graffiti; that would be redundant.

Even with some experience, certain Graffiti letters tend to stay finicky and hard to enter accurately. Make your Graffiti characters as large, square, and vertical as possible.

Another trick is to figure out which letters can be entered by writing a number on the letter side of the Graffiti area and a letter on the number side of the Graffiti area. If you write the number 3 on the letter side of the Graffiti area, for example, the letter *B* turns up more reliably than it does if you draw the actual Graffiti letter *B*. Table 2-1 shows a list of letters that are often a problem and how to get your Palm device to recognize them more reliably.

Table 2-1	Tricks of the Graffiti Trade
To Get This Character	*Perform This Keystroke*
B	Draw the number 3 on the letter side of the Graffiti area.
G	Draw the number 6 on the letter side of the Graffiti area.
K	This one is the trickiest Graffiti character. Just draw the "legs" on the side of the *K,* joined by a little loop. Leave out the vertical bar. To me, it looks a little like a fish swimming from right to left. I describe this subject in greater detail later in this chapter.
P	Begin at the bottom of the *P* and make the loop at the top pretty small.
Q	Draw an *O* with a long tail at the top.
R	Do this just like the *P* I describe, but make the tail of the *R* extra long.
V	Draw the *V* backward (start from the top right).

(continued)

Table 2-1 (continued)

To Get This Character	Perform This Keystroke
Y	Just draw the lower loop of a cursive capital Y. It's just a loop, like the letter K, except that the fish is swimming down.
2	Draw the letter Z on the number side of the Graffiti writing area.
4	Draw the letter C on the number side of the Graffiti area.
5	Draw the letter S on the number side of the Graffiti area.
7	Draw a backward letter C on the number side of the Graffiti area.

The amazing Graffiti fish loop

One Graffiti character has no counterpart in the normal alphabet, although knowing how to draw this character can help you enormously when you use Graffiti. Because the character doesn't have an official name, I just call it the *fish loop.*

I know that my fish story is a dopey explanation, but I bring it up for two reasons. First, because Graffiti seems to recognize this loop symbol more reliably than most other letters or numbers, finding out how to use it certainly makes you a quicker and slicker graffitiist.

The second reason for my fish story is that I find stupid explanations the easiest to remember. By that measure, you'll *never* forget this explanation.

If you draw a little loop that looks like a fish swimming from right to left, as shown in Figure 2-12, Graffiti translates that loop as the letter K.

Figure 2-12:
Did you
have your
Special K
today?

If you make the fish look like he's swimming downward, as shown in Figure 2-13, Graffiti translates that loop as the letter *Y*.

Figure 2-13:
No YMCA here; just *Y*.

If you make the fish look like he's swimming from left to right, as shown in Figure 2-14, Graffiti translates that loop as the letter *X*.

Figure 2-14:
X marks the spot, sometimes.

If you make the fish look like he's swimming upward and you begin drawing from the left, as shown in Figure 2-15, Graffiti translates that loop as the shortcut symbol, a useful tool that I discuss in the next section, "The Graffiti Shortcut Symbol."

Figure 2-15:
Little Red Riding Hood shoulda had a shortcut like this!

By the way, I apologize for referring to the fish as a male in all instances; because the fish has no eyes, though, he appears to have no idea where he's going — a situation in which I find myself regularly. That makes me assume that the fish is male, like me. Feel free to draw your own conclusions. About the fish, that is.

The Graffiti ShortCut symbol

Another compelling reason to use Graffiti is that you can create and use ShortCuts. *ShortCuts* are abbreviations that automatically expand themselves into longer blocks of text or automated entries, such as the current date and time.

When you buy your Palm device, a few ShortCuts are already built in. Some of the preprogrammed ShortCuts are for useful words, such as *meeting, breakfast, lunch,* and *dinner.* You also get some useful time-stamp ShortCuts for entering the current date and time.

To add a time stamp to a memo or note, write the Graffiti ShortCut symbol, followed by the letters **TS,** as shown in Figure 2-16.

Figure 2-16:
"It's Greek to me," you say? Nope, it's a time stamp!

As soon as you finish writing the letter *S,* the three characters you entered disappear, and the current time appears.

The three preprogrammed time-stamp ShortCuts are

- ✔ **TS:** Time stamp; enters the current time
- ✔ **DS:** Date stamp; enters the current date
- ✔ **DTS:** Date-time stamp; enters the current date and time

Other preprogrammed ShortCuts include

- ✔ **ME:** For the word *meeting*
- ✔ **BR:** For the word *breakfast*
- ✔ **LU:** For the word *lunch*
- ✔ **DI:** For the word *dinner*

(In Chapter 3, I show you how to create ShortCuts of your own.)

The On-Screen Keyboard

Perhaps you don't want to spend time finding out about Graffiti. You may just want to get down to business. That's fine. You can call up the on-screen keyboard to enter letters by tapping on a tiny picture of a keyboard, as shown in Figure 2-17.

The on-screen keyboard is too small for touch typing. You definitely need the stylus to pick out those tiny little keys. I use the on-screen keyboard as little as possible because I think that I type more slowly when I'm trying to find those tiny little keys. I know plenty of people who stick exclusively with the on-screen keyboard, though, and they do just fine.

Figure 2-17: The on-screen keyboard is a handy way to enter text.

To make the on-screen keyboard appear, tap the dot in one of the two lower corners of the Graffiti area. When you tap the dot on the letter side of the Graffiti area, the alphabet keyboard appears. When you tap the dot on the number side, a numeric keypad appears, as shown in Figure 2-18. After you've entered the text you want, tap Done to make the on-screen keyboard go away.

The on-screen keyboard appears only when it's possible for you to enter text. If you're looking at your list of memos, for example, the on-screen keyboard doesn't appear because you have to open a memo or create a new memo before you can enter text.

On the on-screen keyboard, you can also see a button labeled Int'l that unlocks a special set of keys for entering those festive international characters that English sadly lacks.

Other Text-Entry Tricks

I've seen some other promising methods of entering text into your Palm device. All of them involve buying a product and adding it to your Palm device. If you have to enter text on the run fairly often, one of these programs can help you.

Other writing systems

T9, from Tegic Communications, is an on-screen telephone-style keypad that lets you enter text the way you would dial one of those famous alphabetic phone numbers, such as 1-800-FLOWERS. It works surprisingly well, although I generally find that using Graffiti is quicker. For more information about the T9 keyboard, check out the manufacturer's Web site, at www.tegic.com.

You can install another writing system, named Jot, if you don't like Graffiti. Jot is quite similar to Graffiti, and some people think that it's easier to understand. You have to pay extra for Jot, of course; Graffiti is built into your Palm device at no extra cost. If you want to know more about Jot, the manufacturer's Web site is at www.cic.com.

GoType

I got a GoType as a Christmas gift, and I must say, I'm crazy about it. The only gizmo I'm more excited about is the Palm device itself. A company named LandWare makes GoType, which includes a docking port for the Palm device. It enables you to enter text the old-fashioned way — by typing. I love using my GoType because it combines the instant availability of a Palm device with the speed of a keyboard. I've been to meetings where I finished typing my notes before the person next to me finished booting up his laptop. Although I still use Graffiti about 90 percent of the time, my GoType makes that other 10 percent a breeze. Although a Palm device still isn't the ideal platform for word processing, if you want to enter extensive text quickly on the spur of the moment, GoType is a time-saver. The company's Web site is at www.landware.com.

Chapter 3

Making Your Palm Device Your Own

- -

In This Chapter

▶ Setting preferences

▶ Using the Security program

▶ Setting passwords

▶ Hiding and showing private items

▶ Saving time with ShortCuts

▶ Using Palm Computing hacks

- -

As Palm devices sell by the million, you can be sure that everyone uses them a little differently. Some people think of their Palm devices as glorified date books, and they're happy with that. Other people install programs that do things you'd never guess, such as track their location by satellite, send e-mail messages by radio, and heaven knows what else.

Because everyone uses a Palm device a little differently, many people want to personalize the way theirs work. In this chapter, I show you some of the easier ways to make your Palm device work the way you do, by using the preference and security settings that are standard on Palm devices.

Setting General Preferences

When you start up your Palm device for the first time, the General Preferences screen appears automatically as an invitation to set the time and date accurately. You may also want to reset the time, if you travel frequently to different time zones.

Follow these steps to access the General Preferences screen:

1. Tap the Applications soft button.

The list of applications appears on the screen.

2. Tap the Prefs icon.

The Preferences application is launched, as shown in Figure 3-1.

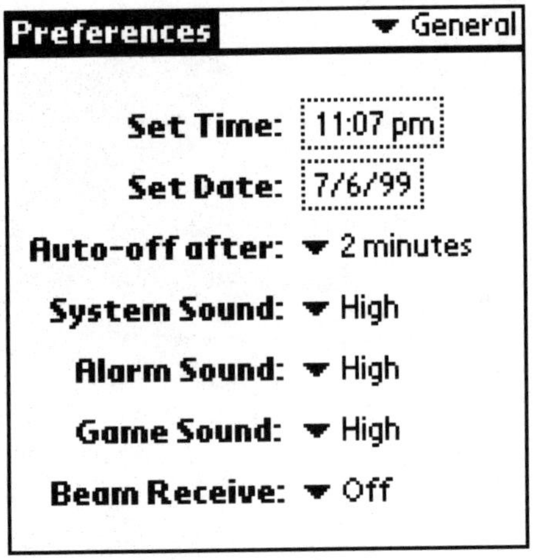

Figure 3-1:
The
Preferences
application
enables you
to make
your Palm
device
your own.

Preferences	▼ General

Set Time: 11:07 pm

Set Date: 7/6/99

Auto-off after: ▼ 2 minutes

System Sound: ▼ High

Alarm Sound: ▼ High

Game Sound: ▼ High

Beam Receive: ▼ Off

3. Tap the word in the upper-right corner of the screen.

The Preferences program has eight options for setting up different types of preferences: Buttons, Digitizer, Formats, General, Modem, Network, Owner, and ShortCuts. The name of the section you're looking at appears in the upper-right corner of the screen. The triangle next to the name of the section means that you can tap the name of the section to see a pull-down list of the other available sections.

4. Choose General.

The General Preferences screen appears.

To change the individual settings of the General Preferences screen, continue with the following sections.

Setting the time

I like having my Palm device remind me of my appointments shortly before they occur, just to avoid missing anything I've scheduled. The Palm device is a little like an alarm clock, though: Alarms can't go off at the right time if I don't set mine to the right time in the first place.

Follow these steps to set the time on your Palm device:

1. **With the General Preferences screen visible, tap the time shown in the Set Time box.**

   The Set Time dialog box opens, showing the time for which the Palm device is now set, along with a pair of triangles for changing the time. The top triangle sets the time later, and the bottom triangle sets the time earlier, as shown in Figure 3-2.

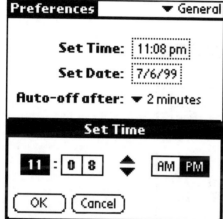

Figure 3-2:
In the Set Time dialog box, tap the triangles to set the time.

2. **Tap the hour in the Set Time dialog box.**

   The hour is highlighted to show that you've selected it.

3. **Tap the triangles repeatedly until the hour you want appears.**

   The hour changes as you tap the triangles.

4. **Set the minutes by following Steps 2 and 3 for each of the two minute boxes.**

   The minutes change as you tap the triangles.

5. **Tap the AM or PM box to choose the appropriate setting.**

   The box you tap is highlighted to show that you've picked it.

6. **Tap OK.**

   The Set Time dialog box closes.

If you like to show the time in a different format than the standard 1:35 PM format, I show you how to change the time format in the section "Setting Format Preferences," later in this chapter.

Setting the date

If you use the calendar frequently or if you enter lots of tasks with due dates assigned, you may want your Palm device to know what day it is.

Follow these steps to set the date on your Palm device:

1. **With the General Preferences screen visible, tap the date shown in the Set Date box.**

   The Set Date dialog box opens, as shown in Figure 3-3.

Figure 3-3:
You can set the date on your Palm device by finding the current date on a calendar in the Set Date dialog box.

Set Date
◀ **1999** ▶

Jan	Feb	Mar	Apr	May	Jun
Jul	Aug	Sep	Oct	Nov	Dec

S	M	T	W	T	F	S
				1	2	3
4	5	(6)	7	8	9	10
11	12	13	14	15	16	17
18	19	20	21	22	23	24
25	26	27	28	29	30	31

(Cancel) (Today)

2. **Tap one of the triangles on either side of the year to set the current year.**

   After you tap the triangle on the left, the year shown moves one year earlier. Tapping the triangle on the right moves the year shown to the next year. Keep tapping until the current year appears.

3. **Tap the month you want.**

   The name of the month you tap is highlighted to show that you've selected it, and a calendar for the month you tap appears.

4. **Tap the day of the month you want to set.**

   The Set Date dialog box closes, and the date you chose appears on the Preferences screen.

After you've set the date, your Palm device remembers and keeps track of the date automatically, unless you let the batteries go dead. If you go around the world for 80 days and come home to a dead Palm device, just change the batteries or recharge your Palm V, HotSync, and reset the date and time. (For more info about batteries, see Chapter 1.)

Setting the Auto-off interval

Your Palm device goes a long way on a pair of AAA batteries; mine usually runs for the better part of a month before I have to replace them. One method the Palm device uses to stretch battery life is to turn off automatically, if you haven't pressed a button for a few minutes.

Although you don't have many choices about how long the Palm device waits before shutting off, here's how you can choose from what's available:

1. **With the General Preferences screen visible, tap the triangle next to the words *Auto-off after.***

   The pull-down list of Auto-off intervals appears. You can choose either 1-, 2-, or 3-minute Auto-off intervals, as shown in Figure 3-4.

2. **Choose the Auto-off interval you want.**

   The interval you tap appears in the Auto-off After box.

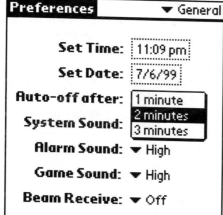

Figure 3-4: The Auto-off feature saves batteries by turning off your Palm device when you're not using it.

REMEMBER

You don't need to worry much about having your Palm device turn off too fast; you only have to press the green power button to switch right back to the program you were working on when the Palm device turned off.

Setting the sound volume

A tiny little speaker inside your Palm device makes little chirping sounds when you tap the screen and plays a squeaky little fanfare when you run the HotSync program. If you think that a Palm device should be seen and not heard, you can turn the sound off. If you have a Palm III or later model, you can also change the volume.

You can adjust three volume settings:

✔ **System:** System sounds are those the Palm OS is programmed to make in certain events. For example, when you want to do something specific that your Palm device can't do at that moment, you may get an error beep, just like when your desktop PC protests one of your actions.

✔ **Alarm:** An alarm sounds when you set a reminder for an appointment. You can also get some third-party Palm Computing programs that use the alarm sound.

✔ **Game:** Game sounds work only with games that are programmed to use them. Although most games are more fun with sounds, those game-like boinks and bleeps are a dead giveaway that you're not using your Palm device for serious work. If you plan to secretly play a shoot-'em-up game at the weekly staff meeting, a good career move may be to turn off your game sounds.

If your Palm device goes off when you're at the movies, you may get some dirty looks, so be a good sport and turn off the sounds when you go to the MegaMultiplex. Follow these steps to adjust the volume for all three types of sounds:

1. **With the General Preferences screen visible, tap the triangle next to the type of sound you want to change.**

   A pull-down list of volume choices appears. On a Palm III or later model, you can choose either Off, Low, Medium, or High, as shown in Figure 3-5. Earlier Palm devices offer only a check box so that you can turn the sound on or off.

Figure 3-5:
The Palm III and later models have adjustable system sound volume. Earlier Palm devices enable you only to turn sounds on and off.

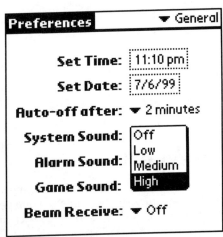

2. **Choose the volume level you want.**

   The volume level you tap appears in the System Sound box.

The term *Palm device volume* is an oxymoron, like *military intelligence, postal service,* and *athletic scholarship.* The minuscule speaker inside the case can only make sounds that I'd describe as soft, softer, and softest. You may want to adjust the volume anyway, so it's good that you have a way to do so.

Turning off beaming

A Palm III or later can send or receive all sorts of things by *beaming,* which is the rather neat process of sending data between Palm devices via an invisible light beam across the air. (Sounds kind of magical, doesn't it? To demystify beaming, see Chapter 9.) The Palm III doesn't distinguish between truly useful information and useless junk when it sends stuff out over the air; it's a little like television in that way.

If you want to avoid having unwanted junk beamed to your Palm III, you can elect not to receive beamed items by following these steps:

1. **With the General Preferences screen visible, tap the triangle next to Beam Receive.**

   The pull-down list of choices appears.

2. **Choose either On or Off.**

   The choice you tap appears in the Beam Receive box.

Turning off beam receiving doesn't stop you from beaming items to others. If you've turned off beam receiving and you try to beam something, though, a dialog box opens up to ask whether you want to turn beam receiving back on. Switching beam receiving back on, in order to exchange business cards with another Palm device user, makes sense. You don't want to be unsociable, do you?

Setting Button Preferences

You may use some programs more than others. As a result, you may want to assign a different program to one of the hard buttons at the bottom of your Palm organizer case.

Here's how to switch the programs assigned to the Applications buttons:

1. **Tap the Applications soft button.**

   The list of applications appears, showing icons for all the programs installed in your Palm device.

2. **Tap the Prefs icon.**

   The Preferences screen appears.

3. **Tap the word in the upper-right corner of the screen.**

   A pull-down list of preferences options appears.

4. **Choose Buttons.**

   The Buttons Preferences screen appears and displays five icons, one for each of the buttons at the bottom of your Palm device and one for the Calculator soft button (the other soft buttons aren't up for grabs). The name of the assigned program shows up next to each icon.

5. **Tap the triangle next to the button whose program you want to change.**

   A pull-down list of all the applications installed in your Palm device appears in alphabetical order, as shown in Figure 3-6. Your applications list may be long. When the list gets too long to fit on the Palm organizer screen, little arrows appear at the top and bottom of the list to indicate that more programs are available. You can scroll up and down the list by either tapping the arrows at the top and bottom of the list or by pressing the scroll-up and -down buttons.

6. **Choose the name of the application you want to assign to that button.**

   The name of the application you tap appears on the Buttons Preferences screen next to the button to which it's assigned.

Figure 3-6: You can make your Application buttons start any program you want by changing the settings on the Buttons Preferences screen.

Now when you press that particular button, your Palm device runs the newly assigned program. All your programs still appear after you tap the Applications soft button, although only the assigned programs run from the hard buttons.

Setting Format Preferences

Because people express time and numbers differently in different places, your Palm device has settings to suit a variety of local customs.

Here's how to change the way dates and numbers appear:

1. **Tap the Applications soft button.**

   The list of applications appears, showing icons for all the programs installed in your Palm device.

2. **Tap the Prefs icon.**

   The Preferences screen appears.

3. **Tap the word in the upper-right corner of the screen.**

   A pull-down list of Preferences options appears.

4. **Tap Formats.**

   The Format Preferences screen appears.

5. **Tap the triangle next to Preset To.**

   A pull-down list of countries appears, as shown in Figure 3-7. When you choose a certain country, the date, time, and number presets for that country appear.

Figure 3-7:
Use the
number
of your
favorite
country by
choosing
from the
Preset To
list.

Preferences	Iceland ▲
Preset to:	Ireland
	Italy
Time:	Japan
	Luxembourg
Date:	Mexico
	Netherlands
	New Zealand
	Norway
Week starts:	Spain
	Sweden
Numbers:	Switzerland
	United Kingdom
	United States

6. **Choose the country whose presets you want to use.**

   The name of the country you tap appears in the Preset To box, and all the number formats on the Format Preferences screen change to the formats common to the country you chose.

7. **If you want to change an individual type of formatting, tap the triangle next to the example of that type.**

   A pull-down list of formatting choices appears. If you choose the United States, for example, the entry in the Time box says HH:MM am/pm, which means that all time entries on your Palm device appear the way people write them in the United States; 11:13 am, for example. If you want the time to appear the way it's displayed in Italy — 11.13, for example — choose the HH.MM entry.

   The format you tap appears on the Format Preferences screen, as shown in Figure 3-8.

Figure 3-8:
You can pick different types of time and number formats on the Format Preferences screen.

Changing your format preferences changes the way numbers appear in all Palm Computing applications. If you want to use one format in one application and another format in a different application, you're out of luck. One format per customer, please.

Using the Security Application

If you keep lots of sensitive business data on your Palm device, you're wise to take advantage of the security features built in. You can hide items you want to protect from unauthorized eyes, and you can even assign a password to lock your Palm device from any unauthorized use.

Follow these steps to access the Security screen:

1. **Tap the Applications soft button.**

   The list of applications appears on your screen.

2. **Tap Security.**

   The Security screen appears, as shown in Figure 3-9.

```
┌────────────────────────────────┐
│ Security                       │
│                                │
│                                │
│  Private Records: [ Show  Hide]│
│                                │
│        Password: ⌐-Unassigned-⌐│
│                                │
│                                │
│  Password Features:            │
│  ┌──────────────────────────┐  │
│  │   Forgotten Password...   │ │
│  └──────────────────────────┘  │
│  ┌──────────────────────────┐  │
│  │  Turn Off & Lock Device... │ │
│  └──────────────────────────┘  │
│                                │
└────────────────────────────────┘
```

Figure 3-9:
Keep your
secrets
secret with
the Security
application.

To change the individual settings on the Security Preferences screen, read the following sections.

Setting your password

Although you can keep confidential information on either a desktop computer or a Palm device, few people misplace their desktop computers in airports or restaurants the way they misplace their Palm devices. That makes password-protecting your Palm data all the more important.

Follow these steps to set a password:

1. **With the Security Preferences screen visible, tap Unassigned in the Password box.**

   The Password dialog box opens.

   If the word *Assigned* appears, you already have a password. If you want to delete your password, see the following section, "Deleting a forgotten password."

2. **Enter the password you want to set by using Graffiti (refer to Chapter 2 for more information about entering text).**

   The password you enter appears in the Password dialog box, as shown in Figure 3-10. Don't forget to remember your password.

Figure 3-10:
Enter your
password
in the
Password
dialog box.

3. **Tap OK.**

   The Password dialog box opens again, asking you to verify your password.

4. **Reenter the password you entered in Step 4.**

   The password you enter appears again in the Password dialog box. By the way, did I mention that you should remember your password?

5. **Tap OK.**

   The Password dialog box closes, and the word *Assigned* appears in the Password box.

Deleting a forgotten password

It happens. You've been asked to supply 1,001 passwords for various systems, your Palm device is the 1,002nd, and you forgot your password. The easiest way to avoid this problem, of course, is simply to remember your password. If you can't, you can delete the old password, as long as you can turn on the power and get to the Security application:

1. **With the Security screen visible, tap the Forgotten Password button.**

The Delete Password dialog box opens, as shown in Figure 3-11, bearing a stern warning that all the items you've marked as private are removed until the next HotSync.

2. **If you want to proceed, tap Yes.**

   After a short pause, the word *Unassigned* appears in the Password box. You can then reassign a new password — just try not to forget it this time, okay? Geesh!

Figure 3-11: Try not to forget your password; the Security program won't be amused.

If you've locked down your Palm device by tapping Turn Off & Lock Device in the Security application and then forgotten your password, you're cooked. You can get back into your Palm device only by performing a hard reset, which wipes out all your data (refer to Chapter 1 for more information about resetting it). You can recover all the items you entered before your last HotSync by doing another HotSync. Whatever you entered after the last HotSync but before you reset is gone for good, however, so, guess what you had better do. . . .

Remember your darn password!

Okay, this is the last time, just in case I haven't said it enough in this section.

Hiding private items

It may not be *Saving Private Ryan,* but *Hiding Private Items* can be heroic stuff, too. The main reason to mark items as private is so that you can hide them from the prying eyes of supervisors, paparazzi, and secret agents (or if you want to hide all the phone numbers of the Bond girls from Miss Moneypenny — but I digress).

Follow these steps to hide private items:

1. **With the Security screen visible, tap the Hide button next to the words *Private Records*.**

   The Hide Records dialog box opens, as shown in Figure 3-12, telling you what happens when you hide records.

2. **Tap Hide.**

   The Hide Records dialog box closes, and the Security screen reappears. The word *Hide* is highlighted, and your private items are hidden, as they should be!

Figure 3-12: You can hide your private items by tapping Hide in the Hide Records dialog box.

After you've hidden your private items, you may want to make them appear again later. Just follow the preceding steps, and tap Show rather than Hide. If you've assigned a password, the Palm device makes you enter your password before revealing your private items. You can mark any item as private by tapping the Details button and then tapping the Private check box.

Setting Up ShortCuts

One cute feature in the Palm Computing world is the ShortCut. A *ShortCut* is an automatic abbreviation. If you write the words *New York* frequently, for example, you may make a ShortCut named NY. Then, whenever you want to write "New York," just enter the Graffiti ShortCut symbol (which looks like a cursive, lowercase *L*) and enter the letters **NY**. The words *New York* appear automatically. (For more info about entering Graffiti ShortCuts, see the section about the Graffiti ShortCut symbol in Chapter 2.)

ShortCuts can save you lots of tapping and scribbling when you want to enter information. I like to use the date-time stamp ShortCuts to measure how long I've worked on projects, especially when I'm billing for those projects by the hour. You can create or edit your own collection of ShortCuts in a jiffy.

To access the ShortCuts screen, follow these steps:

1. **Tap the Applications soft button.**

   The list of applications appears, showing icons for all the programs installed in your Palm device.

2. **Tap the Prefs icon.**

   The Preferences screen appears.

3. **Tap the word in the upper-right corner of the screen.**

   A pull-down list of Preferences options appears.

4. **Choose ShortCuts.**

   The ShortCuts screen appears, listing all your current ShortCuts.

Read the following sections to figure out how to add, change, or delete your ShortCuts.

Adding a new ShortCut

A collection of ShortCuts is already set up for your use when you first buy a Palm device. To get your money's worth from ShortCuts, create some of your own.

Adding a new ShortCut is this simple:

1. **With the ShortCuts screen visible, tap New.**

   The ShortCut Entry dialog box opens, as shown in Figure 3-13.

2. **Use Graffiti to enter the ShortCut name you want (refer to Chapter 2 for more information about entering text).**

   The text you enter appears on the ShortCut Name line.

   You can also use the on-screen keyboard to enter your ShortCut name, but be sure that you can enter the characters you want in Graffiti because you can't use ShortCuts from the on-screen keyboard — only from Graffiti.

3. **Tap the first line of the ShortCut Text section.**

   An insertion point appears at the point where you tap.

Figure 3-13:
Enter the
name of
your
ShortCut on
the first
line in the
ShortCut
Entry dialog
box, and
enter text in
the lower
area.

Preferences	▾ ShortCuts

ShortCut Entry ⓘ

ShortCut Name:

nwj ....

ShortCut Text:

No way, Jose! ....
....
....
....
....

(OK) (Cancel)

4. **Enter the text of your ShortCut by using either the on-screen keyboard or Graffiti.**

   The text you enter appears in the ShortCut Text section.

5. **Tap OK.**

   Your new ShortCut appears on the list of ShortCuts.

Don't use a period as the first character of your ShortCut name. For some reason, ShortCuts whose names begin with a period ("dot ShortCuts," to Palm Computing programmers) do nothing useful for you and me, although they can do nasty things, such as erase all your data or drain your batteries. Try to stick to names made up of letters and numbers when you're creating ShortCuts. Also, ShortCut names can't contain spaces.

Editing a ShortCut

At some point, you may want to change either the name or the contents of a ShortCut.

Follow these steps to edit a ShortCut:

1. **Tap the name of the ShortCut you want to edit.**

   The ShortCut you tap is highlighted to show that you've selected it, as shown in Figure 3-14.

2. **Tap Edit.**

   The ShortCut Entry dialog box opens.

3. **Select the part of the ShortCut you want to replace.**

   The text you select is highlighted to show that you've selected it.

4. **Enter the new text by using either the on-screen keyboard or Graffiti (refer to Chapter 2 for more info about entering text).**

   The text you enter replaces the text you selected.

5. **Tap OK.**

   The ShortCut Entry dialog box closes.

Your revised ShortCut is ready to use at the drop of a stylus.

Figure 3-14: Choose a ShortCut to edit.

Deleting a ShortCut

If you know how to edit a ShortCut, you know how to delete a ShortCut. Just follow the same steps I describe in the preceding section, "Editing a ShortCut," but tap the word *Delete* rather than *Edit.* Zap! Your ShortCut is long gone.

Hacking Up Your Palm Device

No, the heading for this section isn't the latest sequel to *Halloween.* In the Palm Computing universe, *hacks* are applications you can install on your Palm device to add features or to make it behave differently from a normal one. I'm not getting into hacks in any great degree here, although I do want you to know that they exist. Palm devices are catching on in the corporate world in a big way, and some big outfits customize their Palm devices to suit the work they expect people to do. That means that you may have a company-issue Palm device with hacks installed that make it behave in a totally different way from the way I describe in this book.

You can install hacks that change the functions of your buttons, change the way your screen looks, change the things you can do with cut and paste, and lots more. Programmers are coming up with new Palm Computing hacks all the time. Most hacks are useful, such as AppHack, a program that enables you to assign as many as six different programs to each of the four hard buttons. Other hacks are less useful, such as BackHack, which reverses the spelling of all text on your Palm device, so that the word *Record,* for example, comes out as *droceR*. I can't begin to explain why someone would want a program to do that, but rest assured, one does.

One of the most important hacks is HackMaster, the hack that manages other hacks. (Geesh, can this stuff get any more complicated?) Many hacks require you to install HackMaster before installing other hacks. If you're adventurous, check out the Palm Computing-related Web sites listed in Appendix A, and download some hacks to install to your Palm device. When I say "adventurous," I mean that you should be ready to deal with some problems because some hacks are very experimental. In my experience, hacks tend to be fussy and problematic, so I avoid them. Fortunately, they're easy to uninstall.

Chapter 4

Saving Time with Palm Device Time-Savers

*U*sing your Palm device is pretty easy to begin with, and, if you know the ropes, you can save steps here and there and whiz through your work by using the following tips. You may even become a member of the elite ranks of Palm organizer power users. Don't worry — you don't have to buy a uniform or memorize a secret handshake; just be ready for plenty of *esprit de corps*.

I focus on a handful of features that can make you a speedier Palm device user without making you try out anything difficult. I also try to stick to tricks that are part of the Palm Computing operating system and don't require any add-on programs. I deal with accessories and add-on software in Chapters 19 and 20. I've organized all these time-savers into categories so that you can easily find what you need. Enjoy!

General Time-Savers

General time-savers are those you can do at any time or in any application.

Using ShortCuts

The best time-savers are cleverly named *ShortCuts*. You can expand short abbreviations into words and phrases of as many as 45 letters (including spaces) by entering the Graffiti ShortCut symbol, which looks like a cursive letter *L,* and then the abbreviation. (For more info about the Graffiti ShortCut symbol, see Chapter 2.)

When you first buy a Palm device, several ShortCuts are already installed. (To find out how to create your own ShortCuts, see Chapter 3.)

Beaming a business card quickly

If you have a Palm III, Palm IIIx, Palm V, or Palm VII and you've set up your business card for beaming, just hold down the Address Book button for about two seconds. The Beam dialog box opens, and your Palm device searches for a nearby Palm device that's ready to receive your card. (For more info about beaming, see Chapter 9.)

Using your finger rather than the stylus

You can't do anything with a stylus that you can't do with your finger. Because the PalmPilot screen is touch sensitive, your finger can serve as a perfectly good stylus at times. The only reason for a stylus is that many Palm organizer programs contain buttons that are too small to tap with a finger (unless you have very small fingers). A gentle tap with a fingernail can sometimes do just as well as a stylus tap. Be gentle, though; you don't want to scratch the screen.

Checking the time

If you tap the Date tab at the top of the Date Book display area, the current time pops up for a few seconds.

If you use a Palm III, Palm IIIx, Palm V, or Palm VII, the current time is always displayed at the top of the applications list when you tap the Applications soft button. If you want to enter the current time in a memo, you can call on the time stamp ShortCut. Just enter the Graffiti ShortCut symbol, which looks like a cursive, lowercase *L,* and then enter **TS**. I like to use the time stamp as a primitive way to "punch in" when I'm trying to measure time spent on a job. I create a memo, enter a time stamp when I begin, and then enter another time stamp in the memo when I'm finished.

Reassigning a hard button to your favorite program

If you use another program more often than one of the standard Palm organizer applications, you can reassign one of the four application hard buttons to start that program. Many people don't use the Memo Pad or To Do List nearly as much as the Date Book or Address Book, so they reassign the Memo Pad button to make it run another program. Because my girlfriend didn't find the Memo Pad especially useful, she reassigned the Memo Pad button to make it run the game Boggle. You can also get a hack named AppHack that enables you to launch as many as 24 different programs from the hard buttons by pressing two buttons at one time (for more info about hacks, see Chapter 3). I still just go to the Applications screen to start my programs, although you can take your pick.

Application Time-Savers

These time-savers apply directly to the four main applications that come with your Palm device. They can save you loads of time.

Pressing hard buttons to change categories

When you first press the Memo hard button, you see all your memos. If you press the Memo button a second time, the memos in the Business category appear. Each time you press the Memo button again, you see a different category until you've cycled around to the All category. All four standard application hard buttons behave in the same way; push the button several times to run through several different categories. The Date Book button is slightly different in that it shows you different views of the Date Book each time — day and then week and then month. If you don't have any items filed in a particular category, your Palm device conveniently skips that category, of course.

Viewing different dates by pressing buttons

Whenever you want to check your schedule in a jiffy, remember that you can get to any date by pressing buttons so that you don't have to dig for your stylus. Just press the Date Book button once to see Daily view, twice to see

Weekly view, or three times to see Monthly view. After you see the view you want, press the up or down scroll buttons to move to the next day, week, or month. By cleverly combining button clicks, you can see your schedule for any day on the calendar. Granted, whipping out the stylus and picking the date you want is sometimes easier, but when your hands are full, the stylus can be one too many things to hold.

Uncluttering the Date Book

The Date Book shows a blank for every hour of your workday. That can make your schedule look cluttered and hard to read. If you set up your Date Book preferences to have your day begin and end at the same time, the display area shows only entries for the times at which you've scheduled appointments; the rest of the screen is blank, as shown in Figure 4-1.

Figure 4-1:
To make your screen easier to read, set your workday to both begin and end at the same times every day. Drag and drop to change appointment times.

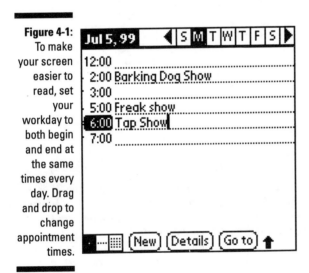

If you press the Date Book hard button twice, you see the Weekly view of the Address Book. Weekly view shows a collection of bars representing appointments for the week. If you want to change the scheduled time of an appointment, just drag the bar representing that appointment to the time you prefer, as shown in Figure 4-2. Sad to say, you can't drag an appointment from one week to another.

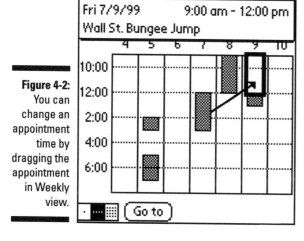

Figure 4-2:
You can
change an
appointment
time by
dragging the
appointment
in Weekly
view.

Cut, copy, and paste

Windows and Macintosh users have been cutting, copying, and pasting text for years. You can do the same trick with your Palm device. Just select some text by drawing an imaginary line through the text with your stylus, and then tap the Menu soft button and choose Edit⇨Cut or Edit⇨Copy. Although cutting makes the text you select disappear, don't worry — it's not gone forever. The text goes to a place named the *clipboard*. The same thing happens when you choose Copy, except that the original text stays put and a copy of that text goes to the clipboard. To make the text reappear in another place, just tap where you want to place the text and choose Edit⇨Paste. Even if you turn off your Palm device, the last text you put on the clipboard stays on the clipboard, so you may find that you can paste text you copied weeks or months ago. Be aware, however, that every time you cut or copy text, that text replaces whatever text was previously on the clipboard.

Adding multiple items to a category

If you want to add a series of new items to a single category, simply display that category and begin creating items. Whatever category you display before creating new items becomes the category assigned to the new items. If I want to make a list of things I need to do at PC Expo, for example, I press the To Do List hard button several times until my PC Expo category appears (assuming that I created a PC Expo category), and then I just start adding items. Because every new item I create while in a certain category turns up in that category, I can see everything in the category as I add items.

Graffiti Time-Savers

If you've really taken to Graffiti, you may appreciate the quick time-savers in this section.

Start writing to create new items

If you want to add a new item to any standard Palm organizer application except for the Address Book, press the hard button for that application and begin entering text in the Graffiti area. This trick works only if you use Graffiti. Whenever the Palm device senses that you're entering Graffiti, it naturally does the right thing — it opens a new item in which to store the new text.

Open Graffiti Help with a single stroke

You can open Graffiti Help by drawing a line with your stylus from the Graffiti writing area to the top of the display area. If you've already earned your black belt in Graffiti, you can assign that stroke to perform one of four other tasks: turn on the backlight, display the on-screen keyboard, beam the current item to another Palm device, or turn off and lock your Palm device. To reassign the upstroke command, tap the Applications soft button, tap Prefs, choose Buttons from the pull-down menu in the upper-right corner, and then tap Pen; the Pen dialog box appears, as shown in Figure 4-3. (For more info about customizing the functions of your Palm device, see Chapter 3.)

Figure 4-3: Customize what happens when you use the Graffiti upstroke.

Part II
Getting Down to Business

The 5th Wave
By Rich Tennant

Mitch would never be sure it was laughter he heard that day at the airport but he never again traveled with his Pez handheld computing device.

In this part . . .

The programs that come with your Palm device can do a great deal if you know all the options. You can create and manage appointments, addresses, tasks, and memos by following the steps in this part. You also find out how to beam data to other Palm devices with just the touch of a button.

Chapter 5

Names and Addresses in a ZIP

I find it incredibly handy to have all the names and addresses I need in electronic form rather than on paper. I love being able to find names in a flash, change details, and keep track of bits and pieces of information about everyone in my social and professional life.

You'd get pretty uncomfortable if you had to walk around with a desktop computer stuffed in your pocket or purse — and you'd look pretty funny, too. Just because I want you to be comfortable (and because I *know* that you're good-looking), I show you how to do all your address keeping on a Palm device because it can always be with you.

Accessing the Address Book

To call up the Address Book on your Palm device, just press the Address Book hard button (the second button from the left at the bottom, as shown in Figure 5-1), which calls up the Address List. My sample Address List is shown in Figure 5-2. Then read the rest of this chapter.

Address Book
hard button

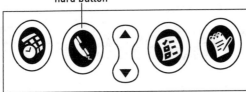

Figure 5-1:
The Address
Book hard
button.

Address List	▼ All
Alifont, "Bull"	555-6597 W
DeDark, Fredda	555-9875 W
Early, Otto B.	555-1324 W
Fergus, Freddie	555-5689 W
Palm III Accessories	801-431-1536 W
Snivel, Heather	555-6127 W
Technical Support	847-676-1441 W
Turpentine, Snidely	800-555-9724 W
Veblen, Thorstein	555-3467 W
Zarathustra, Jake	555-9712 W
Look Up:	(New)

Figure 5-2:
Your
address list
shows all
the names
you've
collected.

Putting Names in Your Palm Device

I know more than a few people who enter and make changes to their Address List on a desktop computer and then transfer the whole shebang to their Palm device just to look up names while they're traveling. That's okay. Actually, most of those folks have employees who enter the information for them; that's the easiest method, although most of us don't have that luxury. (See Chapter 12 for more info about keeping up the Address List in the Palm Desktop program.) The fact is that you can enter all the information you need right on the Palm device, no matter where you are.

Adding a new name

Many people have relied on a Little Black Book since even before Casanova. The paper kind served well until the computer came along and enabled you to find one name from a list of thousands faster than you can say "What's-his-name." Speed isn't the only advantage of electronic address lists; the Palm device looks up a name from your list and plugs that name into an item on the To Do List, Memo Pad, or Date Book to save you the trouble of retyping. Before you can look up a name, however, you have to add the name to the Address Book.

Use these steps to store a name in the Address Book:

1. **With the Address List visible, tap the New button at the bottom of the Address List.**

   The Address Edit screen appears.

2. **Tap anywhere on the Last Name line.**

   The words *Last Name* become highlighted to show that you've selected the Last Name line, as shown in Figure 5-3.

Figure 5-3:
The name of
the line you
tap is
highlighted
to show
where
you're
working.

Address Edit	▼ Unfiled
Last name: Alifont	
First name:	
Title:	
Company:	
▼ Work:	
▼ Home:	
▼ Fax:	
▼ Other:	
▼ E-mail:	
Address:	

(Done) (Details...) (Note) ▓

3. **Enter the last name of the person you're adding by using Graffiti or the on-screen keyboard (see Chapter 2 for more info about entering text).**

   The letters you enter appear on the Last Name line.

4. **Follow Steps 2 and 3 to enter information on the First Name, Title, and Company lines.**

   The text you enter appears on the lines you choose.

5. **Tap anywhere on the Work line.**

   The word becomes highlighted to show that you've selected it.

6. **Enter the person's work telephone number.**

7. **Follow Steps 5 and 6 to enter the person's home phone number.**

8. **If you want to enter a type of phone number that isn't shown, tap Other.**

   A list appears, showing the different types of phone numbers you can enter, including pager and mobile numbers.

9. **Tap the name of the phone number type you want to enter, such as Mobile.**

   The type you choose replaces the word *Other,* as you see in Figure 5-4.

Figure 5-4: Choose the type of phone number you want to enter if it's not shown.

10. **Enter the phone number in the Graffiti number area.**

    The text you enter appears on the new line.

11. **If you want to enter your contact's mailing address, press the scroll-down hard button at the bottom-center of the Palm device.**

    The lower half of the contact form appears, enabling you to enter mailing address information, as shown in Figure 5-5.

12. **Enter mailing address information on the appropriate lines, just as you did in the preceding steps.**

    The information you enter appears on the appropriate lines.

13. **When you finish entering the information, click Done at the bottom of the Address Edit screen.**

    The Address Edit screen disappears, and the Address List reappears.

Now you're ready to find anyone in your personal *Who's Who* faster than you can say "Who?"

Figure 5-5:
Wait! You
can find
more at the
bottom of
the form.

```
┌─────────────────────────────────┐
│ ▐Address Edit▌        ▼ Unfiled │
│  ▼ Other:                       │
│  ▼ E-mail: phinmcfink@farley.com│
│  Address: 1 Abacus Road         │
│     City: Zoopville             │
│    State: AK                    │
│ ▐Zip Code▌ 99912                │
│  Country:                       │
│ Custom 1:                       │
│ Custom 2:                       │
│ Custom 3:                       │
│ Custom 4:                       │
│ ( Done ) (Details...) ( Note )  ↑ ▼│
└─────────────────────────────────┘
```

You probably noticed the downward-pointing triangle next to each phone number line. Whenever you see that character on a Palm screen, it means that a pull-down list is hiding behind that button, where you can choose other options simply by tapping the triangle and then tapping your choice. Although every address record contains three phone number lines and an e-mail line, you can use any of the phone number lines to store any of seven different types of phone numbers or an e-mail address. For example, if you want to save one person's work number and pager number but not his home number, tap the triangle next to Home and pick Pager from the list. Now the number you enter is shown as a pager number.

If you have a list of names and addresses in another contact program on a desktop or laptop computer, you can enter them in the desktop program as a list and then HotSync the whole bunch to your Palm device. As you can see, entering names and addresses in the Palm device is easy, but when you have a large collection of names, you save time by letting your computers take care of the job. For more info about installing and operating the desktop programs for either Windows or Macintosh, see Chapters 12 and 13.

What's in a name? Editing an address record

It seems that some people change their addresses more often than they change their socks. You can't very well tell them to stop moving, but you can keep up with their latest addresses by editing their address records in your Palm device. You may want to say something to them about their socks, though.

These steps help you to change an entry in the Address Book:

1. **With the Address List visible, enter in the Graffiti box the first few letters of the last name you want to edit.**

   The letters you enter appear on the Look Up line at the bottom of the display area. If the name you're looking for is visible to start with, you don't have to look it up, of course.

2. **Tap the name of the person whose record you want to edit.**

   The Address View screen appears, as shown in Figure 5-6, showing details about the contact you chose.

Figure 5-6:
Address view shows you what's already in the Address Book.

Address View screen:

Address View — Unfiled

Magnolia Thunderblossom
President
Clemtexx

Work: **555-3200**

Planning to purchase 9000 lbs of french fries next month.

(Done) (Edit) (New)

3. **Tap Edit at the bottom of the display area.**

   The Address Edit screen appears.

4. **Enter new information the same way you did when you first created the address record (see the preceding section, "Adding a new name.")**

   New information appears on the appropriate lines of the screen.

5. **If you want to replace existing information, select the text you want to replace by drawing a horizontal line through it.**

   The text is highlighted.

6. **Enter new text in the Graffiti box at the bottom of the display area.**

   As in your favorite word processor, the text you enter replaces the text you selected. (For more info about entering text, see Chapter 2.)

7. **When you've made all the changes you want to make, tap Done.**

   The Address Edit screen disappears and the Address List screen reappears.

A Palm device saves all your changes as soon as you tap Done. If you want to change the person's address or other details back to the way they were, you have to go through the whole edit process again. In other words, you don't have an Undo feature to put things back the way they were.

Attaching a note to an address record

You want to know lots of things about a person — where she likes to go, what he said to you the last time you spoke to him, how much she owes you — whatever. You can attach all sorts of information to a person's address record in the form of a note.

To attach a note to an address, follow these steps:

1. **With the Address List visible, tap the name of the person to whose record you want to add a note.**

   The Address View screen appears, showing details about the contact you chose.

2. **Tap the Menu soft button at the bottom of the display area.**

   The menu bar appears at the top of the display area, as shown in Figure 5-7.

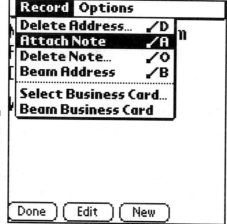

Figure 5-7:
You can order from the menu to create a note.

3. **Choose Record⇨Attach Note.**

   A blank note screen appears.

4. **Enter the note text in the Graffiti box at the bottom of the display area, or use the on-screen keyboard.**

   The text you enter appears, as shown in Figure 5-8.

Thunderblossom, Magnolia

Planning to purchase 9000 lbs of
french fries next month.

(Done) (Delete...)

Figure 5-8:
Enter plain
old text on
the Note
screen.

5. Tap Done at the bottom of the Note screen.

The Note screen disappears, and the Address View screen reappears.

6. Tap Done again.

The Address View screen disappears, and the Address List reappears.

If you enter information in a note and want to find the info again, you can use the Palm Find tool to search all the data on your Palm device. For example, if you add a note to someone's record that says "drives a Studebaker," you can tap the Find soft button in the bottom-right corner of the screen and then enter **Studebaker** to find the person who drives one.

Marking your business card

Now that everybody who's anybody has a Palm device (after all, you have one and I have one, and that's all that matters to me), we can take advantage of the Palm infrared port to exchange our business cards. Before you beam your business card to anyone, you have to enter an address record containing your own name and contact information, as I describe in the section "Adding a new name," earlier in this chapter.

An *infrared (IR) port* is standard equipment on your Palm III and later models. The port is optional on the PalmPilot Professional and earlier models. Infrared lets you *beam* information from one Palm device to another. *Beaming* is when you point two Palm devices at each other and send data across the air using an invisible beam of light. (See Chapter 9 for more info about beaming.) You can even buy software that lets you change the channels on your TV with the Palm infrared feature, (which sounds cool but doesn't really work that well). In the normal course of business, you can beam your business card (as well as other addresses, to-do items, memos, and appointments) to other Palm users.

When I send my business card to you via a Palm device, what I'm really doing is beaming a name from my Palm device Address Book to the Address Book on your Palm device. The name I send you just happens to be my own.

Here's how to set up your Palm device to send your business card:

1. **With the Address List visible, enter the first few letters of your last name in the Graffiti box.**

   The letters you enter appear on the Look Up line at the bottom of the display area.

2. **Tap your name in the Address List.**

   The Address View screen appears, showing details about your contact record.

3. **Tap the Menu soft button at the bottom of the display area.**

   The menu bar appears at the top of the display area.

4. **Choose Record⇨Select Business Card.**

   The Select Business Card dialog box opens, as shown in Figure 5-9.

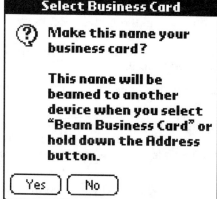

Figure 5-9: Mark your own name to serve as your business card.

5. **Tap Yes at the bottom of the Select Business Card dialog box to close it.**

   A small icon that looks like a file card appears at the top of the Address View screen.

6. **Tap Done at the bottom of the display area.**

   The Address View screen disappears, and the Address List reappears.

You don't absolutely have to mark a business card if you don't plan to use this feature. If you use the beaming feature frequently, you save time if you mark your business card because you don't have to spend time looking up your own name when you want to send a card. I owned a Palm device for several months before I ever beamed my business card, but I had my name marked anyway. If deep-space aliens had showed up like they do in the movie *Independence Day,* I'd have been ready to beam them my friendly greetings (for all the good it would do — they all use Macs).

Using the Names You've Entered

If you're one of those lucky folks who has an assistant to enter your Palm data so that all you do is use what's been entered, the rest of this chapter is for you. After you know how to find the stuff you've collected, you're in business!

Finding Mr. Right (or whomever)

If you took the time to enter a bunch of names in your Palm device, I'd guess that you want to find the names again. Call me crazy, but that's what I thought.

Here's the quickest way to find a name in the Address Book:

1. **With the Address List visible, enter in the Graffiti box the first few letters of the last name you want to find.**

   The letters you enter appear on the Look Up line at the bottom of the display area, as shown in Figure 5-10.

   If you don't like messing with Graffiti, you can press the hard scroll-down button on the Palm device to scroll through your address list. The Address Book can hold thousands of names, so if your list is long, scrolling can be laborious.

2. **Tap the name of the person whose record you want to view.**

   The Address View screen appears, showing details about the contact you chose.

3. **When you're finished, tap Done at the bottom of the display area.**

   The Address View screen disappears, and the Address List reappears.

Figure 5-10: Your Palm device figures out who you're looking for when you enter the first few letters of a last name.

Address List	▼ All
DeDark, Fredda	555-9875 W
Dogg, Pat D.	555-5474 W
Early, Otto B.	555-1324 W
Fergus, Freddie	555-5689 W
Palm III Accessories	801-431-1536 W
Snivel, Heather	555-6127 W
Technical Support	847-676-1441 W
Thunderbloss..., Magnoli	555-3200 W
Turpentine, Snidely	800-555-9724 W
Veblen, Thorstein	555-3467 W
Zarathustra, Jake	555-9712 W

Look Up: za   (New)

If you want to make finding addresses easier, you can assign categories to names on the Address List. Then when you press the Address Book button several times, you cycle through the different address categories until you see the category you want to use. For example, you can assign the category Business to some names and the category Personal to other names. When you press the Address Book button the first time, you see all the names in your collection. The second time you press the button, you see the names assigned to the Business category; and the third time, you see the names assigned to the Personal category; and so on. You may be completely happy keeping all your names uncategorized. That's fine, too.

To assign a category to any name in your list, open the record for editing, as I describe in the section "What's in a name? Editing an address record," earlier in this chapter, and then pick the category you want to assign to your contact in the upper-right corner of the form. You can manage Address Book categories in exactly the same way as you manage categories of to-do items. (See Chapter 6 for more info about managing to-do item categories.)

The Quicklist category is preset in the Address Book to make room for addresses you use frequently and need to find in a hurry. You can use the category for the most important people in your life.

Deleting a name

The main reason to add a name to the Address Book is to help you remember important things about a person. However, sometimes you'd rather forget some people in your list. I won't mention any names.

To delete an unwanted name from the Address Book, follow these steps:

1. **With the Address List visible, enter in the Graffiti box the first few letters of the last name you want to delete.**

   The letters you enter appear on the Look Up line at the bottom of the display area.

2. **Tap the name of the person whose record you want to delete.**

   The Address View screen appears, showing details about the contact you chose.

3. **Tap the Menu soft button at the bottom of the display area.**

   The menu bar appears at the top of the display area.

4. **Choose Record⇨Delete Address.**

   The Delete Address dialog box opens, as shown in Figure 5-11. The dialog box asks whether you want to archive the item. (For more info about archived items, see Chapters 12 and 13.)

Figure 5-11: Deleting the names of those who no longer interest you is easy.

5. **Tap OK.**

   The Address List reappears, minus one name.

If you delete a name in a fit of pique and then wish that you could bring it back, all is not entirely lost. If you haven't used HotSync between the time you deleted the name and the time you want it back, you can find the name in the archive on your desktop computer. You can make a slight change in the address information and then resynchronize to make the offending name a part of your list again. Then you can kiss and make up. (I discuss synchronization in Chapter 11 and archiving in Chapters 12 and 13.) Fractured friendships are another issue altogether.

Deleting a note from an address record

Sometimes the note you've attached to someone's address becomes out of date. You can change the contents of the note by using the same steps you used to create the note, or you can just delete the entire note.

Here's how to delete a note attached to an address:

1. **With the Address List visible, tap the name of the person from whose record you want to delete a note.**

   The Address View screen appears, showing details about the contact you chose.

2. **Tap the Menu soft button at the bottom of the display area.**

   The menu bar appears at the top of the display area.

3. **Choose Record⇨Delete Note, as shown in Figure 5-12.**

Figure 5-12: You can delete a note from a record, too.

   The Delete Note dialog box opens.

4. **Tap Yes at the bottom of the Delete Note dialog box.**

   The Delete Note dialog box closes, and the Address View screen reappears.

5. **Tap Done at the bottom of the Address View screen.**

   The Address View screen disappears, and the Address List reappears.

Zap! Your note is gone for good. (Well, not really for good; see Chapter 12 for details about how to recover an address from your archive.)

Setting Address Book preferences

If you don't like the way the Address Book looks when it first opens, you can change its appearance . . . a little. I think that the Address Book is just fine as it is, but if you simply must rearrange your list, here's how:

1. **With the Address List visible, tap the Menu soft button at the bottom of the display area.**

   The menu bar appears at the top of the display area.

2. **Choose Options⇨Preferences.**

   The Address Book Preferences dialog box opens, as shown in Figure 5-13.

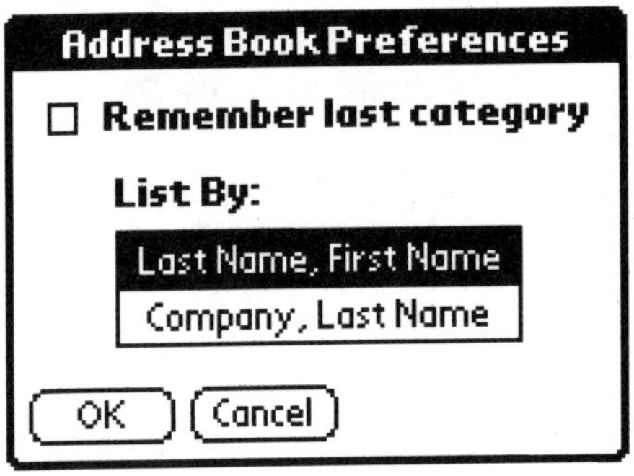

Figure 5-13:
You can express your preferences in the Address Book Preferences dialog box.

> **Address Book Preferences**
>
> ☐ **Remember last category**
>
> **List By:**
>
> | Last Name, First Name |
> | Company, Last Name |
>
> (OK) (Cancel)

3. **From the List By box, choose either Last Name, First Name or Company, Last Name.**

   The choice you make is highlighted.

4. **Tap the Remember Last Category box if you normally want the Address Book to open to the last category you used.**

   If you don't check the Remember Last Category box, the Address Book always opens to show all names. I think that it's better to leave the box unchecked, but that's a matter of personal preference.

Setting up custom fields

Sometimes you need to keep track of something about the people you know that doesn't already have a line (or *field*) on the Address List. For example, if your job involves selling merchandise to retail stores, the Address Book probably contains the names of all the store buyers to whom you sell. The Address Book includes four lines at the end of the Address Edit screen that you can rename to fit your needs. These four lines are *custom fields.* You may want to set up one custom field to keep track of which type of merchandise each buyer buys, such as housewares, appliances, and shoes. You can rename one of the custom fields to Specialty to show each buyer's area of interest.

To set up your custom fields, follow these steps:

1. **With the Address List visible, tap the Menu soft button at the bottom of the display area.**

   The menu bar appears at the top of the display area.

2. **Choose Options⇨Rename Custom Fields.**

   The Rename Custom Fields dialog box opens, as shown in Figure 5-14.

3. **Select the field you want to rename.**

   The text you select is highlighted.

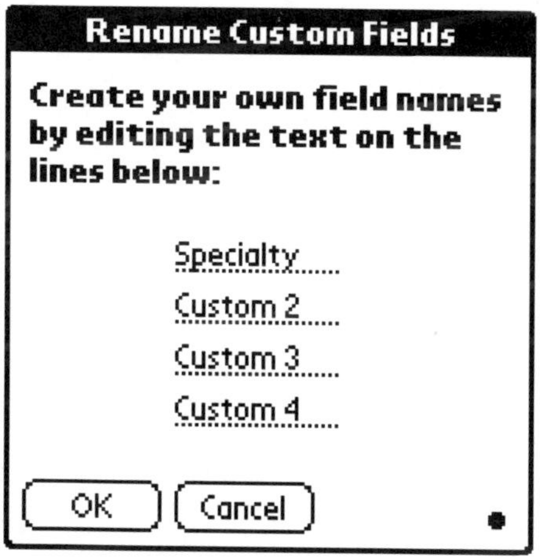

Figure 5-14: Just replace the name Custom 1 with the field name you want.

> **Rename Custom Fields**
>
> **Create your own field names by editing the text on the lines below:**
>
> Specialty
> Custom 2
> Custom 3
> Custom 4
>
> (OK) (Cancel)

4. **Enter the name you want for the field with either the on-screen keyboard or Graffiti (see Chapter 2 for more info about entering text).**

   The text you enter appears as the new field name.

5. **Rename the other custom fields by following Steps 3 and 4.**

   The text you enter appears as the new field name.

6. **When you've renamed all the fields you want to rename, click OK.**

   The Rename Custom Fields dialog box closes, and the Address List reappears.

You don't absolutely have to rename custom fields to use them. You can just enter information in the fields and remember that the field named Custom 1 contains a certain type of entry. Renaming the custom fields just makes them a little more useful and easier to understand. When you rename a custom field, the field name is changed in all address records.

Chapter 6

To-Dos That YOU Do!

*W*ho doesn't have a zillion things to do these days? Just keeping track of the tasks you need to take care of is a full-time job. The only thing worse than keeping track of your tasks is actually doing all those things. And even if you use a computer for many of your daily tasks, you probably can't stay chained to the desk all day; you need to move around, while keeping track of all the things you did in all the places you went.

The To Do List on your Palm device can help you keep a handle on all those little errands and projects that take up all your time. You can add a task when you think of it rather than wait to get back to your computer. By the time I get back to my desk, I usually forget that terribly important detail I need to take care of.

I assume in this chapter that you're using your Palm device exactly the way it comes out of the box. Although that's what most people do, that's not your only choice. A couple of other chapters in this book tell you how to find other programs to replace the To Do List and how to install them. If you've replaced the To Do List with some other program, such as To Do Plus, many of the instructions in this chapter won't work for you. I don't want to discourage you from trying other programs — lots of good ones exist — but, unfortunately, I can't cover all the third-party software that's out there for Palm devices.

Just push the To Do List hard button (it's the second one from the right at the bottom of your Palm device, as shown in Figure 6-1) to call up the To Do List. Then do whatever you want to do with your to-dos!

To Do List
hard button

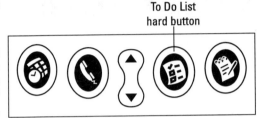

Figure 6-1:
Press the To
Do List
button to
bring up
your list of
to-dos.

Adding New To-Dos

Adding items to the To Do List is as easy as you want to make it. If you want to keep track of short lists of simple projects, you can go a long way with the tools that come with a Palm device. If your planning process involves long lists of elaborate plans and projects and goes beyond the capability of the Palm organizer's To Do List, you may need some extra help in the form of extra software or a daily download from your desktop computer. You can always rely on a desktop program, such as ACT! or Goldmine, to do all the heavy lifting, and you can just HotSync your Palm device to your desktop every day to keep a handy portable copy of your information. For more info about using your Palm device with third-party software, see Part III.

Creating a to-do item

You can take advantage of the powers of the To Do List only if you've entered the to-dos you have to do. No voodoo is involved with To Do — just press a button, tap with a stylus, and you're in business.

Here's how to add a new item to the To Do List:

1. **With the To Do List open, tap New at the bottom of the To Do List.**

   A new, blank line appears on the To Do List.

2. **Enter the name of your task with either the on-screen keyboard or Graffiti (see Chapter 2 for more info about entering text).**

   The name of the task you enter appears on the new line, as shown in Figure 6-2.

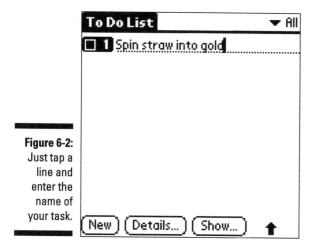

3. Tap any blank area of the screen or press the Scroll Down button.

The highlighting next to your new item disappears.

Ta-da! It's new task to call your very own.

You can use an even simpler way, of course, to enter a new to-do: Press the To Do List button and enter the name of your task by using either the on-screen keyboard or Graffiti (see Chapter 2 for more info about entering text). Your Palm device automatically creates a new to-do with the name you enter.

Entering details for a to-do item

You may not be satisfied with a To Do List that keeps track of only the names of your tasks. Knowing what a productive, demanding person you are (or could be, if you really wanted to), the To Do List enables you to assign priorities, categories, and due dates to each task.

To add details to your tasks, follow these steps:

1. With the To Do List open, tap the name of the task to which you want to add details.

Highlighting appears next to the name of the task you chose.

2. Tap Details at the bottom of the display area.

The To Do Item Details dialog box opens.

3. **To set the priority of your item, tap one of the numbers (1 through 5) next to the word** *Priority.*

   The number you tap is highlighted.

   If the only detail you want to change about your task is the priority, you can simply tap the priority number on the To Do List and pick the priority number from the drop-down list.

4. **To assign a category to your task, tap the triangle next to the word** *Category.*

   A list of available categories appears. Although the option of assigning categories helps you organize your to-do list, you don't have to assign a category to a task. I explain how to use categories in the section "Viewing Items By Category," later in this chapter.

5. **Tap the name of the category you want to assign to your task.**

   The list disappears, and the name of the category you chose appears.

6. **To assign a due date to your task, tap the triangle next to the words** *Due Date.*

   A list appears, giving you these choices: Today, Tomorrow, One Week Later, No Date, and Choose Date, as shown in Figure 6-3.

Figure 6-3:
Pick the due date for your to-do in the To Do Item Details dialog box.

7. **Tap the name of the due date you want for your task.**

   The list disappears, and the date you chose appears, unless you tapped Choose Date. Tapping Choose Date opens the Due Date screen, which looks like a calendar, as shown in Figure 6-4.

8. **If you tapped Choose Date, tap the desired due date for your task on the calendar on the Due Date screen.**

   The Due Date screen disappears, and the date you chose appears in the To Do Item Details dialog box.

Due Date

◀ **1999** ▶

Jan	Feb	Mar	Apr	May	Jun
Jul	Aug	Sep	Oct	**Nov**	Dec

S	M	T	W	T	F	S
	1	2	3	4	5	6
7	8	9	10	11	12	13
14	15	16	17	18	19	20
21	22	23	24	25	26	27
28	29	30

(Cancel) (Today)

Figure 6-4:
You can choose a date from the calendar, if you want.

9. **If you want to mark your entry as private, tap the check box next to the word *Private*.**

   A check appears in the check box to show that the task is private.

   Private entries normally appear with your other entries, but you can also hide your private entries. Just tap the Applications soft button to call up the applications list, choose Security, and tap the word *Hide*. (For more info about privacy and passwords, see Chapter 3.)

10. **Tap OK.**

    The To Do Item Details dialog box closes, and the To Do List reappears with the changes you made visible on the screen.

You may have noticed when you were creating a new task that the Details button was available on-screen the whole time. If you want to add all sorts of details while you're adding a new task, nothing can stop you. However, if you're in a hurry and just want to enter the task quickly, you can enter just the name of the task and then add details later.

Attaching notes to items

A popular book by Robert Fulghum tells us that we learn everything we need to know in kindergarten. That's okay, I guess, but if you didn't get past kindergarten, don't mention it in your next job interview.

In the same way, many tasks need a bit more explanation than a quick subject line can describe, so you may need to add a note to your task if you want to keep track of a detailed explanation along with a task.

Here's how to add a note to a to-do item:

1. **With the To Do List open, tap the name of the task to which you want to add a note.**

   The check box to the left of the item is highlighted to show which task you've selected.

2. **Tap Details at the bottom of the To Do List.**

   The To Do Item Details dialog box opens.

3. **Tap Note at the bottom of the To Do Item Details dialog box.**

   A blank Note screen appears.

4. **Enter text by using either the on-screen keyboard or Graffiti (see Chapter 2 for more info about entering text).**

   The text you entered appears, as shown in Figure 6-5.

Figure 6-5:
If you have
more
detailed
instructions
about your
task, add a
note.

> **Spin straw into gold**
>
> Find out the name of that little troll before tomorrow
>
> (Done) (Delete...)

5. **Tap Done at the bottom of the Note screen.**

   The Note screen disappears and the To Do List reappears. A small, square icon appears to the right of the item you chose, to show that a note is attached. If you want to view a note attached to a to-do, just click the note icon.

The Note screen also has a Delete button that lets you delete a note after you read it. I discuss another way to delete notes attached to to-do items in the section "Deleting a note," later in this chapter, although deleting a note from the Note screen is as good a method as any.

If you've created a note on the Memo List or attached a note to an entry in the Address Book, you find that the general idea of creating notes stays the same throughout your Palm device. Unfortunately, notes attached to different types of Palm Computing items don't have anything to do with each other. For example, you can't move a note from the Memo List to the To Do List or from the To Do List to the Address Book. Not now, at least; maybe in the future.

Viewing Items By Category

To-do items always belong to a category of one type or another. If you don't assign a category yourself, your Palm device automatically assigns the category Unfiled. You can see in the upper-right corner of the screen the name of the category you're viewing. When you first press the To Do List button, the word in the corner is *All,* which means that you're viewing all your tasks, regardless of category. You can change your view to a different category in two ways: the short way and the even shorter way. (Geesh, they make these things easy to use!)

I start with the short way:

1. **With the To Do List open, tap the name of the category in the upper-right corner of the screen.**

   The list of available categories appears. The first time you use your Palm device, the list has four categories: All, Business, Personal, and Unfiled. After you have used your Palm device for the first time, a fifth option, Edit Categories, is available, as shown in Figure 6-6. I talk about that option later in this section.

2. **Tap the name of the category you want to display.**

   The To Do List changes to display only the items assigned to the category you chose. The name of the category you're viewing appears in the upper-right corner of the screen.

The shorter way to change the category you're viewing is — you guessed it — even shorter. Just press the To Do List button more than once. Each time you press the To Do List button, you see the next category for which you've created entries. The categories appear in alphabetical order, including any categories you may have added yourself (see the following section, "Adding categories"). Neat, huh?

```
┌─────────────────────────────────┐
│ ┌─────────────┐┌──────────────┐  │
│ │To Do List   ││All           │  │
│ └─────────────┘│Business      │  │
│ ☐ 1 Spin straw into│Personal  │  │
│ ☐ 1 Call Prince abou│Unfiled  │  │
│ ☐ 1 Open a savings│Edit Categories...│
│ ☐ 1 Get new fillings└──────────┘  │
│                                   │
│                                   │
│                                   │
│                                   │
│ ┌────┐ ┌────────┐ ┌──────┐        │
│ │New │ │Details...│ │Show...│     │
│ └────┘ └────────┘ └──────┘        │
└─────────────────────────────────┘
```

Figure 6-6:
To switch
categories,
just pick
from the list.

Adding categories

People who use Palm devices are often busy people with scads of things to do. If you're usually juggling too many tasks to fit on one little screen, you'll find assigning categories to your tasks useful. You can look through them all with a few clicks of the To Do List button. Sooner or later, you'll want to create categories of your own.

Follow these steps to create a new category:

1. **With the To Do List open, tap the name of the category in the upper-right corner of the screen.**

   The list of available categories appears.

2. **Tap the words *Edit Categories.***

   The Edit Categories screen appears.

3. **Tap New.**

   The Edit Categories dialog box opens.

4. **Enter the name of the category you want to add by using either the on-screen keyboard or Graffiti (see Chapter 2 for more info about entering text).**

5. **Tap OK.**

   The name you entered appears in the Edit Categories dialog box, and the dialog box closes.

6. **Tap OK again.**

   The Edit Categories screen disappears.

Remember that you're better off if you stick to a few well-used categories rather than dozens of categories you never look at. A to-do list should focus on the things you really plan to do; otherwise, you could just call it a Round Tuit list — things you'll do if you ever get around to it.

Deleting categories

If you've gone hog-wild and created categories you never use, delete some of them. You can also create a category for a special event and then delete the category when the event ends. I do that for trade shows sometimes; I create a category for things I have to do during the show and then delete the category when the show is over.

Follow these steps to delete a category:

1. **With the To Do List open, tap the name of the category in the upper-right corner of the screen.**

   The list of available categories appears.

2. **Tap Edit Categories.**

   The Edit Categories screen appears.

3. **Tap the name of the category you want to delete.**

   The category you tap is highlighted to show that you've selected it.

4. **Tap Delete.**

   The Remove Category dialog box opens, warning you that all the items in that category will be reassigned to the Unfiled category. If no items are assigned to the category you picked to delete, the Remove Category dialog box doesn't open.

5. **Tap Yes.**

   The Remove Categories dialog box closes and your category is deleted.

6. **Tap OK.**

   The Edit Categories screen disappears.

The All and Unfiled categories don't show up on the Edit Categories screen because they're not really categories. You can't get rid of the view that shows all your tasks (a mistake you probably wouldn't want to make) because finding things you categorized by mistake would be harder.

Renaming categories

What's in a name? Shakespeare's Romeo thought that it didn't matter, but look what happened to him. Sometimes you want your categories to make sense, so you change the names to fit your style.

To rename a category, follow these steps:

1. **With the To Do List open, tap the name of the category in the upper-right corner of the screen.**

   The list of available categories appears.

2. **Tap Edit Categories.**

   The Edit Categories screen appears.

3. **Tap the name of the category you want to rename.**

   The name of the category is highlighted to show that you've selected it.

4. **Tap Rename.**

   The Edit Categories dialog box opens.

5. **Enter the name of the category you want to add by using either the on-screen keyboard or Graffiti (see Chapter 2 for more info about entering text).**

6. **Tap OK.**

   The name you entered replaces the preceding name of the category in the Edit Categories dialog box, and the dialog box closes.

7. **Tap OK again.**

   The Edit Categories screen disappears.

Because your categories can be sorted and displayed in alphabetical order, you may want to pick category names that fall in line a certain way. Business tasks come before Personal tasks in more ways than alphabetical order. On the other hand, you can cycle through all your categories with a few clicks of the To Do List button so that you can see all your tasks without much fuss.

What to Do with the To-Dos You Do

Even if you don't enter to-do items yourself, you may wind up with a collection of tasks on your list that got sent to you by another person or by a program on your desktop computer. (See the following section and Chapters 9, 12, and 13 for more info about beaming your to-dos and connecting your Palm device to a desktop computer.) After you have to-dos, you need to know what to do. (Anybody else feel a little dizzy?)

Have I got a job for you? Beaming to-dos!

You don't have to keep your to-dos to yourself. If you have a Palm III or later model, you can beam tasks to other people if they're similarly equipped. Although beaming to-dos is reasonably safe and totally sanitary, beaming too many tasks at people can make them sick — that is, sick of all the tasks you're sending. (You can read more in Chapter 9 about beaming.)

To beam a to-do item from one Palm device to another, follow these steps:

1. **With the To Do List open, tap the name of the task you want to beam to another Palm III.**

   The check box to the left of the item is highlighted to show which task you've selected.

2. **Tap the Menu soft button at the bottom of the display area.**

   The menu bar appears at the top of the display area.

3. **Choose Record⇨Beam Item, as shown in Figure 6-7.**

Figure 6-7:
With a Palm III, you can beam your tasks away.

Record	Edit	Options
Delete Item...	/D	tion card
Attach Note	/A	
Delete Note...	/O	
Purge...	/E	
Beam Item	/B	
Beam Category		

[New] [Details...] [Show...]

The Beam dialog box opens.

4. **Tap OK.**

   The Beam dialog box closes, and the To Do List reappears.

Remember that the beaming feature of a Palm device works just like the remote control for your TV. The two Palm devices have to be pointed at each other and reasonably close together, within three feet. If you want to beam a task to someone in the office building across the street or to the driver of an oncoming car, you're out of luck.

Changing to-dos

The French have a saying, *"Plus ça change, plus c'est le même chose,"* which means, "The more things change, the more they're the same." Even if you don't speak French, you know that it makes no sense, although it sounds terribly charming in French.

The charming thing about changing to-do items is that you do pretty much the same things to change an item as you did to enter it in the first place.

To change the priority of a to-do item, follow these steps:

1. **With the To Do List open, tap the name of the task you want to change.**

   The check box to the left of the item is highlighted to show which task you've selected.

2. **To change the priority of your task, tap the number next to the name of the task.**

   A list of numbers 1 through 5 appears, as shown in Figure 6-8.

Figure 6-8: Set priorities to sort out what's *really* important.

3. **Tap the number for the new priority you want to give your task.**

   The highest priority is 1; the lowest is 5. When you tap a number, the list disappears and the new priority number appears next to your task.

If you want to change the name of a to-do item, follow these steps:

1. **With the To Do List open, tap the name of the task you want to change.**

   The check box to the left of the item is highlighted to show which task you've selected.

2. **Select the text you want to change by drawing a horizontal line through it with the stylus.**

   The text is highlighted to show that you've selected it.

3. **Enter new text with either the on-screen keyboard or Graffiti (see Chapter 2 for more info about entering text).**

   The selected text is replaced by the text you enter.

If you want to make further changes to a to-do item, follow these steps:

1. **With the To Do List open, tap the name of the task you want to change.**

   The check box to the left of the item is highlighted to show which task you've selected.

2. **Tap Details at the bottom of the To Do List.**

   The To Do Item Details dialog box opens.

3. **Make whatever changes you want in the To Do Item Details dialog box.**

   You can use the same methods for changing the details of your task as you did to enter the details in the first place (see the section "Entering details for a to-do item," earlier in this chapter).

4. **Tap OK.**

   The To Do Item Details dialog box closes and the To Do List reappears.

The one trick about changing to-do items is that the To Do List almost never displays all the things you can change about a task. That means that because you may change something that's not displayed, at first you may think that your changes didn't take. See the section "Setting preferences for the To Do List," later in this chapter, to find out how to show everything you want to see.

Undoing a mistake

If you make a mistake when you're changing the text in a To Do item, you can fix it in a jiffy by following these steps:

1. **With the To Do List open, tap the Menu soft button.**

   The menu bar appears at the top of the display area.

2. **Choose Edit⇨Undo.**

   The text returns to the way it was before you changed it.

Undo works only when you change or replace text. You can't use the Undo command to recover a to-do item you accidentally delete. If you have archived deleted items, you can go to the archive on the Palm Desktop to recover the item. (See Chapters 12 and 13 for details about recovering items from the archive.)

Marking the to-dos you've done

As you finish the tasks you've assigned to yourself, mark them as completed. Marking to-do items as completed does more than give you a feeling of satisfaction; it can also shorten that depressing list of things left to do. I say "can" because you can set up your Palm device to either display all tasks, completed or not, or hide completed tasks. See the section "Setting preferences for the To Do List," later in this chapter, for information about hiding tasks.

To mark a task as completed, tap the check box next to the name of the task you want to mark. A check mark appears in the check box to show that you've completed the item, as shown in Figure 6-9. If you told your Palm device in the To Do preferences not to show completed items, the item disappears from the To Do List.

Figure 6-9:
When you finish a task, check it off.

```
┌─────────────────────────────────┐
│ To Do List            ▼ All     │
│ ☑ 1  Spin straw into gold......⌐ │
│ ☐ 1  Call Prince about lunch.... │
│ ☑ 1  Open a savings account....  │
│ ☐ 1  Get new fillings..........  │
│                                  │
│                                  │
│                                  │
│                                  │
│                                  │
│                                  │
│ ( New ) ( Details... ) ( Show... )│
└─────────────────────────────────┘
```

Deleting a to-do

Perhaps you added a task to the To Do List and then lost your nerve and decided to erase any trace of it. If you've made it your task to tell what's-his-name that he's a dirty, rotten so-and-so, you may be wiser to delete the thing. If you end up telling him anyway, don't forget that I told you so.

To delete a To Do List item, follow these steps:

1. **With the To Do List open, tap the name of the task you want to delete.**

   The check box to the left of the item is highlighted to show which task you've selected.

2. **Tap the Menu soft button.**

   The menu bar appears at the top of the display area.

3. **Choose Record⇨Delete Item.**

   The Delete To Do dialog box opens, as shown in Figure 6-10.

4. **Tap OK.**

   The Delete To Do dialog box closes and the To Do List reappears.

Figure 6-10:
If you don't
want to
complete it,
delete it.

Some people like to delete tasks rather than mark them as completed because it keeps their list of tasks short. The reason not to delete completed tasks is so that you can brag about all the things you've accomplished. That's a particularly useful approach if you have a job that gives performance reviews. It's up to you: Complete or delete.

The Delete Items dialog box offers to save to your PC an archive copy of each item you delete. By doing so, you can dig up old deleted items through the Palm Desktop on your PC if you need them in the future. If you leave the box checked, each item is archived automatically. If you click the archive check box once, it stays unchecked for every item you delete until you check it again. (For more info about archived items, see Chapter 12.)

Deleting a note

After you've done a task a few times, you may not need a note telling you how to do the task anymore. You can delete a note attached to a to-do item without deleting the item.

To delete a note, follow these steps:

1. **With the To Do List open, tap the name of the task from which you want to delete a note.**

   The check box to the left of the item is highlighted to show which task you've selected.

2. **Tap the Menu soft button.**

   The menu bar appears at the top of the display area.

3. **Choose Record⇨Delete Note.**

   The Delete Note dialog box opens, asking whether you're sure that you want to do this.

4. **Tap Yes.**

   The note is deleted, but the task remains.

When you delete a note, it's gone for good; notes are not archived separately, and the Undo command doesn't bring them back. So, be sure that you *really* want the note you pick to be deleted.

Setting preferences for the To Do List

If you never change a thing about the To Do List, you still get plenty of mileage from your Palm device. Everybody works a little differently, though, so you may want to slice and dice the items on the To Do List in a way that works better for you.

To change the To Do List preferences, follow these steps:

1. **With the To Do List open, tap Show.**

   The To Do Preferences screen appears.

2. **Tap the triangle next to the words *Sort By* to set up your sort order.**

   Your choices, as shown in Figure 6-11, are

   - Priority, Due Date
   - Due Date, Priority
   - Category, Priority
   - Category, Due Date

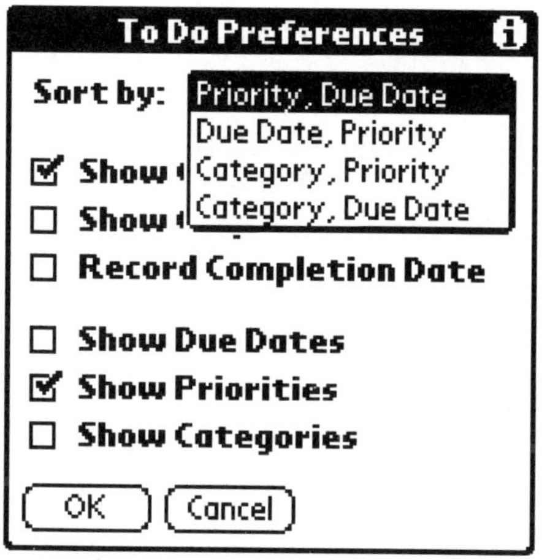

To Do Preferences ⓘ

Sort by: | Priority, Due Date |
| Due Date, Priority |
☑ **Show** | Category, Priority |
☐ **Show** | Category, Due Date |
☐ **Record Completion Date**

☐ **Show Due Dates**
☑ **Show Priorities**
☐ **Show Categories**

(OK) (Cancel)

Figure 6-11:
You can sort
your tasks in
four differ-
ent ways.

3. **Tap the check boxes that correspond to the elements you want dis-played on the To Do List.**

The To Do Preferences screen has a half-dozen check boxes that set your display area to show completed items, due dates, priorities, categories, and other items. If you display everything, your screen can get a bit crowded, but that's your choice.

If you check any of the following boxes, here's what happens:

- **Show Completed Items:** Tasks you complete stay on the list until you delete them. This option is for people who would rather not forget what they did yesterday.

- **Show Only Due Items:** Tasks with due dates set in the future don't show; only tasks with no due date or with a due date set for today or earlier appear. This option is for people who like to wait until the last minute.

- **Record Completion Date:** The due date of a task changes to the date on which you mark the task as completed. For example, if I set the due date of a task for Friday but mark the task as complete on Wednesday, the due date is automatically changed to Wednesday. This one's for people who like to remember when things were really completed rather than when things should have been completed.

- **Show Due Dates:** This option makes a due date appear on the screen along with the name of each task. It's for people who like to put first things first.

- **Show Priorities:** This option makes the priority number appear next to each task. It's for people who put the most important things first.

- **Show Categories:** Use this option to make the category of each task appear next to the name of the task. This one's for people who like to put everything in its place.

4. **Click OK.**

   The To Do Preferences screen disappears, and the To Do List reappears.

If you choose to sort by category or priority, displaying the category or priority is also a good idea. Otherwise, your screen looks confusing.

Looking up an address and phone number

Creating to-do items that involve other people is fairly common, even if the task is something as simple as calling someone on the phone. You can get your Palm device to look up a name from the Address List and plug that person's name and phone number into the to-do item. Phone Number Lookup can save you the trouble of looking up the person's number when it's time to make the call.

Here's how to look up a name and phone number from the Address Book:

1. **With the To Do List open, create or begin to edit a To Do List item.**

   (See the sections "Creating a to-do item" or "Changing to-dos," earlier in this chapter.)

2. **Tap the Menu soft button.**

   The menu bar appears.

3. **Choose Options⇨Phone Lookup.**

   The Phone Number Lookup screen appears. If this screen looks like the Address Book, don't be surprised — that's where the phone numbers come from, as shown in Figure 6-12.

4. **Tap the name of the person whose phone number you want to add to your to-do item.**

   The name is highlighted to show that you've selected it.

5. **Tap Add.**

   The name and phone number of the person whose name you chose appear as part of your to-do item. Bear in mind that only the first phone number of the address record you pick appears in the to-do item, no matter how many phone numbers the address record contains.

Figure 6-12:
Use the
Phone
Number
Lookup fea-
ture to find
important
numbers.

```
┌──────────────────────────────────────┐
│ ▐ Phone Number Lookup: ▌              │
│ Alifont, "Bull"          555-6597 W   │
│ DeDark, Fredda           555-9875 W   │
│ Dogg, Pat D.             555-5474 W   │
│ Early, Otto B.           555-1324 W   │
│ Fergus, Freddie          555-5689 W   │
│ Palm III Accessories  801-431-1536 W  │
│ ▐Rumplestiltskin         555-6666 W▌  │
│ Short, Peg               555-1213 W   │
│ Snivel, Heather          555-6127 W   │
│ Technical Support     847-676-1441 W  │
│ Thunderblossom, Magnoli  555-3200 W   │
│                                    ▲  │
│ Look Up:|........  (Add) (Cancel)  ▼  │
└──────────────────────────────────────┘
```

Unfortunately, you can't get from the To Do List to the person's Address List entry to see other details about the person, such as his street address or other details. You have to press the Address List button and find the name.

Purging to-dos you've done

The reason for keeping a to-do list is to help you get things done. After you've done the things on your list, you have no reason to leave them hanging around. The Purge function automatically deletes items you've marked as completed. You could delete all your completed items one by one, but the purge function deletes them *en masse*.

To purge completed to-do items, follow these steps:

1. **With the To Do List open, tap the Menu soft button.**

   The menu bar appears at the top of the display area.

2. **Choose Record⇨Purge.**

   The Purge dialog box appears. Make sure that a check mark appears in the box that says Save Archive Copy on PC. Otherwise, you won't have a record of all the things you've done.

3. **Tap OK.**

   The Purge dialog box closes, and the items you marked as completed disappear.

If you need to dig up a list of the things you've done to show your boss at review time or as dramatic courtroom testimony ("Just where were you the night of. . . ?"), you can go back to the archives of your to-do items, as long as you checked the archive box in the Purge dialog box. (For more info about retrieving to-do items from the archive, see Chapter 12.)

Chapter 7

Memo Mania

• •

In This Chapter

▶ Creating memos

▶ Reading memos

▶ Changing and categorizing items

▶ Making a memo private

▶ Deleting memos

▶ Setting preferences

▶ Beaming memos

• •

*T*he Memo Pad isn't the flashiest feature on a Palm device, but I must confess that it's my favorite. Like many writers, my best ideas always hit me when I'm farthest from my desk and least able to record them. Now I keep my Palm device nearby 24 hours a day, 7 days a week so that every Brilliant Flash of Insight, along with every Foolish Whim, gets recorded on my Memo Pad. At this point, the Foolish Whims outnumber the Brilliant Flashes by a long shot, but because I can change and delete a memo at any time, I can make myself look foolish less often. As you've probably noticed, I haven't yet figured out how to look brilliant.

When you synchronize your Palm device with a desktop computer, you can copy and paste the text from your memos to regular word-processing programs. That's the best way to format, print, or e-mail the precious prose you've collected on the Memo Pad.

To access the Memo List, just press the Memo Pad button (it's the far-right button at the bottom of your Palm device, as shown in Figure 7-1) and continue with adding, deleting, or whatever you want to do with your memos.

Figure 7-1:
Press the
Memo Pad
button to
bring up
your list of
memos.

Memo Pad
hard button

Take a Memo

If you plan to use the Memo Pad to write down large amounts of information while you're away from your desk, it really pays to understand how to use Graffiti. You can get by in all the other Palm Computing programs by using the little on-screen keyboard to tap out short pieces of text, but that gets tiresome quickly. (I discuss the keyboard and Graffiti in Chapter 2.) Even Graffiti can get a little tiring if you're used to the speed of a standard computer keyboard, but that little keyboard is worse.

Adding items

Many people don't enter memos on their Palm device's Memo Pad; they either enter data from the Palm Desktop program (see Chapter 12) or ignore memos. Take your pick. As I've said, I'm a big fan of the Memo Pad, so I add stuff constantly.

To create a new memo, follow these steps:

1. **With the Memo List open, tap New.**

   A blank note screen appears.

2. **Enter the text you want by using either the on-screen keyboard or Graffiti (see Chapter 2 for more info about entering text).**

   The text you enter appears on the memo screen, as shown in Figure 7-2.

3. **Tap Done.**

   The memo screen disappears, and the Memo List reappears.

What I've just described is the prescribed way of entering a memo. An even easier way is to press the Memo Pad button and just start writing stuff in the Graffiti box. The Memo Pad just assumes that you want to create a new memo and opens a new memo screen. You still have to tap Done to close the new memo.

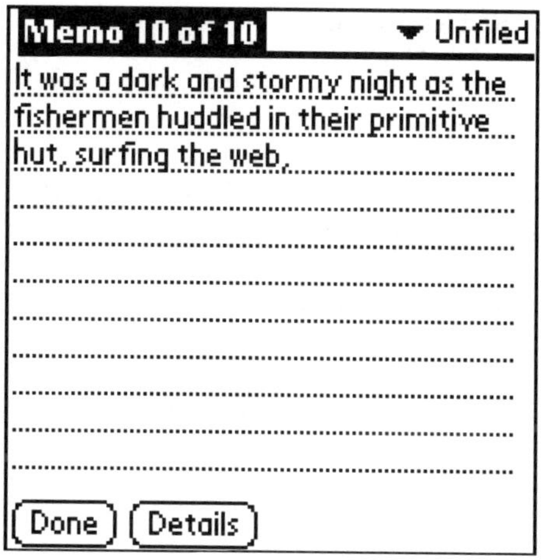

Memo 10 of 10   ▼ Unfiled

It was a dark and stormy night as the
fishermen huddled in their primitive
hut, surfing the web,

(Done) (Details)

Figure 7-2:
Create
memos by
using the
Memo Pad.

Reading memos

The word *memo* looks like someone started to write the word *memory*, but
forgot to finish. You don't have to worry about forgetting how to read your
memos, though; it's just a matter of press and tap. Here's how:

1. **With the Memo List open, tap the name of the memo you want to read,
   as shown in Figure 7-3.**

   The memo you selected opens.

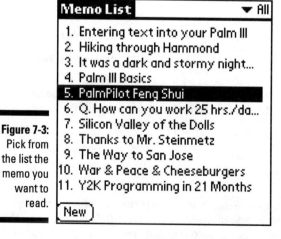

Figure 7-3:
Pick from
the list the
memo you
want to
read.

Memo List   ▼ All

1. Entering text into your Palm III
2. Hiking through Hammond
3. It was a dark and stormy night...
4. Palm III Basics
5. PalmPilot Feng Shui
6. Q. How can you work 25 hrs./da...
7. Silicon Valley of the Dolls
8. Thanks to Mr. Steinmetz
9. The Way to San Jose
10. War & Peace & Cheeseburgers
11. Y2K Programming in 21 Months

(New)

2. **Read your memo to your heart's content.**

3. **Tap Done.**

Your memo closes.

The other sneaky thing I like about memos is that you can read them in the dark. The PalmPilot Professional and later models have a backlight, so you can read (or write) memos after the lights go out. It's just like being back in the days when you used to read comic books under the covers with a flashlight. Don't get caught, though.

Bear in mind that the backlight can drain your batteries rather quickly, so use the backlight sparingly.

Changing items

What's the difference between a Foolish Whim and a Brilliant Insight? Editing! (My editors certainly agree with me about that.) Editing your memos is just as easy as reading and creating them.

The simplest change you can make to a memo is adding new text. I have certain memos to which I add one or two lines every day. Adding more text to a memo takes only a second.

To add new text to a memo you've already created, follow these steps:

1. **With the Memo List open, tap the name of the memo you want to change.**

The memo opens on your screen.

2. **Tap the spot in the memo where you want to add new text.**

A blinking line, the *insertion point,* appears at the spot where you tapped.

3. **Enter the text you want by using either the on-screen keyboard or Graffiti (see Chapter 2 for more info about entering text).**

The text you enter appears in the spot you tapped.

4. **Tap Done.**

Your memo closes.

Another common way to edit a memo is to change the text that's already there. When you select any text you've entered in your Palm device and then enter new text, the text you select is automatically replaced by the text you enter. Most Windows and Macintosh programs work in pretty much the same way, so you should be ready to edit memos in a flash.

To replace existing text in a memo, follow these steps:

1. **With the Memo List open, tap the name of the memo you want to change.**

   The memo opens on your screen.

2. **Select any text you want to replace.**

   The text you select is highlighted to show that you've selected it, as shown in Figure 7-4. (For more info about selecting text, see Chapter 2.)

Figure 7-4:
Get rid of
pesky typos
by highlight-
ing text to
change it.

3. **Enter replacement text by using either the on-screen keyboard or Graffiti (see Chapter 2 for more info about entering text).**

   The text you enter replaces the selected text.

4. **Tap Done.**

   Your memo closes.

If you want to select the whole memo and replace everything in it, you can open the memo, tap the Menu icon, and choose Edit⇨Select All. If you're going to go that far, though, you may as well just delete the memo and start over.

You may have noticed that the first line of the memo is what shows up on the Memo List. If you let your Palm device sort alphabetically, the first word of the first line determines where the memo turns up on the Memo List. You can make sure that a certain memo always ends up at the top of the Memo List by making the first character in the memo 0 (zero).

Categorizing items

After you've created a large enough collection of memos, you may want to start organizing them so that you can quickly find the information you want. You can assign a category to each memo so that it shows up along with other memos with similar content:

1. **With the Memo List open, tap the name of the memo you want to categorize.**

   The memo opens.

2. **Tap the name of the category in the upper-right corner of the display area.**

   If your memo is uncategorized, the word *Unfiled* appears in the upper-right corner of the screen. When you tap the downward-pointing arrow next to the category name or the name itself, a list of categories drops down, as shown in Figure 7-5. (Categories work in pretty much the same way on the Memo Pad as they do on the To Do List, so see Chapter 6 for more information about dealing with categories.)

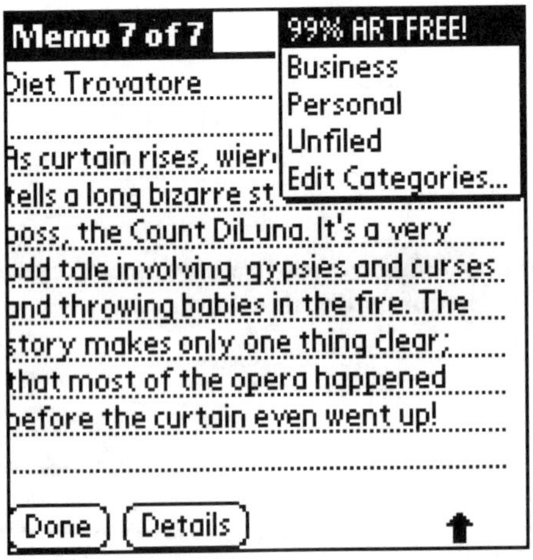

Figure 7-5: Tap the name of the memo category and pick a new category.

3. **Tap the name of the category to which you want to assign your memo.**

   The list disappears, and the category you chose appears in the upper-right corner.

4. **Tap Done.**

   Your memo closes, and the Memo List reappears.

Making a memo private

If you want to be wise about recording your Foolish Whims, you can mark them all as private so that only you know what you've entered. It's a good way to keep from looking foolish if anybody else gets hold of your Palm device. I've thought about marking my sillier memos as private, but I suspect that everybody already knows I'm foolish, so it's probably too late.

Follow these steps to keep private memos to yourself:

1. **With the Memo List open, tap the name of the memo you want to make private.**

   Your memo opens.

2. **Tap Details.**

   The Memo Details dialog box opens, as shown in Figure 7-6.

Figure 7-6:
This dialog box lets you keep your secrets safe.

3. **Tap the check box marked Private.**

   A check mark appears in the check box.

4. **Tap OK.**

   The Private Records dialog box appears if you haven't elected to hide private records. The Private Records dialog box warns you that marking this item as private doesn't matter until you choose to hide private records. (I discuss hiding and showing private records in Chapter 3.) If you have elected to hide private records, the Memo Details dialog box simply closes.

5. **Tap OK in the Private Records dialog box.**

   The Private Records dialog box closes.

6. **Tap Done.**

   Your memo closes, and the Memo List reappears. If you have chosen to hide private records, the memo you marked as private is no longer listed.

You can choose whether to show or hide all private items on your Palm device by going to the Security application and picking either Show or Hide. If you pick Show, all your items can be seen, private or not. If you pick Hide, the items marked as private seem to disappear. If you mark an item as private while hiding items marked as private, the item seems to vanish, only to reappear when you go back to the Security application and pick Show Private Items again. (For more info about hiding private items, see Chapter 3.)

You can also set up a password to protect your private items. That's one more way of keeping your private items private. (Check out Chapter 3 for more information about passwords.)

The tricky thing about items marked as private is that nothing appears on the screen to tell you whether you're seeing them. One way to remind yourself is to create a memo whose first line starts with a zero and says "0 PRIVATE ITEMS SHOWING." That way, you're reminded to check for items you've marked as private.

Using What You Have

Even if you don't enter memos directly into your Palm device, you still want to read the memos you've collected and organize your memo collection in a useful way. The Memo Pad offers a collection of organizing tools that are simple but useful. You can sort your memos in different ways, view different categories, and change the font the Palm device displays to make your memos easier to read.

Deleting items

An old axiom says "When in doubt, throw it out." Deleting a memo takes a few more steps than I wish it did, but not much mystery is involved.

To delete a memo, follow these steps:

1. **With the Memo List open, tap the name of the memo you want to delete.**

   Your memo opens.

2. **Tap the Menu icon.**

   The menu bar appears.

3. **Choose Record⇨Delete Memo, as shown in Figure 7-7.**

   The Delete Memo dialog box opens and asks whether you want to delete the current memo.

Figure 7-7:
You can
delete a
memo when
you don't
want it
anymore.

4. Tap OK.

The Delete Memo dialog box closes, and your memo is deleted. If you've changed your mind about deleting this memo, you can tap the Cancel button in the Delete Memo dialog box to call off the deletion. Be sure that a check mark appears in the box marked Save Archive Copy on PC. That's the only way your deleted memos can be recovered later. (For more info about archiving, see Chapter 12 or 13.)

Boom! It's gone.

Viewing memos by category

My, how memos multiply! In no time at all, you'll probably gather up dozens and dozens of memos, full of stuff that you're sure you want to keep handy at all times. Of course, the catch is this: The more memos you try to keep handy on your Palm device, the less handy they get because you have so doggone many of 'em.

Earlier in this chapter, I show you how to assign categories to your memos (see the section "Categorizing items," earlier in this chapter), although to really use categories, you need to be able to see which memos are in each category.

To view your memos by category, follow these steps:

1. **With the Memo List open, tap the name of the category in the upper-right corner of the screen.**

   The list of available categories appears. When you first use your Palm device, the list has four categories: All, Business, Personal, and Unfiled.

2. **Tap the name of the category you want to display.**

   The Memo List changes to display only the items assigned to the category you chose. The name of the category you're viewing appears in the upper-right corner of the screen.

If you want to really impress your friends with your Palm Computing prowess, you can whip through your memo categories even faster by clicking the Memo Pad button more than once. Each time you press the Memo Pad button, you see a different category.

Changing fonts

When you change the font on your Palm device, you change the size and style of lettering you see on the display area. The itty-bitty letters the Palm device usually displays enable you to show a great deal of information on that tiny little screen, but if your eyes aren't so sharp or if the light isn't just right, your screen can be tough to read. Each new Palm model offers a few more choices in the type of font you can choose to display your text.

The Palm III, Palm IIIx, Palm V, and Palm VII models let you change the font both on the Memo List and in the text of your memos, but you choose the font from the menu bar. Tap the Menu icon, choose Options⇨Font, pick from the Select Font dialog box the font you want to display, and tap OK. These three models also let you choose from among three fonts. You have to choose the font for your memo text and the Memo List separately. If you change the font for the Memo List, you haven't changed the font you see for the text of your memos. You have to open a memo to change the font for the body of memos. When you change the font for the body of one memo, all memos appear in that font until you pick another font.

Setting preferences to organize your memos

When it comes to organizing memos, I believe in freedom of choice: alphabetical or manual. You can either let your Palm device organize your memos by the first letter of the first word in each memo or set up the device to let you drag the titles of memos around the Memo List and drop them off in the order you like. I prefer the alphabetical arrangement.

Follow these steps to let your Palm device know your preferences:

1. **With the Memo List open, tap the Menu icon.**

   The menu bar appears.

2. **Choose Options⇨Preferences.**

   The Memo Preferences dialog box opens, as shown in Figure 7-8.

3. **Tap the triangle next to Sort By.**

   A list appears offering you two choices: Manual and Alphabetic.

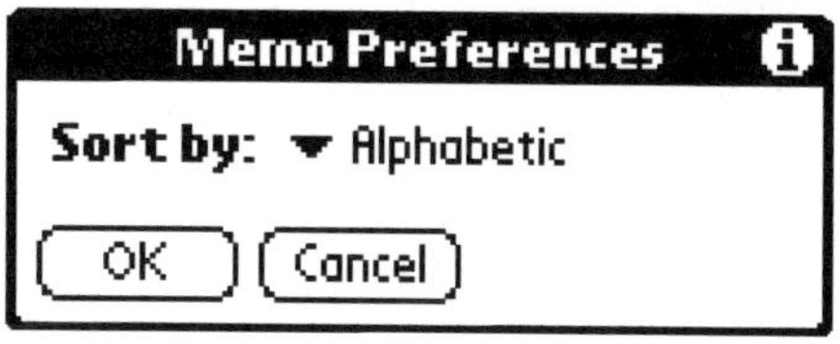

Figure 7-8:
You have
preferences;
so do your
memos.

```
╔══════════════════════════════╗
║ Memo Preferences          ⓘ ║
║ Sort by: ▼ Alphabetic        ║
║ ┌─────┐ ┌─────────┐          ║
║ │ OK  │ │ Cancel  │          ║
║ └─────┘ └─────────┘          ║
╚══════════════════════════════╝
```

4. Tap the choice you prefer.

The list disappears, and your choice appears.

5. Tap OK.

The Memo Preferences dialog box closes, and the Memo List appears in the sort order of your choice.

If you choose to sort your memos alphabetically, you get the result you'd expect: All your memos line up in alphabetical order according to the first word in the memo. If you choose Manual sorting, memos appear in the order in which you created them so that the last memo you created appears at the bottom of the list. When you sort your memos in manual order, you can also drag them to the point on the Memo List where you want them to appear. It doesn't matter what category you're looking at when you set the preferences; the setting you choose applies to all categories.

If you've sorted your memos manually and then switch to alphabetical sorting, your manually sorted arrangement is lost for good. The memos are still there, but you have to re-sort everything.

Beaming your memos

Yes, Virginia, there is a Santa Claus, and if he has a new Palm organizer next Christmas, you can write your gift list on your Palm device's Memo Pad and beam it to Santa. That way, of course, you don't get to sit on his lap.

You can beam nearly anything — not just memos — on one Palm device to another. (For more info about beaming, see Chapter 9.)

To beam a memo, follow these steps:

1. With the Memo List open, tap the name of the memo you want to beam.

Your memo opens.

2. Tap the Menu icon.

The menu bar appears.

3. **Choose Record⇨Beam Memo, as shown in Figure 7-9.**

   The Beam dialog box opens.

4. **Tap OK.**

   Your memo is magically sent to the other Palm III.

You have to set the Palm devices within about three feet of each other, of course, for the beaming process to work, which means that you can't beam your list to Santa as he flies over. Because the Palm devices must also be within line of sight of each other, you can't beam through walls; that's definitely a job for Superman.

Figure 7-9:
Beam
memos to
another
Palm device
at the speed
of light.

> Record Edit Options
> New Memo   /N
> Delete Memo... /D
> Beam Memo   /B ttons
> turns on your Palm III and shows a
> specific screen. The Date Book
> button, for example, displays
> today's schedule.
>
> Select a record and tap the Details
> button to access more options. Some
> settings can be edited directly by
>
> (Done) (Details)

Chapter 8

The Date Game

*T*he Date Book may soon become your favorite Palm Computing feature. Everybody knows how powerful a computer can be at keeping track of your schedule — you may use one at work to keep track of your appointments. A Palm device lets you carry that power around in your pocket and keep your schedule up-to-date while you're carrying it out. Then, when you return to your office or your home, just HotSync to your desktop computer to keep the Date Book current. (For more info about performing a HotSync, see Chapter 11.)

To access the Date Book, just press the Date Book hard button (it's the far-left button at the bottom of your Palm device, as shown in Figure 8-1), and then arrange your appointments as you like.

Date Book
hard button

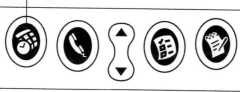

Figure 8-1:
The Date
Book hard
button.

Date Book Views

I think that you'll find the Date Book pretty easy to use after you've tried it a bit. The only tricky part about understanding the Palm Computing Date Book comes from the size of the screen. You can't really show a whole calendar on that itty-bitty display area and still be able to show what's going on each day, so the Palm device breaks the calendar into different views that show a day, a week, or a month.

Each view of your calendar includes three icons at the bottom of the screen representing the three calendar views: day, week, and month. The icon for the view you're seeing appears darkened; if you want to switch to another view, tap a different icon. For example, when you look at Daily view, the left-most icon is darkened. When you tap the middle icon, Weekly view appears.

Another way to switch between Date Book views is to press the Date Book button more than once. Each time you press the button, you see a different view of the Date Book, either Daily, Weekly, or Monthly view. If you don't like the view you see, keep pressing the Date Book button until the view you want appears.

Daily view

The first time you press the Date Book button, you see a daily schedule, as shown in Figure 8-2. It shows a line for each hour of the day, and any appointments on your schedule are listed in order of starting time.

Figure 8-2:
Daily view displays a list of your appointments for a particular day.

Sep 7, 99 ◀ S M T W T F S ▶
8:00
9:00
10:00 Interview
11:00
12:00
1:00 Lunch
2:00
3:00
4:00 Staff meeting
5:00
6:00
▪ ⬚ (New) (Details) (Go to) ↑

Your Palm device usually shows today's appointments first. If you want to see appointments for a date earlier or later in the week, tap the letter for the day of the week at the top of the screen. You can also move from day to day by pressing the scroll buttons on the case of your Palm device.

Weekly view

Weekly view, as shown in Figure 8-3, just shows a diagram of your schedule for the week. It shows a grid of days and times, and shaded bars represent blocks of time when you have appointments scheduled, but the bars don't tell you specifically what's scheduled. If you want to find out what you've scheduled at a certain time, tap the bar representing that scheduled item, and the information regarding the appointment appears at the top of the screen.

Figure 8-3:
Weekly view shows an overview of your appointments over the course of a week.

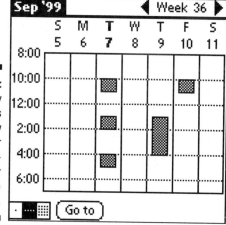

You can look at your weekly schedule for the future or the past by pressing the scroll buttons on the case, just like you can in Daily view. You can also change the week you're looking at by tapping one of the triangles at the top of the screen.

Weekly view has one important feature the other two views don't have: You can change an appointment to a different time in the week by dragging the bar representing the appointment time and dropping it off at another time in the week. Figure 8-4 shows an appointment (represented by the box with the heavy border) being dropped in at 2 p.m. on September 10.

As you're dragging and dropping, the name and time of your appointment appear at the top of the display area to let you know exactly when you've set the new appointment time. You have to be pretty steady with the stylus if you drag and drop this way, but it's the fastest way to change an appointment time.

If you've never done the drag and drop (no, it's not a dance step from the 1960s; that was the Watusi), don't fret. It's very simple:

1. **Put the tip of your stylus on the bar representing an appointment.**

2. **Slide the stylus tip along the screen to where you want the appointment to end up.**

   As you slide the stylus tip along the screen, a little box representing the appointment slides right along with your stylus, as though you were dragging the box along the screen. As you drag, the appointment listed in the banner at the top of the screen changes to show what the new appointment time will be if you "drop" the appointment at the current position by lifting your stylus.

3. **Lift up the stylus when the appointment is where you want it.**

Now you're a drag-and-drop champ!

Monthly view

Monthly view, as shown in Figure 8-5, is the most familiar-looking view in the Date Book because it resembles a regular wall calendar. Unfortunately, Monthly view offers very little information about your schedule; only dots represent your appointments. The main advantage of Monthly view is your ability to navigate through your schedule easily. If you tap any date in Monthly view, you see Daily view for that date.

Again, the scroll buttons change Monthly view from one month to the next. If you need to take a quick look at a date in the distant future (a year or more from now), tap Go To at the bottom of the Date Book screen and pick the date you want to see.

Figure 8-5:
Monthly view shows a general diagram of your appointments for a month.

September 1999						◀ ▶
S	**M**	**T**	**W**	**T**	**F**	**S**
			1	2	3	4
5	6	**7** ▪	8 ▪	9 ▪	10 ▪	11
12	13 ▪	14	15	16 ▪	17	18
19 ▪	20	21	22 ▪	23	24	25 ▪
26	27	28 ▪	29	30		
· ┈▦ (Go to)						

The Go To icon shows a calendar that enables you to tap the date you want to see. If you want to view a date later this month, tap Go To and tap the date you want to see. If you want to see a date in a different month of this year, tap the month you want from the list of months at the top of the screen, and then tap the day you want. If you want to look at a day in a different year, tap Go To, tap one of the triangles next to the year at the top of the screen (depending on whether you want to time-warp into the past or the future), and tap the month you want to see.

Making Dates

You can keep track of a surprising amount of detailed information in the Date Book. Thousands of appointments fit comfortably in the Date Book along with reminders, notes, and other details. You don't have to enter your appointments directly into your Palm device if you don't want to; you can do most of the keyboard work on your desktop computer and then HotSync everything to your Palm device. In some situations, though, you may be better off entering appointments directly in your Palm device.

Adding appointments the simple way

Some folks are into dates; some aren't. You don't have to go crazy entering lots of details when you add an appointment to the Date Book. You can enter many types of appointments with very little effort.

Follow these steps to add a new appointment the simple way:

1. **With the Date Book visible, tap the line next to the hour when your appointment begins.**

   A blinking line, the *insertion point*, appears on the line you tapped.

2. **Enter the name of your appointment by using either the on-screen keyboard or Graffiti (see Chapter 2 for more info about entering text).**

   The name of your appointment appears on the line you tapped, as shown in Figure 8-6.

3. **Tap the blank spot at the bottom of the screen to the right of Go To.**

   The insertion point disappears, and your appointment is set. (If you don't complete this step, nothing terrible happens; your Palm device just waits for you to do something else.)

Figure 8-6: Just write the name of your appointment in the appropriate time slot.

```
Sep 7, 99   ◀ S M T W T F S ▶
  8:00 ........................................
  9:00 ........................................
 10:00 Interview ...........................  ⊡
 11:00 ........................................
 12:00 ........................................
  1:00 Lunch ................................
  2:00 ........................................
  3:00 ........................................
  4:00 ........................................
  6:00 Reception .........................
  7:00 ........................................
 ·····▦  (New) (Details) (Go to) ↑
```

The simple way to enter appointments is to enter the name of the appointment at the time the appointment starts. What could be easier?

Adding appointments the complete way

If all your appointments start right on the hour and last exactly an hour, the simple way to enter appointments (see the preceding section, "Adding appointments the simple way") will suit you just fine. When you have appointments that start at odd times or don't last exactly an hour, you need to resort to the more complete method for entering appointments.

Follow these steps to enter detailed information about an appointment:

1. **With the Date Book visible, tap Go To.**

   The Go To Date dialog box opens.

2. **Tap the date for your appointment.**

   The Date Book appears in Daily view, showing you the appointments you've scheduled for that date.

3. **Tap the hour closest to the starting time of your appointment.**

   The Set Time dialog box opens, as shown in Figure 8-7.

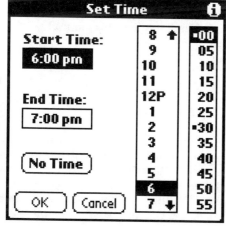

Figure 8-7:
The Set
Time dialog
box accom-
modates
appoint-
ments with
details.

4. **Tap the hour and minute for the starting time of your appointment.**

   The hour and minute you tap appear in the Start Time box.

5. **Tap the End Time box.**

   The End Time box is highlighted to show that you've selected it.

6. **Tap the hour and minute for the ending time of your appointment.**

   The hour and minute you tap appear in the End Time box.

7. **Tap OK.**

   The Set Time dialog box closes, and the Date Book screen reappears.

8. **Enter the name of your appointment by using either the on-screen keyboard or Graffiti (see Chapter 2 for more info about entering text).**

   The name of your appointment appears on the line next to the starting time.

9. **Tap Details.**

   The Event Details dialog box opens.

10. **If you need to make any changes to the details of your appointment, tap the appropriate box and enter that information.**

    Because you've already entered the date and time, you probably don't need to change those details. I explain more about setting alarms, setting private appointments, and repeating appointments later in this chapter.

11. **Tap OK.**

    The Event Details dialog box closes, and the Date Book screen reappears.

There! You've done it! Isn't that satisfying? Okay, maybe not, but you've done all you can do, so take heart. If you didn't find this method helpful or efficient, you can enter your next appointment the simple way by following the steps in the preceding section.

Entering No Time events

Not everything on your schedule happens at a particular hour of the day. Birthdays and holidays, for example, just happen — all day long, even if it rains. If you want to enter an event without a time attached, just open the Date Book to Daily view, and then enter the name of the event in the Graffiti box. (For more info about using Graffiti, see Chapter 2.) Your new event appears at the top of the screen. You can also use the complete method of entering an appointment (see the preceding section) and tap No Time on the Set Time screen in Step 6.

Setting alarms

I'm the first to admit that I need lots of reminding. Fortunately, my Palm device is always around to gently pester me into doing what needs to be done when it needs to be done. It's sort of a like an electronic mother-in-law.

Even if your Palm device is turned off, the alarm wakes it up and makes a series of tiny beeps. You have to turn off the alarm by tapping OK on the screen.

Follow these steps to set an alarm:

1. **With the Date Book visible, tap the name of the appointment for which you want to set an alarm.**

   The insertion point appears on the line with your appointment's name.

2. **Tap Details.**

   The Event Details dialog box opens.

3. **Tap the Alarm check box.**

   A check mark appears in the check box, and the alarm setting appears to the right of the check box, as shown in Figure 8-8. Normally, the alarm setting is five minutes. That means that the alarm will go off five minutes before the scheduled appointment time.

Figure 8-8:
In the Event Details dialog box, set your Palm device to remind you of an important appointment.

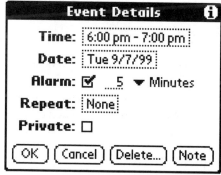

4. **If you want to change the alarm time, tap the word *Minutes*.**

   A list appears with the choices Minutes, Hours, and Days.

5. **Tap your choice of Minutes, Hours, or Days.**

   The list disappears, and the choice you tapped appears.

6. **Enter the number of minutes, hours, or days before the appointment that you want the alarm to sound with either the on-screen keyboard or Graffiti (see Chapter 2 for more info about entering text).**

   The number you enter appears next to the Alarm check box.

7. **Tap OK.**

   The Event Details dialog box closes.

I usually check the Alarm check box *while* (rather than after) creating it.

Adding notes to appointments

Every Date Book item can also contain a note explaining details about the appointment. Date Book notes work exactly the same way as the notes you can attach to to-do items. (See Chapter 6 for more info about attaching notes.)

Using Address Book Lookup

Another feature shared by the Date Book and the To Do List is the ability to look up a name in the Address Book and automatically copy that person's name and phone number into the appointment. To look up a name, tap the Menu soft button and choose Options⇨Phone Lookup. When the Address Book appears, tap the name you want to include in the appointment and then tap the Add button.

Setting up repeating appointments

You certainly don't want to forget that important weekly meeting of Electronics Shoppers Anonymous. Rather than enter each of those meetings individually, you can set up a repeating appointment.

To mark an appointment as a repeating appointment:

1. **With the Date Book visible, tap the name of the appointment you want to set up as a repeating appointment.**

   The insertion point appears on the line with your appointment's name.

2. **Tap Details.**

   The Event Details dialog box opens.

3. **Tap the Repeat box.**

   The Change Repeat dialog box opens, as shown in Figure 8-9.

4. **Tap one of the interval pattern buttons to set the frequency you want.**

   Your choices are None, Day, Week, Month, and Year. When you tap one, the screen changes to show intervals that are suitable to your choice. If you choose nothing, your Palm device assumes that you mean None.

Figure 8-9:
Come
again? Set
up your
recurring
appoint-
ments in the
Change
Repeat
dialog box.

5. **Enter a number to indicate how often you want the appointment to repeat.**

   If you enter nothing, your Palm device assumes that the number is 1, meaning that the appointment occurs every day, week, month, or year, depending on which frequency you chose. If you change that number to the number 2, your appointment occurs every two days, two weeks, two months, or two years, and so on.

6. **If your appointment repeats until a certain date, tap the End On box.**

   Some appointments repeat for a certain period of time. If you go to night school, for example, your class may occur once a week for ten weeks. When you tap the End On box, a menu appears, giving you two choices: No End Date and Choose Date.

7. **Tap Choose Date from the End On box.**

   The Ending On screen appears.

8. **Tap the end date you want on the calendar on the Ending On screen.**

   The Ending On screen disappears, and the date you chose appears in the End On box.

9. **Tap the appropriate box to indicate other information about your repeating appointment.**

   You have one other choice to make if your appointment repeats on either a weekly or monthly basis. You can set weekly appointments to recur on several days of the week (such as Monday, Wednesday, and Friday) by simply tapping the various days. Notice that the days are set on a *toggle*, meaning that you must tap them again to deselect them. If you're setting up a monthly appointment, tap either Day (for example, the third Monday of every month) or Date (for example, the 15th of every month).

When you make any of these choices, text describing your recurrence pattern (such as "The third Monday of every month") appears in the box at the bottom of the Change Repeat dialog box. Keep an eye on this text to be sure that you've set up your appointment correctly.

10. Tap OK.

The Change Repeat dialog box closes, and the Event Details dialog box opens.

11. Tap OK.

The Event Details dialog box closes.

When you create a repeating appointment, each instance of the appointment looks like a separate item, but the occurrences are all connected in the mind of your Palm device. If you change or delete one occurrence of the appointment, your Palm device wants to know whether you're changing every occurrence or just that one. When it asks, just tell it what you want.

Marking items as private

You can enjoy the thrill of a secret rendezvous with your Palm device. I suppose that you can enjoy the rendezvous without your Palm device, too, but it helps you remember the rendezvous while keeping it a secret from anyone else who looks at your Palm device:

1. With the Date Book visible, tap the name of the appointment you want to make private.

The insertion point appears on the line with your appointment's name.

2. Tap Details.

The Event Details dialog box opens.

3. Tap the check box next to Private.

A check mark appears in the check box to show that you've marked the appointment as private.

4. Tap OK.

The Event Details dialog box closes. If you haven't chosen to hide all private records, you see a dialog box telling you how to hide all private records. (In case you forgot, see Chapter 3 for more info about hiding private items.)

Of course, there is such a thing as too much secrecy. If you mark an appointment as private and then tell your Palm device to hide all Private Records, the appointment doesn't show on the screen, so *you* can't even see your private records. That's a problem. To prevent keeping your secrets secret from yourself, tap the Applications icon, choose the Security icon, and then pick Show Private Records.

Putting Appointments in the Past

You may be the type of person who rarely enters anything directly into your Palm device. If you enter everything via a HotSync from your desktop computer, you still want to be able to delete existing appointments and set up your Palm device to suit your fancy.

Deleting appointments

Sooner or later, all your appointments become history. Perhaps you want to save all your appointment records for posterity. Perhaps you think that posterity is baloney, and you want to get rid of the stuff after it's over. I go for the second choice.

Here's how to delete an appointment:

1. **With the Date Book visible, tap the name of the appointment you want to delete.**

   The insertion point appears on the line with your appointment's name.

2. **Tap Menu.**

   The menu bar appears at the top of the display area, as shown in Figure 8-10.

3. **Choose Record⇨Delete Event.**

   The Delete Event dialog box opens.

4. **Tap OK.**

   The Delete Event dialog box closes, and your appointment disappears. Simple as that. If you check the box that says Save Archive Copy on PC, a wonderful thing happens: The next time you HotSync, the HotSync Manager saves a copy of the deleted item on your desktop computer. Who'd have thunk it? (For more information about archived items, see Chapter 12 or 13; for more about HotSyncing, see Chapter 11.)

Another way to delete an appointment is to tap the appointment name, then tap Details, and then tap Delete. You get the same result either way: No more appointment.

```
┌─────────────────────────────────────┐
│ Record  Edit  Options               │
│ New Event        /N ·················│
│ Delete Event...  /D ·················│
│·Attach Note      /A ·················│
│·Delete Note...   /O ·················│
│·Purge...         /E ·················│
│ 1:00 ································│
│ 2:00 Staff meeting ·················│
│ 3:00 ································│
│ 4:00 ································│
│ 5:00 ································│
│ 6:00 ································│
│ ·[:::] (New) (Details) (Go to)      │
└─────────────────────────────────────┘
```

Figure 8-10: Want to delete an appoint-ment? Choose Delete Event from this menu.

Setting preferences

You can change the Date Book in two ways: the number of hours it displays for each day and the type of alarm. If you feel compelled to customize the Date Book, here's how to do it.

To set Date Book preferences:

1. **With the Date Book visible, tap Menu.**

   The menu bar appears at the top of the display area.

2. **Choose Options➪Preferences.**

   The Preferences screen appears, as shown in Figure 8-11.

3. **To change the start time, tap one of the triangles next to the Start Time box.**

   Tapping the top triangle makes the start time later. Tapping the bottom triangle makes the start time earlier.

4. **To change the end time, tap one of the triangles next to the End Time box.**

   The End Time box works just like the Start Time box (see Step 3).

5. **To change the default alarm preset, tap the Alarm Preset check box.**

   A check mark appears in the check box, and the alarm setting appears to the right of the check box. Normally, the alarm setting is five minutes.

6. **If you want to change the Alarm preset time, tap the word *Minutes*.**

   A list appears with the choices Minutes, Hours, and Days.

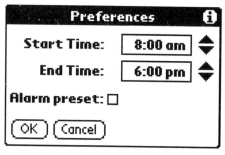

Figure 8-11:
Express
your prefer-
ences here.
Otherwise,
keep them
to yourself,
thank you.

7. **Tap your choice of Minutes, Hours, or Days.**

   The list disappears, and the choice you tapped appears.

8. **Enter the number of minutes, hours, or days before the appointment you want the alarm to sound with either the on-screen keyboard or Graffiti (see Chapter 2 for more info about entering text).**

   The number you enter appears next to the words *Alarm Preset.*

9. **To change the type of alarm sound you hear when the alarm goes off, tap the triangle next to the words *Alarm Sound.***

   A list of all the possible alarm sounds appears.

10. **Tap the type of the alarm sound you want.**

    You have several squeaks and squawks to choose from. The sound that you tap plays, and its name appears in the Alarm Sound box.

11. **Tap the Remind Me box to choose the number of times you want to be reminded of your appointment.**

    A list appears, offering choices ranging from Once to 10 Times.

12. **Tap the number of times you want to be reminded.**

    The choice you tap appears in the Remind Me box.

13. **Tap the Play Every box to choose how often to replay the Alarm.**

    A list appears, offering choices ranging from 1 to 30 minutes.

14. **Tap the choice you want in the Play Every box.**

    The choice you tap appears in the Play Every box.

15. **Tap OK.**

Maybe I'm boring, but I've never changed my Date Book preferences. Maybe you're different. If I could get the alarm to play "Tea for Two," I might change my mind.

Purging the Date Book

Your Palm device can hold as many as 10,000 appointments. That sounds like a great deal, but sooner or later you want to clear out some space and make room for more items. The fastest way to make room is to purge old Date Book items. Purging the Date Book is quick and easy, and it doesn't hurt a bit.

To purge the Date Book, follow these steps:

1. **With the Date Book visible, tap Menu.**

   The menu bar appears at the top of the display area.

2. **Choose Record⇨Purge.**

   The Purge dialog box opens, as shown in Figure 8-12. By default, your Palm device is set to purge appointments older than one week. If you want to change the age of purged appointments, tap the words *1 Week* and choose from the list that appears.

3. **Tap OK.**

   The Purge dialog box closes.

Figure 8-12: Is your schedule too full? Purge it to make room for more appointments.

Now you're rid of all the great things you've done, and you can move on to the great things you're going to do. Isn't that inspiring?

Chapter 9

Beaming Data from Your Palm Device through the Air with Infrared

. . . .

In This Chapter

▶ Sending and receiving items

▶ Sending and receiving categories

▶ Sending and receiving applications

. . . .

*P*eople often will pay more for something cool than they'll pay for something useful. At the moment, the ability to *beam* (or send) information between two Palm devices is very cool but only beginning to be useful. In fact, I would call this feature ultracool, and, fortunately, it doesn't cost you anything extra. However, you may find yourself in very few situations in which you can use it — at least not until most people you encounter are carrying a suitably equipped Palm device. In this chapter, I give you the skinny on beaming so that you're ready when that first momentous beaming occasion presents itself.

The Beaming Thing

Beaming is a Palm Computing feature that enables you to send information from one Palm device to another by directly pointing the two units at one another. As long as the units are within about three feet of one another, the process is quick and simple. My informal tests show that two Palm devices lose sight of each other when they're four feet apart, and they also have some trouble communicating at less than three inches or so. At a typical meeting table, you should have no trouble beaming information to a Palm device across from you.

Only the Palm III and later models have the capability to beam information, but you can easily upgrade whatever Palm device you have by adding a Palm 2MB memory card that turns any earlier PalmPilot model into a Palm III for about 50 bucks. (For more info about upgrading your Palm device, see Chapter 16.)

The Palm beaming feature uses *infrared* (or *IR*) light, which is what the remote control for your TV uses. Computer manufacturers have begun to include IR communications on laptops and printers. You also can find IR capability on certain advanced pagers and cellular telephones.

Not all applications have been built to use the beaming feature. Even the Palm Mail and Expense programs can't beam items. I think that forwarding e-mail by beaming would be useful. Maybe next year.

In the following sections, I show you how to beam individual items, categories, and even applications.

Sending an item

Whenever you beam information between a pair of Palm devices, you're copying information from one unit to the other. The data you send remains on your unit and is duplicated on the second unit. Think of the process as sending a fax: Before you send a fax, only you have a copy of the information; after you're done, you and the receiver both have a copy of the information (and a week later neither of you can find either copy).

Here's how to send an item:

1. **Make sure that both Palm devices are turned on and pointed at one another.**

   Keep the two Palm devices within three feet of one another.

2. **Select the item you want to beam.**

   The item appears on your screen. You can send a memo, an address, a to-do item, or an appointment.

3. **Tap Menu.**

   The menu bar appears.

4. **Choose Record⇨Beam.**

   The menu indicates Beam Event for a Date Book appointment (as shown in Figure 9-1), Beam Address for an Address Book entry, and so on.

The Beam dialog box opens for a short time, first telling you that it's preparing to beam and then that it's searching for another Palm device. After your Palm device finishes beaming the item, the dialog box closes.

Record	Edit	Options

New Event	✓N
Delete Event...	✓D
Attach Note	✓A
Delete Note...	✓O
Purge...	✓E
Beam Event	✓B

2:00
3:00
4:00
5:00 Big Whoop!
6:00

(New) (Details) (Go to)

Figure 9-1:
This event
will be on
the air.

If all goes well, both Palm devices beep to let you know that the item reached its destination. Your recipients actually know more about the transfer than you do because dialog boxes pop up on their Palm devices to say what's been received. If the transfer fails, your Palm device displays a message saying that something's wrong and that you should try again.

If you enter your own address in your Palm Address Book and mark it as your business card, all you need to do when you want to beam your business card is hold down the Address Book button for about two seconds until the beaming process starts.

Receiving an item

Just because you're receiving an item rather than sending one doesn't mean that you can just stand there and do nothing. You can stand there and do *almost* nothing. Just watch the screen and tap Yes when the time comes, like this:

1. **Make sure that both Palm devices are turned on and pointed at one another.**

   The two Palm devices should be within three feet of one another.

2. **When your buddy sends an item to you, wait for the Beam dialog box to open.**

   The Beam dialog box tells you what's being beamed to you and asks whether you want to accept the item.

3. **Tap Yes or No.**

   If you tap No, the Beam dialog box closes, and that's the end of the process. If you tap Yes, the application to which the beamed item belongs opens and shows you details of the item. For example, if the beamed item is someone's business card, your Address Book screen appears, showing the new address record you're about to add to your Address List.

4. **Make any changes you want to the beamed item.**

   You may want to change the category of the item or just make a note about when or where the beamed item originated. For example, if someone beams you her business card at a trade show, you may want to make a note of the trade show at which you met.

5. **Tap Done.**

   The item closes, and you see the main screen of the application to which the beamed item belongs.

In theory, people can beam unsolicited items to you, but you can always refuse them by tapping No. My only gripe about how the routine works is that after you say Yes, your Palm device buries the item in the list of items in the Unfiled category. If I want to go through the items I received today, I have to guess which item came in when. If you assign categories or add a note to everything promptly, you don't have trouble figuring out what's new. (For more info about using categories, see Chapter 6.)

Sending a category

You don't have to beam items one at a time; you can send an entire category at one time. You're limited, of course, to sending bunches of items that can handle categories; for example, because the Date Book has no categories, you can beam only one appointment at a time. (For more info about using categories, see Chapter 6.)

To beam an entire category, follow these steps:

1. **Make sure that both Palm devices are turned on and pointed at one another.**

   Keep the two Palm devices within about three feet of one another.

2. Display the category you want to beam.

The category appears on your screen.

3. Tap Menu.

The menu bar appears.

4. Choose Record⇨Beam Category, as shown in Figure 9-2.

The Beam dialog box opens for a moment and then closes.

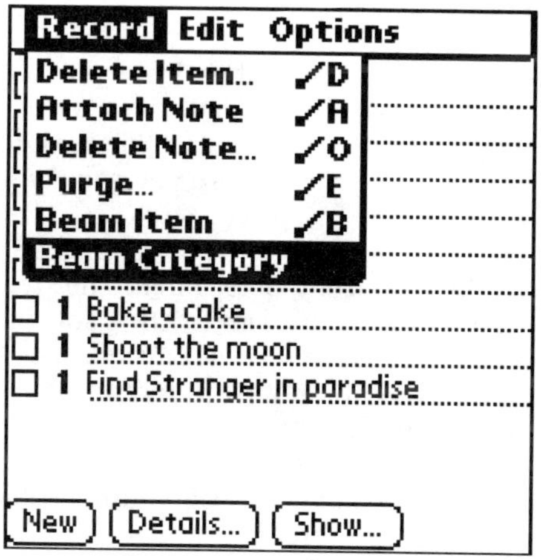

Record	Edit	Options
Delete Item...	✓D	
Attach Note	✓A	
Delete Note...	✓O	
Purge...	✓E	
Beam Item	✓B	
Beam Category		

☐ 1 Bake a cake
☐ 1 Shoot the moon
☐ 1 Find Stranger in paradise

(New) (Details...) (Show...)

Figure 9-2: Beam a whole category of tasks for someone else to do. That's how I spell *relief.*

Before the Beam dialog box closes, it tells you very briefly the name of the category you're sending. A little Cancel button in the dialog box enables you to cancel the transfer if you've sent the wrong thing, but the dialog box closes so quickly that you really can't stop the transfer. Therefore, be sure that you really want to send the items you're beaming.

Receiving a category

The process of receiving a whole category of items works just like receiving a single item (see the section "Receiving an item," earlier in this chapter). Receiving a category of items is a problem, however, for two reasons:

✔ The first reason is that when you tap Yes to accept incoming items, the Palm device opens only one of the items you received. If you want to edit or categorize the incoming items, you can only do so to the first item; all the others get mixed up with your unfiled items, so you have to dig them out one by one. Because you have no way of knowing exactly which items the other person sent, you may have trouble figuring out which items were sent by whom.

✔ The second reason is that the category markings are removed from incoming items; they're all marked Unfiled. There's a good reason for that: A Palm device can handle only 15 categories. If you were able to accept categorized items from lots of different people, you'd end up with a messy collection of categories. On the other hand, if someone sends you a category, you logically expect to get that category. I figure that the Palm people will address this issue in a future upgrade.

Sending an application

Believe it or not, you can beam an entire application from one Palm device to another. Frankly, beaming programs between Palm devices is much easier than installing programs from your desktop computer. You have to install the program first on your Palm device, of course, before you can share it with anyone else.

Some Palm Computing applications refuse to be beamed. The standard applications, for example, appear on the Beam list with a little padlock next to them, which means that you can't beam those programs because they're locked. In the future, many other Palm Computing programs will be locked the same way to prevent software piracy.

At the moment, though, you can beam most Palm Computing software between Palm devices, by following these steps:

1. **Make sure that both Palm devices are turned on and pointed at one another.**

   Keep the two Palm devices within about three feet of one another.

2. **Tap the Applications soft button.**

   The Applications screen appears.

3. **Tap Menu.**

   The menu bar appears.

4. **Choose App⇨Beam.**

   The Beam screen appears, as shown in Figure 9-3, listing all your applications. The applications with a little padlock next to them are locked and can't be beamed.

5. **Tap the name of the application you want to beam.**

   The application you tap is highlighted to indicate that you selected it.

6. **Tap Beam.**

   The Beam dialog box opens, indicating which program you're sending. If you change your mind, tap Cancel.

Beam		
Address	🔒	2K
AirCalc		45K
BrainForest		80K
Date Book	🔒	1K
DietLog		87K
DigiPet		21K
EEToolkit		30K
Flash!		61K
Mail	🔒	2K
Memo Pad	🔒	2K

(Done) (Beam)

Figure 9-3: The locks show the programs that can't be beamed.

Because programs normally take longer to beam than individual items, keep the Palm devices pointed at each other until the Beam dialog box closes, indicating that the process is complete. Programs take longer to beam because they're bigger, and bigger programs take longer to beam than smaller ones. You can see how big a program is by checking the number next to the name of the program on the Beam screen. I've never seen the process of beaming a program between Palm devices take more than a few minutes.

Receiving an application

The process of receiving a beamed application is just like receiving anything else (see the section "Receiving an item," earlier in this chapter, for details). After you agree to receive the application by clicking Yes in the Beam dialog box, your display area switches to the Applications screen, showing the new program.

Here's the big catch to beaming applications: Only the actual program is copied to the receiving Palm device. Files created or used by the program don't come over with the program. For example, if you beam AportisDoc — a document-reading program — from a Palm device that has several text files in AportisDoc, those files aren't copied; only the program itself is. You can't beam AportisDoc files; you have to install the documents from a desktop through the regular Palm Install Tool. The problem is even worse if you want to beam a program that requires an additional file, such as a dictionary, in order to run. If you beam Bogglet (the Palm version of the word game Boggle), the dictionary file Bogglet relies on to create puzzles doesn't transfer along with the program, so the program doesn't work unless you use Palm Desktop to install the dictionary.

Beaming into the Future

Naturally, plenty of people want to write Palm Computing programs that take advantage of the capability to sling data through the air, but only a few programs are finished so far. A couple of products I've tried are pretty interesting.

IrPrint, from IS/Complete, Inc. (www.iscomplete.com), offers a program that enables you to print via infrared to any suitably equipped printer. At this point, HP, Canon, and other companies have printers with IR capability. With the IrPrint program, you can point your Palm device at a printer and print a memo, task, or appointment on the spot.

Several software vendors offer IR HotSync products, which enable you to point your Palm device at a desktop or laptop computer and perform a HotSync without placing your Palm device in a cradle. IBM (www.ibm.com) has a utility named IR Sync that's designed to synchronize a Palm device with an IBM ThinkPad, but it works with other brands of laptop as well.

I've even tried products that enable you to use your Palm device as a remote control for your TV or VCR. Unfortunately, the tiny IR transmitter in the Palm device is too weak to get all the way from your couch to your TV. If you have to get off the couch to move within three feet of your TV, I think that you may as well make the rest of the journey, right? But I like the idea anyway.

Chapter 10

Special Delivery: Using Palm Mail

*R*omantic movies always have a scene where a character moons over a letter from his Special Someone. Romantic Reader ambles down the streets of Paris reading the letter and hearing Special Someone's voice as the movie soundtrack swells.

That scene would be difficult to imagine if Special Someone had sent Romantic Reader an e-mail. Imagine poor Romantic Reader trying to drag a desktop computer through the Left Bank with an endless extension cord, or trying to balance a laptop on his knee while overlooking the Seine, hoping that the laptop batteries don't go dead in ten minutes.

Although e-mail is convenient, the business of sitting in front of a computer to read and write e-mail isn't so convenient. Your Palm device includes a rather basic e-mail program that enables you to carry a little bucket of messages wherever you go. You can read messages and compose replies while you're sitting on the Seine or riding the subway. I have to admit that the program has its limits, although I often find it handy to deal with my e-mail on my Palm device; plugging in my desktop computer on the crosstown bus can be a bit difficult.

Making Sense of the Palm Postal System

The Palm Mail program doesn't exchange messages like a desktop e-mail package does. Like the Palm device itself, the Mail program acts as an accessory to the programs on your desktop; in this case, your e-mail program. When you perform a HotSync, the Palm Mail program copies the messages in your desktop e-mail program's Inbox and stores those copies on your Palm device. You can read or reply to those messages or compose new messages on your Palm device when you're away from your desktop computer. When you get back to your desktop computer, you have to perform another HotSync to move your outgoing messages to your desktop e-mail program, which does the work of actually delivering the messages.

The Palm VII includes a second, totally separate e-mail program, named iMessenger. It works much like the Palm Mail program, except that it does send messages directly from your Palm VII to the recipient without connecting to any other computer. This chapter is about the original Palm Mail program, which is not that clever. (You can read more about the Palm VII in Chapter 14.)

The Palm Mail program can't send messages directly to their recipients without a desktop e-mail program acting as a middleman (or middleperson, for all you politically correct readers out there). That's not what it's designed to do.

You can overcome this limitation by taking a few extra steps. If you want to send e-mail directly from your Palm device, you need something that connects it to the Internet: either the PalmModem or one of those very cool wireless modems, like the Minstrel Modem I mention in Chapter 15. You also need to buy an independent e-mail program for your Palm device, such as HandMail, which I mention in Chapter 16.

In the following sections, I focus on showing you how to use what comes out of the box with your Palm device.

Working with Your Messages

You can use the built-in Palm Mail program only if you have a desktop mail program with which to synchronize it. You can do many of the same tasks with Palm Mail that you can with your desktop e-mail program, such as read and write messages, reply to messages, and forward messages. However, some popular e-mail features aren't available in Palm Mail, especially the ability for you to attach files or read files attached to incoming messages. You may be willing to trade those features for the ability to read your e-mail on a bicycle built for two (preferably on the back seat), but the choice is up to you.

To access your Palm e-mail program, tap the Applications soft button and then choose the Mail application. The Mail program's Inbox opens.

Creating a message

Creating a new e-mail message is much like writing a regular paper letter. All you need is an address and a message. Actually, all you need is an address; but sending a message as well is a sign of good manners.

Follow these steps to create a new message:

1. **With the Mail program open, tap New.**

   The New Message screen appears. If you know your recipient's e-mail address by heart, enter that address by using Graffiti or the on-screen keyboard. If you do that, skip ahead to Step 7.

   If you don't know your recipient's address, you can look it up in the Address Book. Continue with Step 2 if you're in this particular boat.

2. **Tap the word *To*.**

   The To screen appears.

3. **Tap Lookup.**

   The To Lookup screen appears, as shown in Figure 10-1, showing the e-mail addresses of the people you entered on the Address List. It doesn't show everyone in the Address Book, just those who have e-mail addresses. Convenient, eh?

Figure 10-1: If you don't know your recipient's e-mail address, you can pick a name from the Address Book on the To Lookup screen.

To Lookup:

Alifont, "Bull"	bsalifont@somewhere....
DeDark, Fredda	fredda.dedark@nigh...
Dogg, Pat D.	pdog@bells.org
Early, Otto B.	obearly@snoozer.com
Fergus, Freddie	fergus@sniff.net
Short, Peg	pshort@medalcast.com
Technical Support	support@palm.com
Thunderbl..., Magn	Thunder@clemte...

Look Up: .... (Add) (Cancel)

4. **Tap the name of the person to whom you're sending your message.**

   The name you tap is highlighted to show that you selected it.

5. **Tap Add.**

   The e-mail address of the person you selected appears on the To screen. You can repeat Steps 3 through 5 for each person to whom you want to send copies of the message.

6. **Tap Done.**

   The New Message screen reappears, showing the names of the people to whom you've chosen to send your message.

7. **If you want to send copies of your message to additional people, tap the line to the right of CC.**

   CC is highlighted to show that you selected it. If you know your recipient's e-mail address, just write it by using Graffiti or the on-screen keyboard. If you don't know the e-mail address and want to check your Address Book, repeat Step 2 (tap CC rather than To) through Step 6 for each CC addressee you want to add.

8. **Tap the line to the right of Subj.**

   A blinking line, the *insertion point*, appears, and Subj is highlighted, as shown in Figure 10-2.

Figure 10-2: On the New Message screen, enter the subject of your message as you would any other text.

```
┌────────────────────────────────────┐
│ New Message                          │
│   To: fredda.dedark@night.com ...... │
│   CC: obearly@snoozer.com .......... │
│ Subj: ...............................│
│ Body: ...............................│
│       ...............................│
│       ...............................│
│       ...............................│
│       ...............................│
│       ...............................│
│       ...............................│
│       ...............................│
│ (Send) (Cancel) (Details...)     ↑   │
└────────────────────────────────────┘
```

If you tap Subj itself, the Subject screen appears. Opening the Subject screen is an extra step you don't really need to take because you can enter your subject on the New Message screen. If you prefer to use the Subject screen, tap Done when you finish entering your text and continue to Step 10.

9. **Enter the subject of your message by using either the on-screen keyboard or Graffiti (see Chapter 2 for more info about entering text).**

   The text you enter appears on the Subject line.

10. **Tap to the right of Body.**

    The insertion point appears, and Body is highlighted.

    If you tap Body itself, the Body screen appears. Just like with the Subject line, you don't really have to take this extra step. If you prefer using this screen to enter your message, just tap Done when you finish and continue to Step 12.

11. **Enter the text of your message by using either the on-screen keyboard or Graffiti.**

    The text you enter appears on the screen.

12. **Tap Send.**

    Your message closes and moves to the Outbox.

Even though you tapped Send, your message isn't on its way to your recipient. Tapping Send simply moves your message to the Outbox. The next time you HotSync your Palm device, everything in the Outbox moves to your desktop e-mail program, which then sends off your message.

Reading a message

A true boon to humanity, a Palm device now enables me to read my e-mail while waiting for the bus, so I can waste time two ways at one time. While I'm at it, I can also do some deep knee bends to make myself look foolish in public. (I don't need a Palm device to make me look foolish; I do that quite nicely on my own, thank you very much.)

To read your messages:

1. **With the Mail program open, tap the pull-down list in the upper-right corner of the Mail screen to see the list of available folders.**

   The list includes Inbox, Outbox, Deleted, Filed, and Draft. You can expect to find new messages in the Inbox.

2. **Tap the name of the folder you want to view.**

   The folder you tap appears on the screen, showing a list of messages.

3. **Tap the message you want to read.**

   The text of the message you tap appears.

4. **After you finish reading the message, tap Done.**

Your message closes, and the list of messages reappears. A check mark appears next to the message you just read.

If you want to cycle through your messages but don't want to return to the message list, just use the two left- and right-pointing triangles at the bottom of each message screen. Tapping one of those triangles enables you to see the next message or the preceding message. Although that feature is useful, for some reason I think of the next message as being *below* the current message, rather than to the right. Anyway, that's what those triangles do, in case you were wondering.

While you're reading a message, you may also notice a pair of icons in the upper-right corner of the message screen. One looks like a tiny message containing a great deal of text, and the other looks like a tiny message with only a little bit of text. If you tap the icon that looks like it holds a great deal of text, you reveal the message *headers,* the information that comes before the body of the message, including whom the message is to and from, the subject of the message, and the date the message was sent. The other icon conceals everything except the name of the person who sent the message and the subject of the message. You can tap either icon at any time to see as much or little header information as you want. I prefer to see less header information.

Replying to a message

The simplest way to address a message to somebody is to reply to a message he sent you. Here's what to do:

1. **With the Mail program open, tap the message you want to reply to.**

The text of the message you tap appears.

2. **Tap Reply.**

The Reply Options dialog box opens, as shown in Figure 10-3.

3. **Tap either Sender or All.**

If you choose Sender, your reply goes only to the person (or persons) listed on the To line of the message. If you choose All, your reply goes to the person (or persons) on the CC line too. To see what happens when you tap Forward, see the following section, "Forwarding a message."

You probably will notice two additional options: Include Original Text and Comment Original Text. If you check the first option, the text of the message you're replying to is included with the message you're sending. Checking the second box puts a caret symbol (>) in front of every line of the original text so that the person getting your reply can quickly see which text she wrote and which text you added. You can check the first box, neither box, or both boxes; if you just check the second box, though, nothing happens. You can't add comment marks to the original text unless you include the original text. Normally, I leave both boxes checked.

Figure 10-3:
Reply to just the person who sent the message or to everyone it was sent to.

4. **Tap OK.**

   The New Message screen appears. Your recipient's e-mail address appears on the To line, and the Subject line shows Re: followed by the subject of the original message. If you chose in Step 3 to include the original message text in your reply, that text appears in the body of your new message.

   You can change any of this text by deleting and adding text as you normally would.

5. **If you want to add new addresses to either the To or CC line of the message, enter the new addresses on those lines.**

   You can add an address to a message you're replying to in the same way as you do when you create a new message. See the section "Creating a message," earlier in this chapter, for details.

6. **If you want to add text to your message, tap to the right of *Body.***

   The insertion point appears. If you chose to include the original message's text, your Palm device conveniently leaves you a blank line to start writing your reply text.

   If you tap the word *Body* itself, the Body screen appears with the subject of your message at the top. If you enter your text on the Body screen rather than on the New Message screen, just tap Done when you finish entering your text and continue to Step 8.

7. **Enter the text you want to add by using either the on-screen keyboard or Graffiti (see Chapter 2 for more info about entering text).**

   The text you enter appears with the original message's text.

8. **Tap Send.**

   Your message closes and moves to the Outbox to await delivery.

Forwarding a message

Forwarding a message is just like replying to a message (see the preceding section), except that rather than send a message back to the person who sent you the original message, you send a message to a third person.

To forward a message:

1. **With the Mail program open, tap the message you want to forward.**

   The text of the message you tap appears.

2. **Tap Reply.**

   The Reply Options dialog box opens.

3. **Tap Forward.**

   When you forward a message, the text of a message you received from one person is sent to another person.

4. **Tap OK.**

   The New Message screen appears, containing the text of the message you're forwarding. On the Subject line, you see Fwd:, followed by the subject of the original message.

5. **On the To line, enter the e-mail address of the person to whom you're forwarding the message.**

   You address a message you're forwarding in the same way as you do when you create a new message. See the section "Creating a message," earlier in this chapter, for the lowdown.

6. **If you want to add text to your message, tap to the right of *Body*.**

   The insertion point appears. If you tap the word *Body* itself, a new screen appears for the body text, with the subject of the message at the top. You can enter text on either this screen or the New Message screen — your choice. If you choose to enter text on the Body screen, just tap Done when you're finished and continue to Step 8.

7. **Enter the text you want to add by using either the on-screen keyboard or Graffiti (see Chapter 2 for more info about entering text).**

   The text you enter appears with the message text.

8. **Tap Send.**

   Your message closes and moves to the Outbox to await delivery.

People seem to enjoy forwarding jokes by e-mail. I guess that forwarding a joke to 25 people is faster than standing around the water cooler and waiting for them to show up so that you can repeat the joke to each of them, one by one. Also, using your Palm device to forward jokes by e-mail makes you look like you're working (except to those who know better).

Deleting a message

Your Palm device seems to have plenty of space until you start loading it with e-mail. You'd be surprised how easily you can collect enough e-mail to fill a couple of megabytes of memory. Fortunately, deleting a message is just as easy. Here's how:

1. **With the Mail program open, tap the message you want to delete.**

   The text of the message you tap appears.

2. **Tap Delete.**

   Your message disappears. If you have the Confirm Deleted Message option checked in the Preferences dialog box (tap the Menu soft button, and then choose Options⇨Preferences), the Delete Message dialog box opens, as shown in Figure 10-4. Just tap Yes to get rid of that pesky message.

Figure 10-4:
Tap Yes to
delete.

Presto! Your message has magically disappeared — sort of. Actually, when you choose to delete messages, they move to the Deleted folder and wait for you to purge them.

If you change your mind after deleting a message, you can undelete a message from the Deleted Items folder. Open the Deleted Items folder by tapping the list of folder names in the upper-right corner of the Mail screen, and then choose Deleted. Tap the message you want to undelete to open it, and then tap the Undelete button at the bottom of the message screen. When you tap Undelete, the message returns to the Inbox.

When you HotSync, your Palm device's Inbox is forced to match the Inbox on your desktop e-mail program. Therefore, if you delete a message from your desktop e-mail program, the next HotSync removes that message from your Palm device's Inbox. You may find it easier to delete messages from your desktop and then HotSync. Most desktop e-mail programs enable you to delete batches of messages all at one time, which is faster and easier than deleting messages one by one on your Palm device.

If you want to take a message out of the Inbox but leave it on your Palm device, you can move the message to the Filed folder. Just tap the Menu soft button and then tap Message⇨File. That way, when all the messages in your Inbox are replaced by a new set during the next HotSync, the ones you sent to the Filed folder stay put. To see the contents of your Filed folder, tap the folder list in the upper-right corner of the Inbox screen and then tap Filed.

Purging deleted messages

Deleting a message doesn't eliminate that message from your collection. A deleted message moves to the Deleted folder until you purge your deleted items, like this:

1. **With the Mail program open, tap Menu.**

   The menu bar appears.

2. **Choose Purge⇨Deleted.**

   The Purge Deleted Message dialog box opens, as shown in Figure 10-5.

3. **Tap Yes.**

   The Purge Deleted Message dialog box closes, and your messages are gone forever.

The Deleted folder exists to save you if you accidentally delete an item and then change your mind and want to undelete it. But the best way to save space on your Palm device is to purge deleted messages frequently.

Figure 10-5:
This dialog box warns you about wiping out your deleted messages.

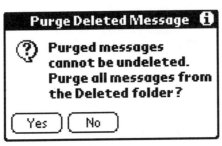

Purge Deleted Message ⓘ

Purged messages cannot be undeleted. Purge all messages from the Deleted folder?

Yes   No

One big difference between deleting e-mail messages and deleting other items on your Palm device is that no archive for deleted messages exists on the Palm Desktop. Your desktop e-mail program serves as the archive, so make sure that you really want those messages to disappear forever before you delete them.

Saving drafts

If you tap Cancel while composing a new message, the Save Draft dialog box asks whether you want to save a draft of the message. If you tap Yes, your incomplete message moves to the Drafts folder, where you can return to it later. Isn't that thoughtful?

Tapping No deletes your incomplete message forever, and Cancel simply returns you to the message itself.

Sending a blind copy

Sending blind copies of your messages is a sneaky way to inform someone about your communications with a third person without that third person knowing. For example, if you need more cooperation from someone in another department of your company, you can send that person an e-mail asking for the help you need and at the same time send a blind copy to the person who supervises both of you. The person you're addressing the message to doesn't know that you've clued in the boss.

Blind copies, or *BCCs,* are so sneaky that the line for them is hidden unless you know how to find and use it. Here, I let you in on the secret:

1. **With the Mail program open, tap New.**

   The New Message screen appears.

2. **Tap Details.**

   The Message Details dialog box opens.

3. **Tap the check box labeled BCC.**

   A check appears in the box, as shown in Figure 10-6.

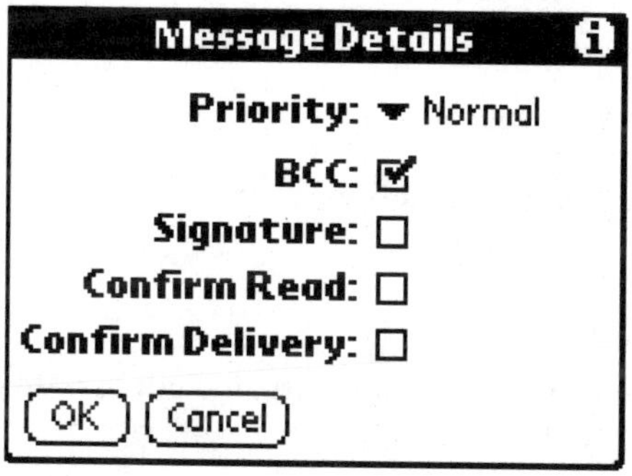

Figure 10-6: To send a secret blind copy of a message, find the secret check box.

Message Details ⓘ
Priority: ▾ Normal
BCC: ☑
Signature: ☐
Confirm Read: ☐
Confirm Delivery: ☐
(OK) (Cancel)

4. **Tap OK.**

   The Message Details dialog box closes, and the BCC line appears on the New Message screen.

5. **Tap BCC on the New Message screen.**

   The BCC screen appears. If you know the e-mail address of your BCC addressee by heart, enter the address by using Graffiti or the on-screen keyboard, tap Done, and continue creating your message. If you need to look up the address of the BCC addressee, continue to Step 6.

6. **Tap Lookup.**

   The BCC Lookup screen appears, showing all the names and e-mail addresses in the Address Book. Not everyone in the Address Book shows up on this list — only the ones with e-mail addresses.

7. **Tap the name of the person to whom you want to send a blind copy.**

   The name you tap is highlighted to show that you selected it.

8. **Tap Add.**

   The name you chose appears on the BCC screen.

9. **Tap Done.**

   The name you chose appears on the BCC line of your message.

10. **Continue creating your message.**

Well, now the secret is out. Don't forget; you saw it here first.

Sorting messages

I like to read messages in the order in which I receive them, although sometimes I like to see all the messages from a certain person lined up in a row. Other times, I want to read all the messages about a certain subject all at once. You can sort your messages in three different ways, depending on what you need.

To change the sort order of your messages:

1. **With the Mail program open, tap Show.**

   The Show Options dialog box opens.

2. **Tap the triangle next to Sort By.**

   A list of ways to sort your messages appears, including Date, Sender, and Subject, as shown in Figure 10-7.

3. **Tap your choice.**

   The sort type appears next to Sort By.

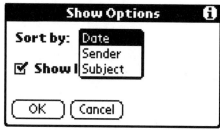

Figure 10-7:
In the Show
Options
dialog box,
you can sort
messages
by category.

4. **If you want to display the date you received each message, tap the check box next to Show Date.**

5. **Tap OK.**

   Your messages appear sorted the way you chose.

This sort order remains in effect until you choose a different sort order.

Customizing Your Palm E-Mail

After you develop a serious Palm e-mail habit, you need to know some techniques for managing the messages you get, customizing the messages you send, and speeding up the process of synchronizing your messages with your desktop. You may never use these tricks, although I want you to know that they're available.

Setting HotSync options

After you gather a healthy-size collection of items on your Palm device, the HotSync process may slow down quite a bit. At first, a HotSync should take only a few seconds, although after a couple of months a HotSync may take several minutes, which is a big deal for people as busy as you and me. You may want to shorten your HotSync time by telling your Palm device to limit e-mail activity to just sending or just receiving messages you haven't read yet. You can ignore the HotSync options if you want, with no ill effect.

To set HotSync e-mail options:

1. **With the Mail program open, tap Menu.**

   The menu bar appears.

2. **Choose Options⇨HotSync Options.**

   The HotSync Options screen appears, as shown in Figure 10-8.

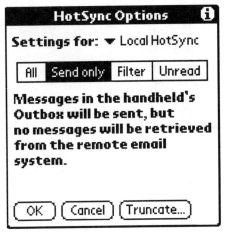

HotSync Options

Settings for: ▼ Local HotSync

| All | **Send only** | Filter | Unread |

Messages in the handheld's Outbox will be sent, but no messages will be retrieved from the remote email system.

(OK) (Cancel) (Truncate...)

3. Tap the triangle next to Settings For.

A list appears that enables you to choose either Local HotSync or Remote HotSync. You may want to make different things happen when you perform a modem HotSync than when you do a local HotSync. Modem HotSyncs are slower than local HotSyncs, so if you download only unread messages, for example, you save time and money when you do a long-distance modem HotSync. On the other hand, you may want to get all your messages when you do a local HotSync, so you need to be able to create different settings for the two types of HotSyncs. If you never attach your Palm device to a modem, you don't need to think about modem HotSync options.

4. Tap either Local HotSync or Remote HotSync.

Your choice appears next to Settings For. You're not limited to setting only local or only remote HotSync options; you just have to set the options for each type of HotSync one at a time.

5. Tap one of the boxes below Settings For.

A definition for each setting appears in the space. Here's the skinny on each setting:

- **All:** All messages in your desktop Inbox are copied to your Palm device and all outgoing messages are transferred to your desktop when you HotSync.

- **Send only:** Only outgoing messages are transferred to your Palm device when you HotSync. Incoming messages stay on your desktop computer.

- **Filter:** You can tell your Palm device to accept certain kinds of messages and reject others. For example, you can set up a filter to accept only messages marked as high priority. I discuss message filtering in greater detail in the following section, "Filtering messages."

• **Unread:** Your Palm device accepts only those messages you haven't read yet. The ones you've read stay on your desktop.

6. **Tap OK.**

The HotSync Options screen disappears, and your message list reappears.

If you frequently perform remote HotSyncs via a modem, you can set remote HotSync options separately from your local HotSync options. Your Palm device automatically picks the options you want depending on which type of HotSync you're doing. For example, you may want to exchange all messages when you're doing a local HotSync and send messages only when you do a remote HotSync.

Filtering messages

Filtering is a fairly sophisticated HotSync option. It enables you to set up rules to limit the messages the system copies to your Palm device, based on the priority of the message, the name of the person whose address appears in the To or From line, or the text on the Subject line.

I know people who get hundreds of e-mail messages every day. If performing a HotSync copied all their messages to their Palm devices, no room would be left for anything except e-mail. Filtering is a good idea for those who get more e-mail than they want on their Palm devices but who still want to take some messages with them.

Here's how to filter your messages:

1. **With the Mail program open, tap Menu.**

The menu bar appears.

2. **Choose Options⇨HotSync Options.**

The HotSync Options screen appears.

3. **Choose either Local or Modem HotSync.**

4. **Tap Filter.**

Options for filtering messages appear, as shown in Figure 10-9.

5. **If you want to copy only high-priority messages to your Palm device, tap the check box next to Retrieve All High Priority.**

Figure 10-9:
You filter the
junk from
your water,
so why not
filter the
junk from
your e-mail
messages,
too!

6. **If you want to create a rule for selecting a type of message to retrieve, tap the triangle at the left edge of the screen.**

   A list appears with two choices: Ignore Messages Containing and Retrieve Only Messages Containing.

7. **Choose the type of rule you want to create.**

8. **If you want to ignore or receive messages according to the address of the person they're sent to, enter that e-mail address on the To line.**

   "Wait a minute," you say. "I'm the recipient of my own e-mail, so if I choose to ignore my own e-mail address, I won't get any messages, right?" Technically, yes. Although filtering messages addressed to yourself may seem silly, you may discover reasons to exclude certain messages. First, you may get e-mail addressed to a mailing list. People on mailing lists often get dozens of messages every day, and you may not want to clutter up your Palm device with that kind of stuff. Besides, you can still look at the excluded messages on your desktop computer. Another reason is that your desktop e-mail program may collect messages from two e-mail addresses. If you have one address for business and another for personal messages, you can filter out one or the other type of message by putting that e-mail address on the To line.

9. **To ignore or receive messages from a particular sender, enter that sender's address on the From line.**

   You can enter multiple addresses on this line; just separate them with a comma.

10. **To ignore or receive messages in which the subject line contains a certain word or phrase, enter that text on the Subj line.**

11. **Tap OK.**

    The HotSync Options screen disappears, and your message list reappears.

If you're used to the more elaborate rules and filters in your desktop e-mail program, you can have your desktop computer do all the filtering for you before you HotSync your Palm device. Remember that only the items in the Inbox of your desktop program are copied to your Palm device, so if you sort your desktop Inbox before running HotSync, only the messages that make the cut on the desktop find their way to your Palm device. Most people I know are perfectly happy without ever using any kind of e-mail rule or filter, so if you ignore filtering, you're probably just as well off.

Using signatures

Lots of people like to personalize their e-mail with a standard bunch of text at the end of each message. Most popular e-mail programs enable you to set up a signature, so why not use signatures on the messages you create with your Palm device?

Why, indeed, when the process is this simple:

1. **With the Mail program open, tap Menu.**

   The menu bar appears.

2. **Choose Options⇨Preferences.**

   The Preferences screen appears, as shown in Figure 10-10.

Figure 10-10:
Individualize
your e-mail
with a flashy
signature.

3. **Enter your signature text by using the on-screen keyboard or Graffiti (see Chapter 2 for more info about entering text).**

   The text you enter appears on the Preferences screen.

4. **Tap OK.**

   The Preferences screen disappears, and your message list reappears. Your signature is automatically added to all your outgoing messages from now on.

One little detail about signatures: You can't see them yourself when you create your messages. The Mail program adds the signature when you send a message, so don't worry if you don't see your signature.

Setting truncating options

One of the limitations of using a tiny gadget device like a Palm device for reading e-mail is severe space limitations. You may not care much about megabytes or RAM until you run out of them. That's why the Palm Mail program automatically truncates, or chops off, messages at a certain length. Although you can determine the length, you're still limited to 8,000 characters. Because the full text of your messages is stored on your desktop computer, you can always look in your desktop e-mail program to see what got lopped off the messages on your Palm device.

Here's how to set the length at which messages are truncated:

1. **With the Mail program open, tap Menu.**

   The menu bar appears.

2. **Choose Options⇨HotSync Options.**

   The HotSync Options screen appears.

3. **Tap Truncate.**

   The Truncate Options dialog box opens, as shown in Figure 10-11.

4. **Tap the maximum message length you want.**

   The choice you tap is highlighted to show that you selected it.

5. **Tap OK.**

   The Truncate Options dialog box closes, and the HotSync Options screen appears.

6. **Tap OK.**

   The HotSync Options screen disappears, and your message list reappears.

The other thing your Palm Mail program chops off is attachments. If someone sends you a file — such as a word-processing document or a spreadsheet — that's attached to a message, you don't see the extra file on your Palm device. You can still see the file on your desktop computer, altough the Palm device just doesn't have space for the extra file. Instead, it simply tells you that a file

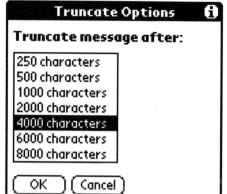

Figure 10-11:
You can
include any-
thing you
want in a
message, as
long as it
has fewer
than 8,000
characters.

Part III
Palm Organizers and the Outside World

"Let's see if I can get a menu any faster from their web site than I can from the waiter."

In this part . . .

Your Palm device isn't meant to be left all alone. You have to hook it up to a regular desktop or laptop computer to take full advantage of a Palm device's features. In this part, you find out how to help your Palm device and your regular computer carry out a meaningful relationship.

Chapter 11

Installing and HotSyncing to the Desktop Program for Windows

. . . .

In This Chapter

▶ Installing the Palm Desktop for Windows

▶ HotSyncing between your Palm device and your PC or Mac

. . . .

*I*n theory, you could use your Palm device all by itself, with no other computer involved. But if you're only interested in doing things the easiest way possible (my favorite way), then the Palm Desktop programs may be the best way to put things in your Palm device. You can carry it around to read your saved data and fiddle with it a little bit, as you see fit. I still prefer to enter most of my Palm Computing data by using Graffiti (refer to Chapter 2), but most people that I know don't. Although you can put information into your Palm device in many clever ways, the desktop program is the simplest and most understandable method for anyone who has used a computer. In this chapter, I show you how to install the Palm Desktop, and I tell you all you need to know about HotSyncing your Palm device to your desktop computer. In Chapter 12, I show you how to do all that cool Palm Computing-type stuff on your desktop computer. If you're a Mac user, see Chapter 13.

Installing Palm Desktop for Windows

Hold up! Stop! Whoa, Nellie! (Did I get your attention?)

Before you install your desktop software, you need to hook up the Palm cradle to your desktop computer.

Different names for the same program? What gives?

Palm Desktop 3.0.1 is the name for the program that manages your Palm organizer from your desktop, Windows-based computer. For those of you who own models earlier than Palm III (or The Device Formerly Known As the PalmPilot), Palm Desktop was once named PalmPilot Desktop. The two programs look a little bit different, but in action they're mostly similar.

You can run Palm Desktop 3.0.1 under Windows 95, Windows 98, or Windows NT. Because the program is on the CD that comes with your Palm device, you need a CD-ROM drive to install the program on your desktop computer. If you don't have a CD-ROM drive, contact 3Com, the manufacturer of your Palm device, and the folks there will send you the program on floppy disks.

You can still get a copy of the Palm Desktop for Windows 3.*x* if you contact 3Com and ask for the old program on floppy disks. Frankly, Windows 3.1 is a perfectly good host for a Palm device. The desktop program works like a champ, and there's absolutely no difference in what you do to make the Palm device do its thing.

Connecting the cradle to your PC

Normally, you can simply plug your Palm cradle into the only plug — or *serial port* — on the back of the PC in which it fits. If you can plug the cradle into the back of your PC easily, you've got it made. Just shout "Hooray!," pass Go, and collect $200 (or just jump ahead to the next section). If you can't plug the cradle right in, you have to do some fiddling around (see the following sidebar, "Cradle connection woes and how to fix 'em").

Now, you get to install Palm Desktop

Palm Desktop for Windows enables your computer to talk to and work with your Palm device through a process named HotSyncing. You have to install the desktop software only once, and then you're through. All you need to do after that is place your Palm device in the cradle and press the HotSync button on the cradle every day or so. More on HotSyncing later in this chapter.

After you connect the cradle to your computer, you can install Palm Desktop by following these steps:

1. **Put the CD that came with your Palm device in your CD-ROM drive.**

   The Palm Desktop Installer menu appears, as shown in Figure 11-1.

Cradle connection woes and how to fix 'em

If your desktop computer is fairly new, chances are that the serial port is unoccupied and working. The serial port is usually a small plug with 9 small pins. However, some serial ports are slightly larger and have 25 small holes rather than 9 small pins. The Palm cradle comes with an extra adapter you can put on the end of your cradle cable so that it plugs into the port with 25 small holes. But don't mistake the larger serial port plug for your printer port, which has 25 small pins. That port doesn't work with your Palm device. Is that clear? Of course not. The collection of ports on the back of a PC often confuse the most experienced technician, so don't be too concerned if the ports seem to make no sense.

Another common problem with PC serial ports is that sometimes they're occupied. You may have a mouse plugged in to your serial port or an external modem or who knows what else.

Most PCs have two serial ports, named COM1 and COM2; if you've filled up both serial ports, you may need to have your friendly local computer technician install a couple of extra serial ports to accommodate your Palm device. Because technicians often own Palm devices themselves, they know what to do.

Because people have been messing up the settings of their serial ports since the first personal computers, Microsoft added a feature to Windows 95 and Windows 98 named Plug and Play. This handy feature saves you the trouble of messing up your serial port settings by messing them up for you automatically. Isn't that thoughtful? If your Palm cradle never, ever manages to communicate with your computer, have your friendly computer technician check to see whether your serial port settings are messed up properly.

Figure 11-1:
The Palm Desktop Installer kicks off the installation process.

2. Click Install.

The Welcome screen appears and tells you what's about to happen, as shown in Figure 11-2.

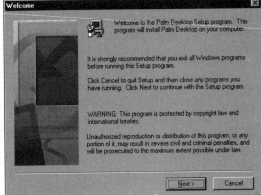

Figure 11-2:
The
Welcome
screen
explains
what you're
getting into.

3. Click Next.

The preinstall screen appears, telling you to connect your HotSync cradle, leave the Palm device out of the cradle for the moment, and install the batteries in your Palm device.

4. Click Next.

The Setup Type dialog box opens, as shown in Figure 11-3. You can choose between a typical installation and a custom installation. I recommend leaving Typical checked.

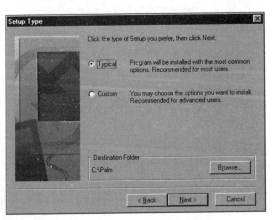

Figure 11-3:
The Setup
Type screen
gives you
a choice
between a
typical or
custom
installation.
Keep it
simple; pick
Typical.

5. **Click Next.**

   The Serial Port Setup dialog box opens. The only reason for this dialog box is to remind you to put your Palm device in the cradle so that the Install program can test the connections between your Palm device and your desktop computer.

6. **Place your Palm device in the cradle and click OK.**

   The Install program copies files for a few moments. If you have a Palm VII, you get to choose which Palm Query Applications you want to install. (See Chapter 14 for more info about Palm VII and its programs.) Otherwise, the Setup Complete dialog box opens.

7. **Click Finish.**

   The Palm Desktop Installer closes.

To HotSync or Not to HotSync . . . Just Do It

When you install the Palm, you end up with a good tool for tracking all your to-dos, addresses, memos, and appointments. That's fine if you're always at your desk. But if you divide your time between sitting at your desk and being on the go (and who doesn't, nowadays?), then keeping track of the data on two different machines can be a real pain. That's where HotSyncing comes in.

HotSyncing your Palm device with your desktop computer is blindingly simple. All you do is make sure that your desktop computer is running, put the Palm device in the cradle, and push the HotSync button. That's it. The HotSync button, as shown in Figure 11-4, is the only button on the cradle and has two arrows pointing at each other, so you can't go wrong. You don't even have to launch the desktop program. Pressing the HotSync button calls the HotSync Manager into action, which coordinates the whole process of swapping data. The HotSync Manager automatically turns on your Palm device, compares the data on it and on your desktop computer, and updates each machine with the most current info. After a few minutes, you end up with the same data on two different machines.

Most of the time, you don't need to know how the HotSync process works. However, every once in a while, you have to deal with HotSync problems, which happen most often when you synchronize your Palm device with other personal information managers, such as Microsoft Outlook, Goldmine, or Act! Then you need to mess around with something called a *conduit,* which moves data between your Palm device and non-Palm Computing programs. I say more about conduits in Chapter 20.

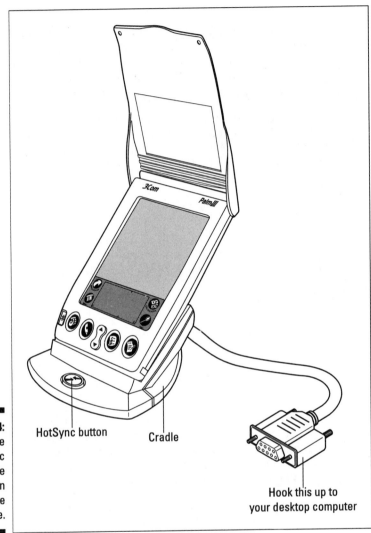

Figure 11-4:
The
HotSync
button is the
only button
on the
Palm cradle.

HotSync button   Cradle

Hook this up to
your desktop computer

Chapter 12

Operating the Palm Desktop Program for Windows

*I*n this chapter, I focus on using the Palm Desktop program for Windows. If you still need to install the desktop program, go to Chapter 11, where I give you the skinny on installing the program. Mac users, your Pilot Desktop is a totally different product from the Windows version, so you get Chapter 13 all to yourselves.

Even for the folks who take to Graffiti like a fish to water, entering data through the Palm Desktop now and then has some advantages. Typing is normally faster than using Graffiti, even for experienced users, and you can do things — such as copy multiple items and perform tricks with drag-and-drop — that a Palm device can't handle just yet. The biggest benefit of the Palm Desktop is that you can manage archived items you've purged or deleted from the Palm device. Near the end of this chapter, I tell you how to manage archived items.

The Palm Desktop isn't your only choice, of course, if you'd rather feed data to your Palm device from your desktop. You can set up many popular personal information managers (PIMs) — such as Microsoft Outlook, Lotus Organizer, and ACT! — to send data back and forth to your Palm device.

Because you may have spent years entering names and dates into another PIM, you may not want to change now. However, you do need a special something, a *conduit*, to be able to HotSync your PIM to your Palm device. I talk a bit about conduits in Chapter 20; for more info about operating your PIM, check out your local bookstore for a ...*For Dummies* book on the subject. Odds are that you'll find one!

Palm Desktop Basics

A Palm device does an amazing amount of work for a little gizmo with a tiny screen and barely a half-dozen buttons. But there's nothing like a big old computer with an old-fashioned keyboard and mouse for whipping off appointments, memos, to-dos, and addresses in a flash. Don't be prejudiced, though: You can use both the Palm Desktop and your Palm device to enter your data — whatever suits your fancy. In this section, I give you an overview of the Palm Desktop interface and take you on a tour of the basic applications of the Palm Desktop.

Understanding the Palm Desktop interface

Interface is a techie term that computer geeks use to describe what you see on your computer screen after you launch a program. The interface of the Palm Desktop is made up of the same elements as the screens of most computer programs, combined with elements of the Palm device screens. You can see the name of the program in the upper-left corner of the screen, in the *title bar* area. Below that is the *menu bar,* which works just like the menu bar in other programs you use on your computer. Below the menu bar sits the *toolbar,* as shown in Figure 12-1, containing a row of icons you can click to perform the tasks you need to do most often.

Figure 12-1:
The Palm
Desktop
toolbar.

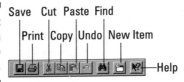

Save Cut Paste Find

Print Copy Undo New Item

———Help

On the left edge of the Palm Desktop screen is a column of buttons named the *launch bar.* The names of the buttons correspond to those of the standard Palm organizer applications: Date, Address, To Do, and Memo. Clicking any of these buttons launches the corresponding application.

Below the four application buttons are two more icons labeled Expense and Install. The Expense icon starts up the special Microsoft Excel spreadsheet that's filled with data from your Palm Expense application (if you use it). If you don't have Excel on your computer, the Palm Desktop Expense button does nothing, although you can still see it.

The Install icon, which is new to Palm Desktop 3.0, launches the Palm Install Tool for installing programs to your Palm device. Users of earlier versions of the Palm Desktop had to search for the Install tool on the Windows Start menu. Now, just one click launches it for you. For more info about installing applications on your Palm device, see the section "Installing applications," later in this chapter.

The main part of the screen looks a bit different depending on which application button you click. Normally, it's divided into two big sections, or two *panes* of the window. The left pane, or the *list pane* (yes, it has a name), displays information in a format that's nearly identical to the way your Palm device displays information. The right pane, named the *Record Pane,* shows you more detailed information. I go into more detail in the following sections about what you see for each application.

Arranging appointments in your Date Book

The Date Book on the Palm Desktop has many of the same parts as the Date Book screens, but the Palm Desktop organizes things a bit differently because your computer screen has more room to display items than your Palm device screen does. Also, your computer monitor probably has a color screen, which is something you can't get on a Palm device (yet).

Along the right edge of the Date Book, you can see three tabs labeled Day, Week, and Month. When you click any of those tabs, the view on the screen changes to the view you clicked. Here's the lowdown on what you see in each view:

- ✔ **Daily:** You may end up using Daily view more than the other views (at least I do). As shown in Figure 12-2, the left side of the Palm Desktop in Daily view shows a list of appointments for a single day. The right side of the screen shows a miniature monthly calendar. When you click a date on that calendar, the list of appointments for that date appears. A list of the months of the year appears above the monthly calendar. Tap the month, and the calendar for that month appears. Above the list of months is a box showing the current year. If you want to see a date in a past or future year, click the triangle on either side of the year display.

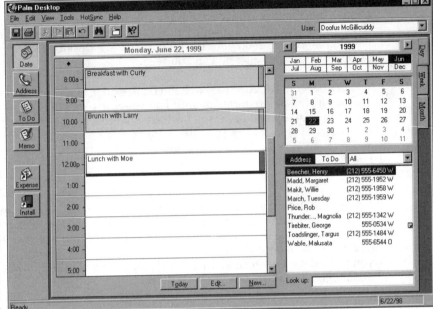

Figure 12-2:
Whaddya
doin' today,
knuckle-
head?
Check your
Date Book!
Nyuk-nyuk!

Below the calendar, Palm Desktop conveniently displays your To Do List and your Address Book so that you don't have to keep clicking the buttons on the left to switch between them. To toggle between your To Do List and Address Book, just click the name of whichever one you want to see.

✔ **Weekly:** Whenever you want to see how your week is shaping up, Weekly view shows a grid representing the whole workweek. Weekly view works just like it does on your Palm device, although Palm Desktop shows you the names of your appointments, whereas your Palm device shows you only bars representing the appointments.

✔ **Monthly:** If you like to think ahead, Monthly view shows you what you're doing for the whole month. Palm Desktop gives you more detail, however, than Monthly view on your Palm device because your computer screen is larger.

For more info about using the Date Book on your Palm device, refer to Chapter 8. To bring up your Date Book in Palm Desktop, just click the Date button on the left side of the screen or choose View➪Date Book, and then continue to the following sections.

Adding appointments

Entering appointments in your Palm Desktop is undoubtedly faster than entering them on your Palm device itself, as long as you're sitting at your big computer. If you're out in the field or at a meeting, it's a different story.

While you're sitting at the keyboard, follow these steps to add an appointment to the Palm Desktop:

1. **With the Date Book visible, click the Day tab on the right edge of the screen (or press Alt+D).**

   Daily view of your Date Book appears.

2. **Click the date of your appointment on the calendar on the right side of the screen.**

   The Date Book shows the appointments scheduled for that date.

3. **Click the line next to the hour when you want your appointment to begin.**

   A box opens where you clicked, and a blinking bar (an *insertion point*) appears. The first line of Daily view, next to the black diamond, has no time assigned to it; you can click there to enter events that last all day or that have no specific time assigned.

4. **Type a subject for your appointment.**

   The subject appears on the schedule.

5. **Click any other part of the screen (or press Tab).**

   Your appointment is displayed in yellow to show that you entered it.

I describe the method of adding appointments to Daily view of your calendar on the Palm Desktop because it is most similar to the way you add appointments on the Palm device itself. You have more flexibility in how you enter appointments on the desktop, though. For example, Palm Desktop enables you to add appointments in Weekly view as well as in Monthly view — something you can't do on a Palm device. Figure 12-3 shows you what Weekly view looks like. Just follow Steps 3 through 5 in the preceding example.

You may have noticed the New button at the bottom of the screen. (No, that doesn't make you a new person — you're fine the way you are.) The New button opens the Edit Event dialog box. You can always use the Edit Event dialog box for entering a new appointment, which is frankly the most complete and detailed way to enter information, but I think that it's a little cumbersome. You can read more about the Edit Event dialog box in the following sections.

Repeating appointments

Anything worth doing is worth doing at least once a week — that's my opinion. Especially days off. Try to make a habit of those, won't you? And note them in your Palm Desktop, like this:

1. **With the Date Book visible, click the Day tab on the right edge of the screen (or press Alt+D).**

   Daily view of your Date Book appears.

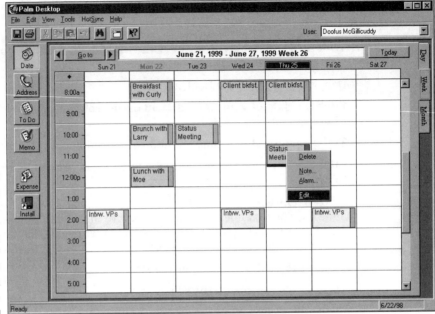

Figure 12-3:
You can add appoint-ments in Weekly view of the Palm Desktop.

2. **Click the date of your appointment on the calendar on the right side of the screen.**

   The Date Book shows the appointments scheduled for that date.

3. **Click the appointment you want to set as a repeating appointment.**

   The appointment's yellow box appears shadowed to show that you selected it.

4. **Click Edit at the bottom of the screen (or choose Edit➪Edit Event).**

   The Edit Event dialog box opens, as shown in Figure 12-4.

Figure 12-4:
Change appointment details in the Edit Event dialog box.

5. Click the button next to Repeat in the Edit Event dialog box.

The Change Repeat dialog box opens, as shown in Figure 12-5.

Figure 12-5:
Do it again!
Set up
appoint-
ments that
repeat as
often as
you want.

6. Click the name of the repeat pattern you want.

The name you choose is selected, and options for that pattern appear.

7. Enter the choices you want for the repeat pattern you chose.

The choices you make appear in the Change Repeat dialog box. Your choices are confirmed by the text box at the bottom of the dialog box.

8. Click OK.

The Change Repeat dialog box closes.

9. Click OK again.

The Edit Event dialog box closes, and a little circle appears next to your appointment to show that it repeats.

One tricky thing about repeating appointments is that every time you change one, the Palm device asks whether you're just changing this one appointment or the whole series. Don't be alarmed; just click the All button if you want to change all instances of the appointment, or click Current if you just want to change this instance of the appointment.

Making appointments private

Private appointments work pretty much the same way as private memos do (see the section "Making a memo private," later in this chapter) except that the check box in which you mark the appointment as private isn't on the main screen; it's hidden. To find the check box to mark an appointment as private, click the appointment to select it and click the Edit button at the bottom of the screen. That action opens the Edit Event dialog box, which contains the Private check box.

Whenever you mark an appointment as private, a tiny key appears in the upper-left corner of the appointment box. You can hide all private records by choosing View⇨Hide Private Records. When you hide private records, a key appears on the toolbar. You can show private records again by choosing View⇨Show Private Records.

Deleting appointments

When you set up an appointment you're not entirely sure about, you may tell a person that you'll "pencil him in," which implies that you may erase him, too. All appointments on your Palm device are "penciled in" in a way because it's so easy to erase them.

Take these steps to delete an appointment from your Palm Desktop:

1. **With the Date Book visible, click the Day tab on the right edge of the screen (or press Alt+D).**

   Daily view of your Date Book appears.

   You can also tap the Week tab. If you prefer to view your whole week at a glance, jump ahead to Step 3.

2. **Click the date of your appointment on the calendar on the right side of the screen.**

   The Date Book shows the appointments scheduled for that date.

3. **Click the appointment you want to delete.**

   The appointment's yellow box opens shadowed to show that you selected it.

4. **Click Delete (or choose Edit⇨Delete).**

   The Delete Datebook Event dialog box opens, as shown in Figure 12-6.

Figure 12-6:
Simply
delete an
undesirable
date.

5. **Click OK if you want your appointment to disappear, or click Cancel if you have a change of heart.**

   If you leave the Archive box checked in the Delete Datebook Event dialog box, the appointment isn't lost forever; it automatically moves to an archive file, where you can look it up later.

Arranging entries in your Address Book

Keeping that little black book on a pocket computer is wonderfully efficient and amazingly quick. Using a little computer for all that crucial stuff has one big drawback: What if you lose the thing? Yikes! Losing a contact lens is nothing compared to losing your personal organizer — not to mention how it can put a crimp into your social life!

Fortunately, you can maintain the whole mess on your desktop computer, where it's all safe and sound and backed up. What are the chances of losing both your desktop computer and your Palm device at the same time? Do you really want to find out? I didn't think so.

To bring up your Address Book, just click the Address button on the left side of the screen, or choose View⇨Address Book, and continue to the following sections. You won't have a problem making sense of the Address Book; when you open it, you see a list of names from which to select on the left side of the screen and full details of the person you select on the right side.

Adding a new Address Book entry

You can keep track of as little or as much information as you want about each person in the Address Book. Just fill out the form.

To add a new entry to your Address Book on the Palm Desktop:

1. **With the Address Book visible, click New at the bottom of the screen (or choose Edit⇨New Address).**

   The Edit Address dialog box opens.

2. **Type the last name of the contact in the Last Name text box.**

   The text appears in the Last Name text box, as shown in Figure 12-7.

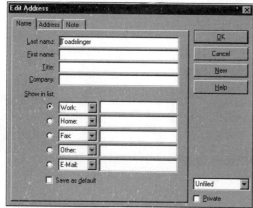

Figure 12-7: To add a new address, fill in the form, please.

3. **Enter the contact's first name, title, and company in the appropriate boxes.**

4. **Enter the contact's telephone number in the appropriate phone number box.**

   Your choices for telephone number are work, home, fax, and other.

5. **Click the radio button to the left of the phone number you want shown on the Address List.**

   The radio button you click is blackened to show that you selected it.

6. **Click the Address tab at the top of the Edit Address dialog box.**

   The Address page of the Edit Address dialog box opens, as shown in Figure 12-8.

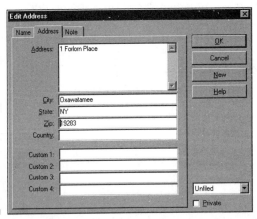

Figure 12-8:
Put the street address in the big box and the city, state, and zip in the little boxes.

7. **Type the street address of your contact.**

   The person's street address appears in the Address box.

8. **Enter the contact's city, state, zip code, and country in the appropriate boxes.**

9. **Click OK.**

   The Edit Address dialog box closes.

Although you can enter plenty of information in an Address Book entry, you can get away with just filling in one blank. If you enter just a phone number and not the name of the person at that phone number, of course, you don't get much benefit other than a way to start a weird party game. It depends on what kind of parties you go to. I probably won't be there, thanks.

Editing an address record

I think that most people who carry Palm devices are upwardly mobile, and so are most of the people that they know. Don't you? Of course. We both carry Palm devices. What else would we think?

As you'd expect, all these upwardly mobile people are continually moving to better jobs and better addresses, so plan on making lots of changes to your Address List. And, please, don't forget the little people.

These steps show you how to edit an address in your Palm Desktop:

1. **With the Address Book visible, double-click the name of the person whose record you want to change.**

   The Edit Address dialog box opens.

2. **Add new information the same way you entered it originally.**

   For more information, see the preceding section, "Adding a new Address Book entry."

3. **Select any information you want to change and type the new information.**

   The text you enter replaces the information you selected.

4. **Click OK when you finish.**

   The Edit Address dialog box closes.

A big advantage to making your changes on the Palm Desktop rather than on the Palm device is that you can save the old address in your archive. Just select the address record, and then press Ctrl+C to copy and then Ctrl+V to paste, and you have two identical records. If you delete one of the two and change the one that's left, you have the old address safely stored for posterity. To dig an old address from your archive, see the section "Archiving Your Palm Computing Stuff," later in this chapter.

Attaching a note to an address record

"Always tell the truth," a wise person said. "It's the easiest thing to remember." If you can't always recall what you said to whom, you could probably benefit from keeping track of what you say along with a record of whom you say it to. The perfect way to store these gems is in the form of notes in your Address Book. That way, you won't get caught.

Follow these steps to attach a note to an address record on your Palm Desktop:

1. **With the Address Book visible, double-click the record you want to annotate.**

   The Edit Address dialog box opens.

2. **Click the Note tab.**

   The Note page of the Edit Address dialog box appears, as shown in Figure 12-9.

3. **Enter the text of your note.**

   The text you type appears in the Note box.

4. **Click OK when you finish.**

   The Edit Address dialog box closes. To view your note, just click the person's name on the Address List; the note appears with the other contact information in the box on the right side of the screen.

If you still can't remember what you said, keep your fingers crossed.

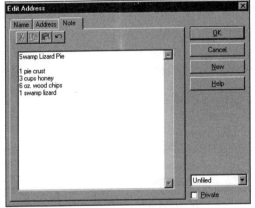

Figure 12-9:
Notes have their own page in the Edit Address dialog box.

Finding the name you want

If you need to find a person's vital statistics quickly, you can just type the first few letters of the person's last name in the Look Up text box at the bottom of the screen. When you type a letter or two in the Look Up text box, the Palm Desktop highlights the first name on the list that starts with those letters. If that's not the exact name you're looking for, the one you are looking for probably isn't far away. Keep typing letters until the name you want to find is highlighted. You can open that person's address record by double-clicking her name.

Deleting a name

Some names just don't make your list anymore. It's sad but true. To gently but firmly remove the name of someone who just isn't close to your inner microprocessor anymore, just click her name on your Address List and press Delete. A dialog box opens to make sure that you really want to do the deed; if you're sure, click OK.

If you change your mind, you can always restore any address record you saved in an archive. See the section "Archiving Your Palm Computing Stuff," later in this chapter, for details.

Setting up custom fields

If you keep track of lots of people who have a few important things in common, it's useful to set up special fields in your Address Book to help you keep track of what you need to know. If you're a teacher, for example, you may want to keep track of each student's age or grade level. If you're a Realtor, you may want to distinguish buyers from sellers and renters from landlords. Whatever your specialty, it's good to know that you can customize four of the Address Book fields for your own use.

These steps help you set up custom fields in the Palm Desktop:

1. With the Address Book visible, choose Tools⇨Custom Field Labels.

The Custom Field Labels dialog box opens, as shown in Figure 12-10.

Figure 12-10: You can customize four fields in your Address Book.

2. Type the name you want to assign to the first custom field.

The name you type appears in the Label 1 box.

3. Press Tab and enter the name you want to assign to each successive custom field.

4. Click OK.

The Custom Field Labels dialog box closes.

After you define the name of a custom field, all your address records have a field by that name. For example, if you rename field 1 Grade Level, every record on your address list has a field by that name, even if the records aren't for students.

Doing stuff with your to-dos

Knowing what to do isn't enough if you don't remember to do it. The To Do List lets you add to your Palm device the items you need to do so that the Palm device can remind you to do them.

To bring up your To Do List, just click the To Do button on the left side of the screen, or choose View⇨To Do List, and continue to the following sections. The left side of the To Do screen looks much like the Palm device To Do screen. It's just a list of your to-dos. The right side shows details of the to-do you selected.

Creating a to-do item

Nothing could be easier than entering a task on your To Do List. If only doing the tasks were so easy!

1. **With your To Do List visible, click New at the bottom of the screen (or choose Edit⇨New To Do).**

    A rectangle appears at the bottom of the To Do List, and the insertion point appears in the To Do text box on the right side of the screen, as shown in Figure 12-11.

2. **Type what you need to do in the To Do text box on the right.**

3. **Click the Apply button.**

    The name of your task appears on the To Do List on the left.

Setting the priority for a to-do item

With so many important things on your To Do List, how do you know what to do first? You need to set priorities. You have only the numbers 1 through 5 to assign as the priority for each task, but that's enough to make sure that you get to the important things first.

Here's how to set the priority of a to-do item:

1. **With your To Do List visible, click the name of the to-do item for which you want to set a priority number.**

2. **Click one of the radio buttons next to Priority on the right side of the screen.**

    The radio button next to the number you click is blackened to show which number you selected.

3. **Click the Apply button.**

    The priority you assign appears next to your to-do item.

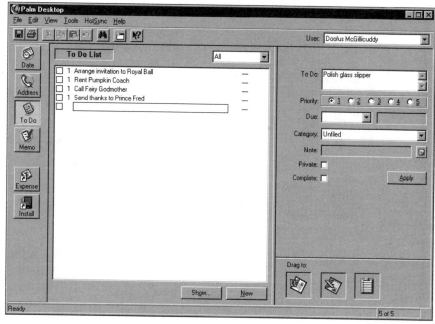

Figure 12-11:
Whatever
you type
appears
in the
rectangle.

Another trick you can try is to simply click the priority number on the To Do List. Clicking a priority number makes a list of priority numbers appear, as shown in Figure 12-12. You can choose the number you want by picking it from the list with a single mouse click.

It's okay to have more than one to-do with the same priority. You can make every task your top priority or your bottom priority. Whatever you pick, it's *your* priority.

Assigning a category to a to-do item

Another way to keep track of what task you need to do next is to assign categories. For example, some tasks must be done at home, and others can be done only at work. When you're at the office, you don't need to remind yourself to mow the lawn (although if it gets you out of the office early, it's worth a try).

To assign a category to a to-do item, follow these steps:

1. **With your To Do List visible, click the name of the to-do item to which you want to assign a category.**

2. **Click the Category box on the right side of the screen.**

   The drop-down list of available categories appears.

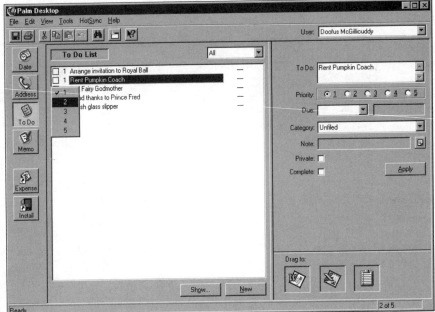

Figure 12-12:
Some tasks
are more
important
than others.

3. **Click the category you want to assign to your to-do item.**

   The category you click appears in the Category text box.

4. **Click the Apply button.**

   The priority you assign appears next to your to-do item.

Adding categories

You can maintain your collection of categories on either your Palm device or the Palm Desktop. Every time you HotSync your data, the categories you set up on your Palm device are mirrored on the Palm Desktop and vice versa.

Follow these steps to create a new category:

1. **With your To Do List visible, click the downward-pointing arrow next to Category on the right side of the screen.**

   The drop-down list of available categories appears.

2. **Click Edit Categories.**

   The Edit To Do Categories dialog box opens, as shown in Figure 12-13.

3. **Click New.**

   The New Category dialog box opens.

Figure 12-13:
Create new
categories
in this
dialog box.

4. **Enter the name of the category you want to add.**

   The name you enter appears in the New Category dialog box.

5. **Tap OK.**

   The new category appears in the Edit To Do Categories dialog box.

6. **Tap OK again.**

   The Edit To Do Categories dialog box closes.

You can have no more than 15 categories on your Palm device or on the Palm Desktop. If you try to exceed 15 categories, the program adamantly (but nicely) refuses to add new categories.

Deleting categories

If you went wild and added some categories you now regret, you can just zap your excess categories and get back to basics.

Follow these steps to delete a category:

1. **With your To Do List visible, click the downward-pointing arrow next to Category on the right side of the screen.**

   The drop-down list of available categories appears.

2. **Click Edit Categories.**

   The Edit To Do Categories dialog box opens.

3. **Select the name of the category you want to delete.**

   The category you tap is highlighted to show that you selected it.

4. **Click Delete.**

   The Delete Category dialog box opens, asking whether you want to move all items in the category to the Unfiled category or delete all items, as shown in Figure 12-14.

5. **Choose either Move All Items to Unfiled or Delete All Items.**

   The circle next to the choice you click appears darkened to show that you selected it.

Figure 12-14:
Rename 'em
or remove
'em. Take
your pick.

6. **Click OK.**

The Delete Category dialog box closes, and your category is deleted.

7. **Click OK.**

The Edit To Do Categories dialog box closes.

At least when you delete a category on the Palm Desktop, you get a choice between deleting all the items in the category or sending all the items to the Unfiled category. On the Palm device itself, you can only send everything to Unfiled.

Renaming categories

Did you know that Whoopi Goldberg changed her name from Caryn Johnson? Go figure. Changing the names of your categories is easier than changing your name for show business, but it won't make you a star.

To rename a category, follow these steps:

1. **With your To Do List visible, click the downward-pointing arrow next to Category on the right side of the screen.**

The drop-down list of available categories appears.

2. **Click Edit Categories.**

The Edit To Do Categories dialog box opens.

3. **Click the name of the category you want to rename.**

The name of the category is highlighted to show that you selected it.

4. **Click Rename.**

The Rename Category dialog box opens, as shown in Figure 12-15.

5. **Enter the new name of the category you want to change.**

The name you type replaces the old name in the Rename Category dialog box.

6. **Tap OK.**

The name you entered replaces the preceding name of the category in the Edit To Do Categories dialog box.

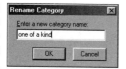

Figure 12-15:
Rename
your cate-
gories at
any time.

Rename Category

Enter a new category name:
one of a kind

OK   Cancel

7. **Tap OK again.**

The Edit To Do Categories dialog box closes.

In case you're interested, Hal Linden started off as Harold Lipshitz, and Peter Marshall was originally named Pierre LaCock. But that's a totally different category.

Assigning a due date to a to-do item

Your To Do List can do more than tell you what tasks to do; it also helps you remember when to do them.

Follow these steps to assign a due date to a to-do item:

1. **With your To Do List visible, click the name of the to-do item to which you want to assign a due date.**

2. **Click the downward-pointing triangle to the right side of the Due text box on the right side of the screen.**

A drop-down menu of available choices appears, including Today, Tomorrow, One Week Later, No Date, and Choose Date.

3. **Click the date you want to assign to your to-do item.**

If you picked anything other than Choose Date, the date you picked appears in the Due text box, so you can click the Apply button and you're done.

4. **Select Choose Date if you need to assign a specific date to your task.**

The Select Date dialog box opens.

5. **Click the date you want to assign as your due date.**

Figure 12-16 shows the date I selected for my to-do item.

Figure 12-16:
Give your
task its due
date in the
Select Date
dialog box.

6. **Click OK.**

   The Select Date dialog box closes, and the date you chose appears in the
   Due text box.

7. **Click Apply.**

Unfortunately, the To Do List doesn't have reminders for the list itself, so you
have to remember to look at your list from time to time.

Marking a to-do item private

You may have things to do that other people shouldn't know about. Shhh!
Keep them under your hat — or at least under a password.

These steps show you how to mark a to-do item private on the Palm Desktop:

1. **With your To Do List visible, click the name of the to-do item you want
   to mark as private.**

2. **Click the Private check box on the right side of the screen.**

3. **Click the Apply button.**

   A little key appears next to your item on the To Do List to show that it's
   now marked as private, as shown in Figure 12-17.

If you want your private items to remain private, you should choose, of course,
View⇨Hide Private Records. That action makes your private items invisible
until you choose View⇨Show Private Records. If you want to password-protect
your private items, you have to set your password on your Palm device. For
more info about setting up passwords, refer to Chapter 3.

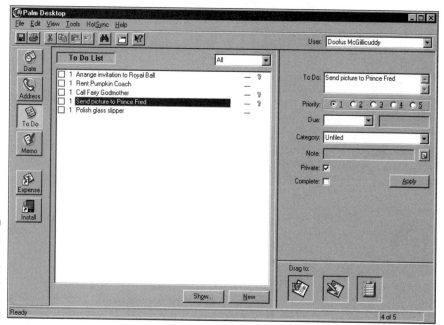

Figure 12-17:
Those little
keys mark
your private
tasks.

Attaching notes to to-do items

You know what you need to do and when you need to do it, of course, but do you always remember how or why? Perhaps you just need a more detailed explanation of some part of the task, such as driving directions or a secret formula. If you need some elaboration on your task, add a note.

To add a note to a to-do item in the Palm Desktop, follow these steps:

1. **With your To Do List visible, click the name of the to-do item to which you want to attach a note.**

2. **Click the Note button to the right of the Note text box on the right side of the screen (it looks like a piece of paper with the bottom-right corner lifted up).**

   The Note Editor dialog box opens, as shown in Figure 12-18.

3. **Type the text of your note.**

   The text you type appears in the Note Editor dialog box.

4. **Click OK.**

   The Note Editor dialog box closes, and the same little piece of paper that's on the Note button appears next to the name of your to-do item to show that the item has a note attached.

Figure 12-18:
Make a note
of what to
do in your
to-do.

You don't have to type lots of text into the note if you don't want to. You can always copy text from another document on your desktop or from a Web page and paste the text into the Note Editor dialog box.

Viewing items by category

If you make the effort to assign categories to your tasks, you get some real mileage from that feature by viewing your tasks according to the categories to which they belong. The name of the category you're viewing is always shown at the top of the To Do List. If you click the name of the category you're viewing, a drop-down list of the other categories appears. Just choose the category you want to see.

Deleting a to-do item

Some tasks become unnecessary before you even do them. If you planned to water the lawn and it rains, you're in luck.

Follow these steps to delete a to-do item on the Palm Desktop:

1. **With your To Do List visible, click the name of the to-do item you want to delete.**

2. **Press Delete.**

   The Delete To Do Items dialog box opens, as shown in Figure 12-19.

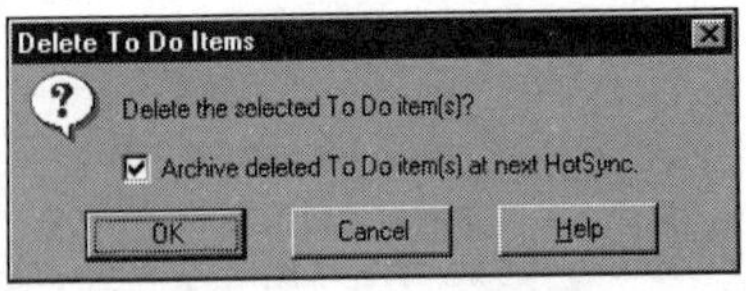

Figure 12-19:
Complete or
delete —
take your
pick.

3. Click OK.

Your to-do item is deleted.

The check box in the Delete To Do Items dialog box enables you to send deleted items to the archive for storage. I discuss how to deal with archived items at the end of this chapter.

If you actually did the task, your best bet, of course, is to mark the task as complete. The little check box next to the name of the task is put there for that very reason. One click and you're the hero! Mission accomplished!

Setting preferences for your To Do List

Setting preferences is, well, a matter of preference. You don't need to make any changes in your To Do List preferences if you don't want to. But if you like your To Do List just so, you can change several little things.

To set your To Do List preferences on the Palm Desktop, follow these steps:

1. With your To Do List visible, click the Show button at the bottom of the screen (or press Alt+O).

The Show Options dialog box opens, as shown in Figure 12-20. Your To Do options for the Palm Desktop are identical to the To Do options on the Palm device itself, which I discuss in Chapter 6.

Figure 12-20: When it comes to sorting tasks, you have several options.

2. Click the downward-pointing triangle to the right of the Sort By text box to see your list of choices.

The drop-down list of sort options for your To Do List appears.

3. Choose the way you want to sort your To Do List.

The choice you click appears in the Sort By text box. The sort options on the Palm Desktop are identical to the choices on the Palm device, as I discuss in Chapter 6.

4. **Click the check boxes next to the options you want for your To Do List.**

5. **Click OK.**

   The Show Options dialog box closes, and your To Do List reflects the preferences you set up, as shown in Figure 12-21.

If you set up your preferences and then decide that you'd prefer something else, just change everything again.

Working with memos

The best reason to enter memos on the Palm Desktop rather than use Graffiti is that memos usually contain lots of text, and typing is much faster than scribbling with Graffiti or punching in individual letters on the Palm device's on-screen keyboard. You can also copy and paste text to a memo from other desktop programs, such as your word processor.

To bring up the Memo Pad, just click the Memo button on the left side of the screen or choose View➪Memo Pad, and continue to the following sections.

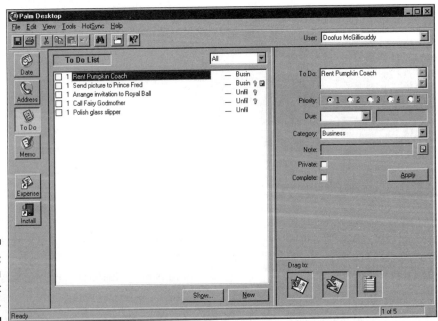

Figure 12-21:
What you
see is what
you set.

Creating a memo

Sometimes, you need certain information that's not exactly an appointment and not exactly a to-do item, but you still need it on your Palm device. The simplest way to keep miscellaneous information on hand is to create a memo. Nothing could be easier.

Use these steps to create a new Memo on the Palm Desktop:

1. **With the Memo Pad visible, click New at the bottom of the screen (or choose Edit⇨New Memo).**

   A new line appears on your list of memos and the insertion point appears in the memo area on the right side of the screen.

2. **Type the text of your memo.**

   The text you type appears in the memo area on the right side of the screen, as shown in Figure 12-22.

3. **Click the Apply button below the memo area.**

   The title of your memo appears on the list of memos on the left side of the screen.

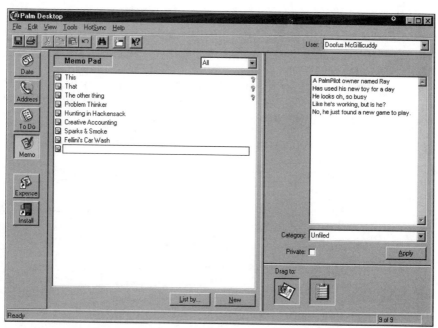

Figure 12-22:
Type or copy whatever you like into a memo.

If you hate to type, you can also copy and paste text into your Memo Pad, too. Just select text from a word-processing document or even from the World Wide Web, press Crtl+C to copy the text, start the Palm Desktop Memo Pad, and then press Ctrl+V to paste the text directly into the memo. You don't even need to create a new memo; the Palm Desktop figures out that you want a new memo and creates one automatically.

Reading a memo

You may not want to hang around reading your memos on the Palm Desktop because you can send them all to your Palm device and then go sit in the park to read them. Even so, you may need to check what you put in your memos now and again, and, fortunately, I can show you a way to do just that.

To read a memo, all you have to do is click the Memo Pad button on the left side of the screen (or choose <u>V</u>iew➪Memo Pad) and then click the memo you want to see. Read away!

If you need to read through all the memos on your desktop quickly, you can whip through the whole list by pressing the down-arrow key. Each time you press the down-arrow key, the next memo on the list appears in the memo area on the right side of the screen.

Printing a memo

Another big thing you can do from the desktop is print things. Yes, some people out there have clever schemes for beaming their Palm organizer data to especially well-equipped printers, but the whole scheme is still tricky, and most printers aren't up to the job. Nearly everybody has printers hooked up to their desktop computers, so printing from the desktop is the quickest way to see your data on paper.

To print a memo from the Palm Desktop, follow these steps:

1. **With the Memo Pad visible, click the title of the memo you want to print.**

   The text of the memo you clicked appears in the memo area on the right side of the screen.

2. **Choose <u>F</u>ile➪<u>P</u>rint (or press Ctrl+P.)**

   The Print dialog box opens.

3. **Click OK.**

   Your memo is printed.

The Palm Desktop doesn't let you do any fancy formatting of your memos; it's all plain vanilla. If you need to format and fiddle around with your text, you can drag the memo you want to work with to the Microsoft Word icon at the bottom of the Palm Desktop for Windows screen. Dragging a memo to the

Microsoft Word icon opens Word and copies your text into a new Word document you can beautify as you please. You can also drag text to Excel if you want, as I mention later in this chapter, in the section "Working with the Drag To icons." If you don't have Word installed on your desktop computer, you have to drag text to the clipboard icon, open any word processor or text editor, and paste the text into another document.

Editing a memo

If you use memos often, as I do, you certainly want to change a few of them now and then. The biggest advantage to keeping memos in an electronic form is that the text is so easy to change.

Follow these steps to edit a Memo on your Palm Desktop:

1. **With the Memo Pad visible, click the title of the memo you want to edit.**

   The text of the memo you clicked appears in the memo area on the right side of the screen.

2. **Click in the memo area on the right side of the screen at the point where you want to edit.**

   An insertion point appears where you clicked your mouse.

3. **Make any changes you want to the memo.**

4. **Click the Apply button below the memo area.**

   Your changes are saved as part of your memo.

If you replace a large amount of the text in a memo, the text you replace is ordinarily gone for good. Normally, that's fine by me, but sometimes you may want to save a copy of the original memo. One thing you can do with memos on the Palm Desktop that you can't do on the Palm device itself is copy whole memos and then just change one of them. To copy a whole memo, click the name of the memo to select it, press Ctrl+C to copy the memo, and then press Ctrl+V to paste it. You then have two identical memos. Just change one, and you have two different memos.

Categorizing a memo

Categories are particularly useful after you've collected more than a few dozen memos. Categorizing not only makes memos easier to find but also lets you see your memo collection more easily on your Palm device because that little screen can show only 11 memos at one time.

Follow these steps to assign a category to a memo on the Palm Desktop:

1. **With the Memo Pad visible, click the title of the memo you want to categorize.**

   The text of the memo you clicked appears in the memo area on the right side of the screen.

2. **Click the category scroll-down button (the downward-pointing triangle) below the memo text and choose the category you want, as shown in Figure 12-23.**

The category you choose appears below your memo text.

If you want to create several memos in the same category, switch to that category and then create the new memos. For example, if you switch to a view of your business memos and start creating new memos, all the new memos are automatically assigned to the Business category.

Making a memo private

I'm sure that you have some things you don't want just anybody to see, but you don't want to forget them yourself. You can mark certain memos as private to protect them from prying eyes.

To mark a memo private in the Palm Desktop, follow these steps:

1. **With the Memo Pad visible, click the title of the memo you want to mark as private.**

The text of the memo you clicked appears in the memo area on the right side of the screen.

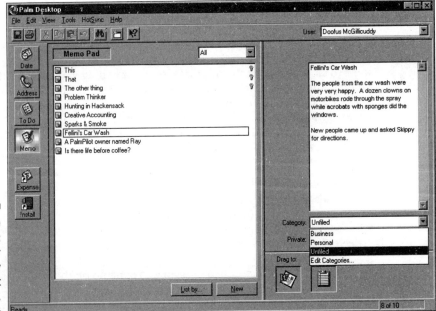

Figure 12-23:
Change your category with just two clicks.

2. Click the Private check box below the memo text.

A check mark appears in the Private check box to show that this memo is private, as shown in Figure 12-24. A key also appears next to the subject of any memo that's marked as private.

You can make all your private items disappear by choosing View↪Hide Private Records. If you want to make them reappear, choose View↪Show Private Records. Presto! If you want to be sneaky, you can set a password on your Palm device to keep anyone from seeing your private records unless they know your password. For more information about setting passwords, refer to Chapter 3.

Deleting a memo

You know how memos are — easy come, easy go. Especially go. Follow these steps to make your memos go away:

1. With the Memo Pad visible, click the title of the memo you want to delete.

The text of the memo you clicked appears in the memo area on the right side of the screen.

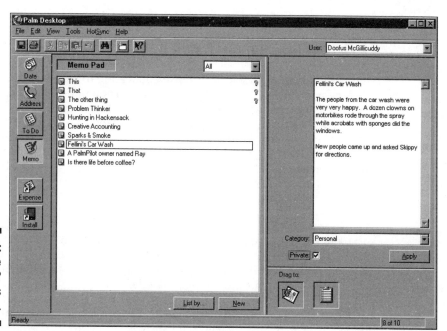

Figure 12-24:
Do you have
a secret?
Mark it as
private.

2. **Choose Edit⇨Delete (or press Delete).**

   The Delete Memo Pad Items dialog box opens, as shown in Figure 12-25. If you put a check mark in the box next to Archive Deleted Memo Pad Items, your memo is stored in an archive file.

3. **Click OK.**

   Poof! Your memo is gone.

If you left the Archive box checked, you can go back and find the deleted memo later. See the section "Archiving Your Palm Computing Stuff," later in this chapter, for more information.

What does that Expense button do?

Your Palm device includes an Expense application to help you track how much money you spend as you spend it. When you perform a HotSync, the information you've gathered is pulled into a file on your desktop. Frankly, the program is limited and is best for people who need to track business spending in order to file expense reports. Even for those people, the program has major drawbacks. It requires you to choose a description of each expenditure from a noncustomizable list of 28 choices ranging from Airfare to Telephone. It's hard to make the Expense application useful if you can't enter the exact type of expenses you incur.

You can start the Expense application by tapping the Applications soft button and tapping the Expense icon on your Palm device. Write in the amounts you spend and pick the description that you think fits best. The program automatically assigns the current date to each expenditure unless you tap the date and pick another one from the calendar.

The Expense button on the Palm Desktop for Windows automatically starts up a special Excel spreadsheet that captures data you've entered in the Expense application on your Palm device. If you don't have Excel installed on your Windows PC, the button is still present, but it doesn't do anything. Plenty of Palm device users have complained that the Expense program is too weak, so I hope that future versions will be more useful.

Working with the Drag To icons

If you use Microsoft Word and Microsoft Excel on your desktop computer, the Palm Desktop for Windows displays a set of icons labeled Drag To in the lower-right portion of the screen. Two of the icons look just like the icons for Word and Excel, and the third icon looks like a little clipboard. When you drag any item from the Palm Desktop to the Word icon, Word opens and creates a copy of the item you dragged and converts it to a Word document. Dragging an item to the Excel icon creates a copy of the item, formatted as an Excel spreadsheet. The most useful thing you can do with this feature is to turn a memo into a Word document so that you can save, format, or print the text of the memo.

If you don't have Word or Excel installed on your computer, the Word and Excel icons don't appear. Even without Word or Excel, you can still drag items to the clipboard icon and then open a document in any word processor and choose Edit⇨Paste to insert the text that's on the Clipboard.

Furnishing Your Palm Device

What is a home, after all, without some furnishings? You may have a lovely breakfast nook, but eventually you want a dinette, at least. You can furnish your Palm device as lavishly (or sparingly) as you'd furnish your home. A few games, a spreadsheet — who knows what may strike your fancy?

Checking memory

Before you start adding things to your Palm device, you'd better make sure that you have room for the stuff. After all, a Palm V, for example, with 2MB of memory has less room for programs than a couple of your average floppy disks. An old PalmPilot Professional has only 1MB of memory, or half the space of a Palm III, and a newer Palm IIIx has 4MB. Sad to say, the super-sleek Palm V and Palm VII models have only 2MB, although they compensate by being terribly hip. So, unlike my hall closet, which I seem to be able to cram anything into, your Palm device protests if you try to put too much stuff on it.

You can see how much space is available on a Palm III or later model by following these three steps:

1. **Tap the Applications soft button.**

   The applications list appears.

2. **Tap the Menu soft button.**

   The menu bar appears.

3. **Choose App⇨Info.**

   The Info screen appears. The line at the top of the Info screen says something like Free Memory: 849K of 960K, as shown in Figure 12-26.

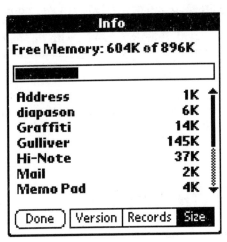

Figure 12-26:
Before you install a new program, check your memory to see whether you have enough room.

Most Palm organizer applications are small, so as long as you have a few hundred kilobytes of memory (abbreviated *K* by computer geeks), you should be okay. Remember, though, that every time you add an item to one of the standard applications, like the Address Book or the Date Book, you tie up a bit more memory. So leave yourself some breathing room. You can free up some memory by either deleting applications, as I describe later in this chapter, or by deleting bunches of items from the standard Palm organizer applications. The easiest way to delete records en masse is to use the Palm Desktop, as I describe in earlier sections of this chapter.

If you're still using a PalmPilot Professional or earlier model, the process for checking memory is a bit different because earlier Palm devices have a separate Memory application. To check how much memory is available on those models, tap the Applications soft button and tap Memory.

You can upgrade the memory on your Palm device fairly easily, but it'll cost you a few bucks. A company named TRG specializes in selling extra memory for your Palm device. Check out Chapter 16 for more info about upgrading.

Installing applications

Thousands of programmers are out there writing scads and scads of programs for Palm devices. You can get many programs over the Internet, and I include a sampling of particularly useful or fun programs on the CD that comes with this book. All you need to do to install an application on your Palm device is to copy the application to your desktop computer from the Internet or from the CD and then locate that file with the Palm Install Tool.

It's important to remember that the Palm Install Tool doesn't install applications; it *prepares* applications for installation. After picking an application with the Palm Install Tool, you have to perform a HotSync. Just place the Palm device in its cradle and press the HotSync button (for more info about HotSyncing, refer to Chapter 11).

Using Palm Desktop for Windows

To install Palm organizer programs by using the Palm Desktop, follow these steps:

1. **Launch the Palm Desktop.**

2. **Click the Install button on the left side of the screen, or choose View⇨Install.**

   The Palm Install Tool dialog box opens.

3. **Click Add (or press Alt+A).**

   The Open dialog box opens.

4. **Click the name of the file you want to install.**

   The filename you click is highlighted to show that you selected it, as shown in Figure 12-27.

   If you downloaded the application from the Internet or are installing applications from the CD, browse until you find the application you want to install.

Figure 12-27: Add new programs with the Palm Install Tool.

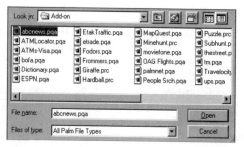

5. **Click Open.**

   The Open dialog box closes, and the filename you picked is now listed in the Palm Install Tool dialog box.

6. **Click Done.**

   Another dialog box opens, telling you that the applications will be installed the next time you HotSync.

7. **Click OK.**

   The Palm Install Tool closes.

8. **Press the HotSync button on the cradle of your Palm device.**

   The HotSync process begins, and the program is installed on your Palm device.

 You have an even easier way to install Palm applications if you're comfortable dealing with files in Windows. Just find a Palm application file in Windows Explorer (Palm files end with .PRC, .PDB, or .PQA). Double-click the name of the file when you find it with Windows Explorer, and your Palm Install program opens, already showing the name of the file you double-clicked. Just click OK in the Palm Install Tool dialog box and your program will be installed on your next HotSync.

Deleting applications

Eventually, you may tire of your once-fashionable furnishings. I mean, orange shag carpet? Lava lamps? Please! Martha Stewart would send you straight to K-Mart!

Discarding unwanted applications from your Palm device is even easier than dumping those old Woodstock posters. You'll also be less embarrassed if someone catches you at it. You don't need to launch Palm Desktop to delete applications, either.

Deleting applications on a Palm III or later

The process of deleting applications differs slightly on the Palm III and later models from the way it works on earlier models. Here's how to delete a program from a Palm III or later:

1. **Tap the Applications soft button.**

   The applications screen appears.

2. **Tap the Menu button.**

   The menu bar appears.

3. Choose App⇨Delete.

The Delete screen appears, as shown in Figure 12-28.

4. Tap the name of the application you want to delete.

The name you tap is highlighted to show that you selected it.

5. Tap Delete.

The Delete Application dialog box opens.

6. Tap Yes if you're sure. If you change your mind, tap No.

If you tap Yes, the application is deleted, and its name disappears from the list of applications on the Delete screen. If you tap No, the dialog box closes, and the application is still there.

7. Tap Done.

The Delete screen closes.

Deleting applications on a PalmPilot Professional or earlier model

On a PalmPilot Professional (or earlier model), you follow a slightly different process, which has an equally charming result: one less program cluttering up your Palm device.

To delete a program from a PalmPilot Professional (or earlier model):

1. Tap the Applications soft button.

The applications screen appears.

2. **Tap Memory.**

    The Memory application opens.

3. **Tap Delete Apps.**

    The Delete Applications screen appears.

4. **Tap the name of the application you want to delete.**

    The name you tap is highlighted to show that you selected it.

5. **Tap Delete.**

    The Delete Application dialog box opens, as shown in Figure 12-29.

Figure 12-29:
Zap pesky
programs
from this
dialog box.

6. **Tap Yes if you're sure. If you change your mind, tap No.**

    If you tap Yes, the Delete Application dialog box closes, and your application is deleted. If you tap No, the dialog box closes, but the application is still there.

7. **Tap Done.**

    The Delete Application screen disappears.

There you are! And there it isn't! Your unwanted application is gone like platform shoes. Oops, I guess platform shoes have made a comeback. Well, you can always reinstall the applications by using the same procedure shown in the section "Installing applications," earlier in this chapter.

Protecting Your Turf

Sometimes the worst does happen; your little Palm device gets lost, stolen, or destroyed. You can always buy a new Palm device — that's the easy part. But what about all your data? You're in luck — the Palm Desktop makes it easy to reinstall all your precious data.

Restoring Palm organizer data

In the best of times or in the worst of times, you may need to restore all your Palm organizer data. The best of times may be when you upgrade to a new Palm organizer model; the worst of times may be when you replace a lost, stolen, or destroyed Palm device. Either way, you can restore everything that was on your old Palm device with a simple HotSync:

1. **Put your Palm device in its cradle.**

   Nothing happens. Surprise!

2. **Press the HotSync button on the Palm device's cradle.**

   The HotSync Manager on your desktop PC is launched, and the Users dialog box opens on your desktop PC's screen.

3. **Click the name of the user whose data you want to install on the Palm device — it's probably your name.**

   The name you click is highlighted to show that you selected it, as shown in Figure 12-30.

Figure 12-30:
Pick the name of the user whose data should go on this Palm device.

4. **Click OK (on the desktop).**

   The HotSync Progress dialog box opens. After a few minutes, the dialog box closes, your Palm device plays some tinny little fanfare, and a button labeled Reset appears on the screen.

5. **Tap the Reset button on the screen.**

   The General Preferences screen appears on your Palm device. You don't need to do anything in the General Preferences screen after a reset; you can either turn off the Palm device or go right on and use any application.

If you use one desktop computer to synchronize more than one Palm device, don't assign the same username to more than one Palm device. The HotSync program can get confused and send the wrong data to the wrong Palm device or, worse, make data disappear.

Backing up your data

If you use only the programs that come in the box with your Palm device, you don't need to worry about backing up. If you HotSync regularly to keep your data current, you're covered. Your data from all the standard Palm organizer applications gets saved and archived by the Palm Desktop every time you HotSync. It's a good idea, of course, to back up the data on the desktop machine regularly.

On the other hand, if you installed programs that don't come preinstalled on your Palm device, those programs may not automatically back themselves up like your standard applications do, so you need a backup program to keep those files safe. One program, Backup Buddy, is available over the Internet to help you back up your nonstandard programs automatically. The program is shareware, which means that the author of the program asks you to send in the $15 registration fee voluntarily. You can contact him via e-mail at ahinds@poboxes.com. It's a good idea to register your shareware.

If all you've added to your Palm device is a few games, I wouldn't worry about backing up. You need to be concerned with backups if you've added programs that add data themselves, like spreadsheets, databases, time and billing applications, or similar programs. If your Palm device was issued to you at work, you should check with your system administrator about whether you need to do anything special with backups.

Archiving Your Palm Computing Stuff

Your Palm device can hold only a fraction of the information your desktop computer can. To save space on the Palm device, clearing things out regularly is a good idea. The Palm device has a Purge function in the Date Book and To Do List that automatically gets rid of unneeded items and moves them to an archive file, if you want. For more info about purging Palm organizer items, refer to Chapter 6.

Viewing archived items

The Palm Desktop is the only place where you can open and view archived items. Even if you use another personal information manager, such as Microsoft Outlook or Lotus Organizer, to put items into your Palm device, you still need to look in the Palm Desktop to view your archived items.

These steps show you how to view your archived items on the Palm Desktop:

1. **Choose from the buttons on the left side of the screen (or from the View menu) the type of archived item you want to look at.**

   Calendar items are archived separately from items deleted from the Address Book, To Do List, or Memo Pad, so you need to open the part of the Palm Desktop that handles the type of item you want to see.

2. **Choose File⇨Open Archive.**

   The Open Archive dialog box opens, as shown in Figure 12-31.

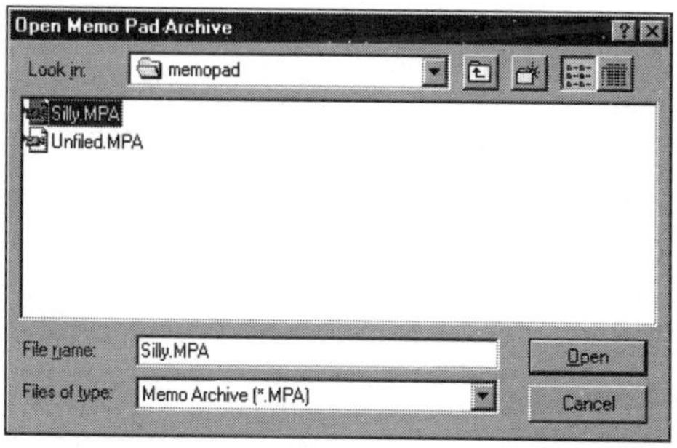

Figure 12-31:
Find those
old deleted
items by
opening an
archive file.

3. **Click the name of the archive file you want to view.**

   Usually, only one file appears on the archive list. If more than one archive file is listed and the archive you open doesn't contain the item you want, repeat Steps 2 and 3 until you find the archive containing the item you want.

4. **Click OK.**

The items in the archive you picked appear as a new list of items on your Palm Desktop.

If you're looking at the archive of items assigned to categories, the archive files are organized by category — personal, business, or whatever you assign.

Returning an archived item to your Palm device

Another benefit of keeping archive files is to help you get back items you accidentally delete. Don't be embarrassed — it happens to everybody.

To recover an item from an archive on the Palm Desktop, follow these steps:

1. **Choose from the buttons on the left side of the screen (or from the View menu) the type of archived item you want to recover.**

   Pick either Date Book, Address Book, To Do List, or Memo Pad.

2. **Choose File⇨Open Archive.**

   The Open Archive dialog box opens.

3. **Click the name of the archive file you want to view.**

   The file you click is highlighted to show that you selected it.

4. **Click OK.**

   The items in the archive file you picked are listed on the Palm Desktop.

5. **Click the item you want to return to your Palm device.**

   The item you click is highlighted to show that you selected it.

6. **Choose Edit⇨Copy (or press Ctrl+C).**

   The item is copied to the Clipboard. Nothing happens on the screen.

7. **Choose File⇨Open Current.**

   Your collection of current items appears.

8. **Choose Edit⇨Paste (or press Ctrl+V).**

   The item appears as part of your collection of current items.

9. **Place your Palm device in its cradle, and press the HotSync button on the cradle.**

   The HotSync dialog box opens and shows the progress of your synchronization.

The whole reason for archiving items is to save space on your Palm device, so don't load old items back on your Palm device unless you really need them.

Accommodating Multiple Users

Most people use a Palm device in conjunction with a desktop computer in order to simplify data entry and keep the data on their Palm devices safe. But you don't have to limit yourself to one Palm device per computer. The Palm Desktop enables you to synchronize Palm devices with different users. The first time you HotSync your Palm device, the HotSync Manager asks for your username. The Palm device username you enter (or choose) is added to the list of usernames on the Palm Desktop. Each time you put a Palm device in the cradle attached to that desktop computer, the program recognizes which Palm device is in the cradle when you press the HotSync button. After you've set up a computer to HotSync a particular Palm device, the desktop computer always knows which Palm device it's dealing with and synchronizes to that particular person's information.

It's not a good idea to set up multiple users on the same computer if you don't use the Palm Desktop program. It's possible to make your Palm device information synchronize to other programs, such as Microsoft Outlook or Act!, but you could encounter some confusion if you try to synchronize more than one Palm device to one of those programs. It's not impossible to use several Palm devices with those programs; it's just not certain that everything will work right if you do it all through the same computer. If you want to host several Palm devices on the same desktop PC, your best bet is to stick with the Palm Desktop.

The Palm Device Name Game

Although all Palm devices look pretty much alike in those little tiny boxes, each one has one important difference: the name of the user. You can find out which name is assigned to the Palm device you're using by tapping the Applications soft button and then tapping HotSync. The HotSync screen displays the name of the user assigned to it. A Palm III shows the username in the upper-right corner of the screen. Older Palm devices say Welcome, username. Also, when you perform a HotSync, the name of the user whose data is being synchronized appears in the HotSync Progress dialog box. You determine the Palm device username the first time you perform a HotSync. If you try to HotSync a Palm device to a computer that hasn't ever seen a Palm device with that username, the HotSync Manager asks whether you want to set up a new account for that user.

Chapter 13

Operating and HotSyncing to the Palm Desktop Program for the Mac

· ·

In This Chapter

▶ Installing Palm Desktop for the Macintosh

▶ HotSyncing between your Palm device and your Mac

▶ Using the Palm Desktop program on your Mac

· ·

*T*he easiest way to enter large amounts of data in a Palm device is by using the Palm Desktop software. To do that, you have to connect your Palm device and your Macintosh. This chapter shows you how.

Installing Palm Desktop for Macintosh

Palm Desktop 2.1 for the Macintosh is the main part of the Palm MacPac Version 2.0, which you have to buy separately; the CD that comes with your Palm device doesn't include this software — it has only Windows software.

If you've just bought your MacPac and it came on a CD, chances are that you have the latest version. If you bought the MacPac some time ago (and it came on floppy disks), you have to download a free copy of the Version 2.1 upgrade from the Palm Web site:

```
http://www.palm.com/custsupp/downloads/macpacv2.html
```

To use Version 2.1, you need a PowerPC. If you have a pre-PowerPC Macintosh, contact 3Com to determine the version you should be using and how to get it. Keep in mind that the older version of the software looks much different from what is described in this chapter.

Before you do anything, though, you have to hook the Palm device cradle to your Macintosh. The following section shows you how.

Connecting the cradle to your Mac

The MacPac comes with a serial port adapter for the Palm device cradle. Don't ask me why PCs and Macs can't have the same type of serial ports — that's just the way it goes. Just hook whichever end of the adapter fits on the end of the cradle's plug. The other end of the adapter plugs into the back of your Mac.

Most desktop Macs have two serial ports — a printer port and a modem port — that enable you to add *peripherals* (other pieces of hardware) to your machine. You can plug the cradle into either one. If you have an internal modem, you have a free port. Rejoice and be happy. However, you may have both a printer and an external modem already using those two ports. Unfortunately, you don't have many options if that's the case. You can purchase a device that lets you use an A/B switch to switch connections from one of your serial ports to either your modem or your printer and your Palm device. Your local Mac guru can help you with this task, or, like many other users, you can tough it out: Unplug one of your peripherals, plug in the cradle, unplug the cradle when you're done, and then plug in the other peripheral again. That routine can get tedious after awhile, though.

If you use the oh-so-not-fun method of continually unplugging and plugging back in, this piece of advice may make life a little easier: Decide which peripheral you use least, and alternate with that one. If you live on the Internet, for example, you may constantly use your modem and may not use your printer very often. The printer port is the perfect choice for you. If you're a graphics designer, though, and you continually print pages showing your latest design masterpiece, the modem port may be a better choice.

Macs, just like PCs, come in all shapes, sizes, and ages. Do a little research to make sure that your Mac's configuration can handle the requirements.

If you own an iMac or one of the new G3 PowerBooks, your Mac has a USB port rather than serial ports. You have to buy a serial-to-USB adapter from a third-party vendor. Luckily, companies named Keyspan (`www.keyspan.com`) and Entrega (`www.entrega.com`) sell these little gizmos.

Installing Palm Desktop

Installing the Palm Desktop software Version 2.1 is easy; you just put the CD in the slot and follow the on-screen prompts, although you do have to tinker a little when you're setting up your Mac to HotSync (read more about that subject in the following section).

If you have downloaded the software from the Internet, you have to "expand" the file before you can install it; follow the directions on the Web page. After you've done that, double-click the Palm MacPac v2 Installer icon and go on to Step 4.

Follow these steps to install Palm Desktop on your Mac; I recommend that you reboot with extensions turned off (restart your computer and hold down the Shift key until you see your desktop again).

1. **Insert in your CD-ROM drive the CD that came with the MacPac.**

   The CD icon appears on the desktop.

2. **Double-click the CD icon to see its contents.**

3. **Double-click the Palm MacPac v2 Installer icon.**

   The Palm Desktop install screen appears.

4. **Click Continue.**

   A Read-Me screen with information about the Palm Desktop and HotSync software appears.

5. **Click Agree.**

   The Software License agreement screen appears.

6. **Click Agree.**

   The Palm Desktop Installer screen appears, as shown in Figure 13-1.

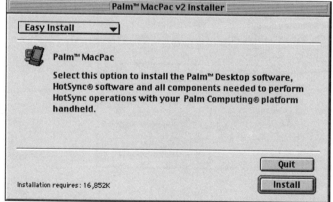

Figure 13-1: Easy Install is the easiest option.

The pull-down menu gives you three options: Easy Install, Custom Install, and Uninstall. Easy Install is (you guessed it) the easiest; it installs everything on the disks to your hard drive. Custom Install enables you to choose which components to install; if you don't want to install the Palm

Tutorial, for example, don't put an X in that box. Uninstall acts just like Custom Install, except in reverse; if you want to uninstall certain components after you install them, you choose this option.

For now, just choose Easy Install.

7. Click Install.

A dialog box appears that lets you select the folder in which you want to install the program. The default setting puts all the files in one folder named Palm on your hard drive.

Most of the time, I just install programs to the default placement and then move them later to wherever I want them, such as to the folder that has all my applications in it.

8. Choose a Destination Folder and click Install.

A dialog box opens, telling you that you must quit all applications before the program can be installed.

9. Click Continue.

Your computer automatically quits all running applications, and the Install Progress dialog box opens. The bar at the bottom of the dialog box shows you the progress of the installation.

When the installation finishes, the HotSync Setup application is launched. The dialog box opens, as shown in Figure 13-2, asking you to select your username and the serial port to which the Palm device cradle is connected.

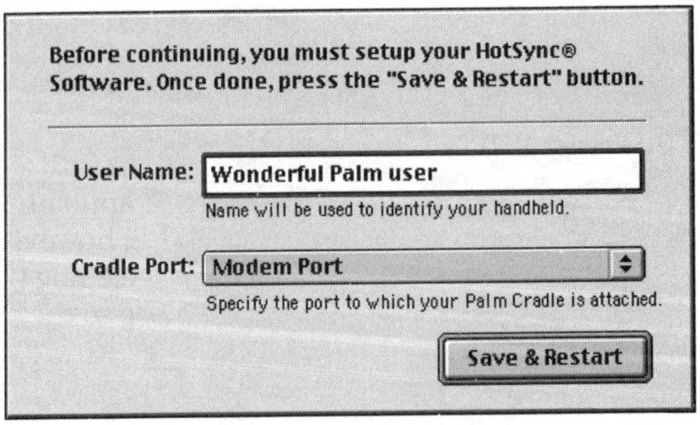

Figure 13-2:
Introduce your Mac to your Palm device: Enter your username and the serial port.

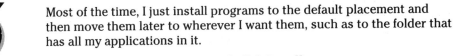

10. Enter the username you plan to assign to your Palm device. Then choose either Printer Port or Modem Port and click Save & Restart.

Your name is the best bet. Spell it with normal capitalization and spacing. Your Mac reboots and is ready to go.

Setting Up Your Macintosh to HotSync

If you hooked up the Palm device cradle to your modem port, you're set. If you plugged the cradle into your printer port because you have an external modem you use all the time, however, you have to turn off AppleTalk before you can HotSync. Follow these steps:

1. **Choose Apple Menu⇨Chooser.**

   The Chooser dialog box opens.

2. **Turn off AppleTalk by clicking the Inactive button in the bottom-right corner of the dialog box.**

   A dialog box telling you to disconnect from your network opens. Don't worry about this message.

3. **Click OK.**

4. **Close the Chooser by clicking the box in its upper-left corner.**

Now, you can simply place the Palm device in its cradle and tap the HotSync button to kick off the HotSync process. The Default setting for HotSyncing is that it always watches the serial port the Palm device cradle is plugged into for any request for a HotSync.

If you own an iMac or a G3 PowerBook, the printer and the modem share a port, so you don't have to turn off AppleTalk to make HotSync work.

Remember that you may have unplugged your printer or external modem so that you could plug in the Palm device cradle. To use either of those peripherals, you have to plug them back in and repeat the preceding steps, tapping Stop in the HotSync control panel first and then turning AppleTalk back on.

When you install Palm Desktop for Macintosh, you end up with a pretty good tool for tracking all your to-dos, addresses, memos, and appointments. That's fine if you're always at your desk. If you divide your time, however, between sitting at your desk and being on the go (don't we all?), keeping track of the data on two different machines can be a pain. HotSyncing to the rescue!

HotSyncing your Palm device with your desktop computer is amazingly easy. Just make sure that your desktop computer is running, put the Palm device in the cradle, and push the HotSync button. That's it. The HotSync button, as shown in Figure 13-3, is the only button on the cradle and has two arrows pointing at each other, so you can't go wrong. You don't even have to launch the desktop program. Tapping the HotSync button calls the HotSync Manager into action, which coordinates the whole process of swapping data. The HotSync Manager automatically turns on your Palm device, compares the data on the Palm device and your desktop computer, and updates each machine with the most current info. After a few minutes, you end up with the same data on two different machines.

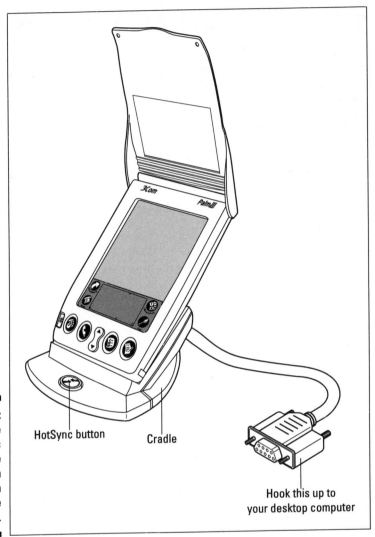

Figure 13-3:
The
HotSync
button is the
only button
on the Palm
device
cradle.

HotSync button   Cradle

Hook this up to
your desktop computer

Most of the time, you don't have to know how the HotSync process works.
Every once in awhile, however, you have to deal with HotSync problems,
which happen most often when you synchronize your Palm device with other
personal information managers. Then you have to mess around with something called a *conduit,* which moves data between your Palm device and
non-Palm Computing programs. (I describe conduits in Chapter 20.)

Operating Palm Desktop for the Macintosh

In this section, I show you how to work with memos, arrange appointments, set up an address book (also called a contact list), track to-do lists, and manage archived items.

Even if you're a Graffiti expert, you occasionally want to enter data by using Palm Desktop. Even if you're an experienced user, you can normally type faster than you can use Graffiti, and you can do things — such as copy multiple items and perform tricks with drag-and-drop — that the Palm device can't handle just yet. The biggest benefit of using Palm Desktop is that you can manage archived items you've purged or deleted from the Palm device. At the end of this chapter, I tell you how to manage archived items.

Palm Desktop isn't your only choice, of course, if you'd rather feed data to your Palm device from your desktop. You can set up many popular personal information managers (PIMs) to send data back and forth to a Palm device. Because you may have spent years entering names and dates into another PIM, you may not want to change now. However, you will need a special something, a *conduit,* to be able to HotSync your PIM to your Palm device. (See Chapter 20 for more info about conduits; to find out how to operate your PIM, check out your local bookstore for a *...For Dummies* book on the subject.)

Palm Desktop Basics

With its tiny screen and barely a half-dozen buttons, a Palm organizer does a ton of work. However, nothing beats a big old computer with an old-fashioned keyboard and mouse for quickly handling your appointments, memos, to-dos, and addresses. Just remember that you can use both Palm Desktop and your Palm device to enter your data — whatever you want. This section gives you an overview of the Palm Desktop interface and describes the basic Palm Desktop applications.

Understanding the Palm Desktop interface

Computer folks use the technical term *interface* to describe what you see on your computer screen after you launch a program. The Palm Desktop interface is made up of the same elements as the screens of most computer programs, combined with elements of the Palm organizer screens. You can see the name of the program in the upper-right corner of the screen, in the area named the *menu bar.* Below that is the *toolbar,* which contains a row of icons you can click to perform tasks you do most often, as shown in Figure 13-4. The icons are grouped into categories for Contacts, Tasks, Notes, and Date Book. You click these icons to launch its corresponding application. The toolbar also has icons for common tasks, such as printing, searching for, and deleting files.

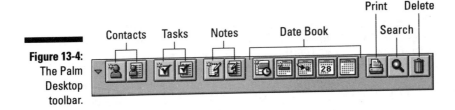

Figure 13-4:
The Palm
Desktop
toolbar.

The main window under the toolbar looks a little different depending on which application button you click. The default is the Daily Calendar window, which corresponds to the Date Book function.

Arranging entries in the Date Book

The Palm Desktop Date Book has many of the same parts as the Palm organizer Date Book screens, except that Palm Desktop organizes things a little differently because your computer screen has more room to display items than a Palm organizer screen does. Also, your computer monitor probably has a color screen, which is something Palm devices don't have (yet).

Along the right edge of the Date Book are three tabs labeled Day, Week, and Month. Click one of those tabs to change the view you see on the screen. This list describes what you see in each view:

  ✔ **Daily:** As shown in Figure 13-5, the left side of Daily view shows a list of appointments for a single day. The right side of the screen shows your Task List for that day. Click the arrows to view the next or preceding day.

  ✔ **Weekly:** Whenever you want to see how your week is shaping up, Weekly view shows a grid representing the entire workweek. Weekly view works the same way it does on a Palm device, except that Palm Desktop shows you the names of your appointments, whereas a Palm device shows you only bars representing the appointments. Clicking the plus and minus buttons adds or deletes days that are visible in the window. Click the arrows to skim easily through preceding and future days.

✔ **Monthly:** Monthly view shows you what you're doing for the entire month. Palm Desktop gives you more detail, however, than Monthly view on a Palm device because a computer screen is larger. Arrows also enable you to view other months easily.

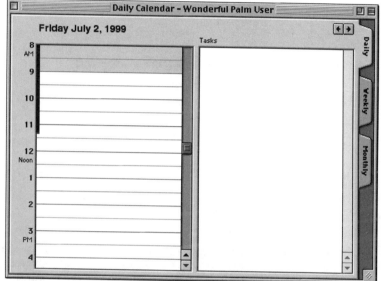

Figure 13-5:
Check the Date Book to see what you're doing today.

For more info about using the Date Book on a Palm device, refer to Chapter 8. To display the Palm Desktop Date Book, just click the View Calendar button on the right side of the toolbar or choose View⇨Calendar from the menu, and then continue to the following sections.

Adding appointments

You can enter appointments on Palm Desktop faster than you can enter them on a Palm device, as long as you're sitting at your big computer. If you're out in the field or at a meeting, it's different. As long as you're sitting at your computer, follow these steps to add an appointment to Palm Desktop:

1. **With the Date Book visible, click the Daily tab on the right edge of the window (or press ⌘+Shift+D).**

   The Date Book appears in Daily view, showing your appointments scheduled for that date. To change the date, click the arrows to move forward or backward.

2. **Double-click the line next to the hour you want your appointment to begin.**

The Appointment dialog box opens, and the Appointment text field is highlighted with the words *New Appointment* inside, as shown in Figure 13-6.

3. Type a subject for your appointment.

The subject appears in the box.

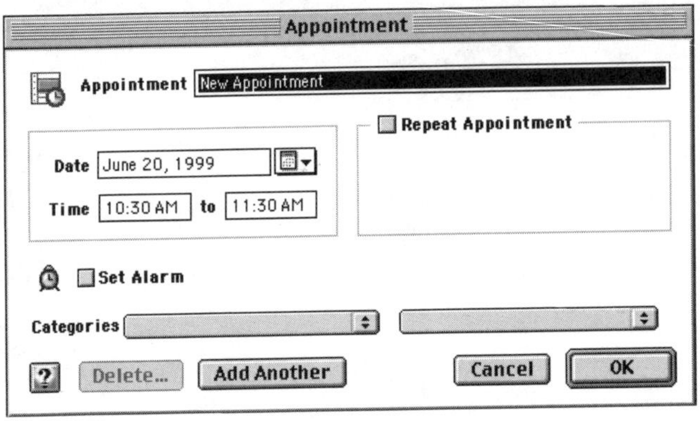

Figure 13-6:
The Appointment dialog box is ready for you to enter the details.

Appointment
Appointment New Appointment
☐ **Repeat Appointment**
Date June 20, 1999
Time 10:30 AM to 11:30 AM
☐ **Set Alarm**
Categories ⬍ ⬍
? Delete... Add Another Cancel OK

4. If you want to change the start or end time or date of your appointment, click in the box next to those fields, respectively, and enter the new information. You can also tab from one field to another.

One helpful way to choose another date is to click the pop-up menu to the right of the date field and pick one from the calendar that pops up.

You can set an alarm to remind you of an appointment, and you can also assign a category to an appointment. The appointment shows up on the calendar in the color in which the category is displayed on the list. You can customize the titles and colors of categories by choosing Edit⇨Categories⇨Edit Categories from the menu. Notice the Add Another button near the bottom of the dialog box. Clicking that button enables you to create another appointment without having to go back to the calendar and click the time.

5. Click OK.

The Appointment dialog box closes, and your appointment shows up on your calendar.

Because the method of adding appointments to Daily view of your calendar on Palm Desktop is most similar to the way you add appointments on the Palm device, that's what I describe here. You have more flexibility in how you enter appointments on the desktop, though. For example, Palm Desktop enables you to add appointments in Weekly view as well as in Monthly view — something you can't do on a Palm device. Figure 13-7 shows what Weekly view looks like. Just follow Steps 3 and 4 in the preceding example.

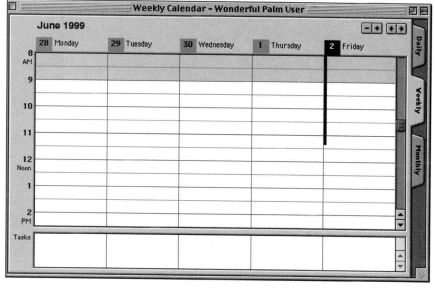

Figure 13-7:
You can add appointments in Palm Desktop Weekly view.

In addition to being able to work with appointments, you can work with the unique feature *event banners,* which are exactly like appointments except that they can span one or more days (up to a year). Vacations, holidays, and conferences are some examples. You can create, edit, and delete, just like you do with appointments.

Repeating appointments

Some tasks require that you pay attention to them once a week. (I wish that all tasks were in that category.) Note them in Palm Desktop by following these steps:

1. **With the Appointment dialog box open, click the box next to Repeat Appointment.**

   A check mark is displayed in the box, and more options appear, showing choices for how often you want to repeat the appointment, as shown in Figure 13-8. A field labeled Until also appears, letting you type the date on which you want the appointments to stop repeating. If you leave this field blank, the appointments repeat forever or until you stop using your Palm device (whichever comes first). If you click the pull-down menu to the right of that field, you can choose from the little calendar a date to stop repeating.

2. **Click OK.**

   The Appointment dialog box closes, and your appointment shows up on your calendar.

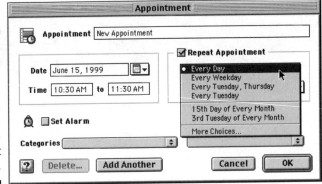

Figure 13-8:
Choices for
repeating
appoint-
ments are
shown
in the
Appointment
dialog box.

Editing appointments

1. **With the Date Book visible, click the Daily tab on the right edge of the window (or tap ⌘+Shift+D).**

   Date Book is displayed in Daily view. It shows the appointments scheduled for that date.

2. **Double-click the appointment you want to change.**

   The Appointment dialog box appears, and you can change any details you want.

3. **Click OK.**

   Your appointment is now changed.

One tricky thing about repeating appointments is that if you double-click one to change it, you're asked whether you want to change just this one, this one and future appointments, or all instances of the appointment. Don't be alarmed; just click the button next to the choice you want.

Duplicating appointments

You may want to set up appointments that are similar to ones you've already created. You can duplicate the appointment without having to type all the information again:

1. **With the Daily Calendar window visible, click the Daily tab on the right edge of the window (or tap ⌘+Shift+D).**

   The Date Book is displayed in Daily view and shows the appointments scheduled for that date.

2. **Click once the appointment you want to duplicate, and choose Edit⇨Duplicate Appointment (or press ⌘+D).**

   The Appointment is shown on top of the original appointment.

3. Double-click the duplicated appointment and edit it.

You can also click the duplicated appointment's box and drag it to another time.

4. Click OK.

You now have another appointment.

Deleting appointments

Appointments that you're not sure you're going to keep are, in a way, "penciled in" on your Palm device because it's so easy to erase them. Follow these steps to delete an appointment from Palm Desktop:

1. **With the Daily Calendar window visible, click the Daily tab on the right edge of the screen (or press ⌘+Shift+D).**

   The Date Book is displayed in Daily view and shows the appointments scheduled for that date.

   You can also choose the Weekly tab. If you prefer to view an entire week at a glance, jump ahead to Step 3.

2. **Click the appointment you want to delete.**

   The appointment becomes highlighted and has a box around it.

3. **Press the Delete key or click the delete button on the toolbar. You can also choose Edit⇨Delete or press ⌘+E.**

   The warning box, as shown in Figure 13-9, opens, asking whether you're sure that you want to delete this appointment. You can uncheck the option for giving you a warning when you want to delete appointments. If it's a repeating appointment, it asks whether you want to delete just this one, this one and future appointments, or all instances of the appointment.

4. **Click OK if you want your appointment to disappear, or click Cancel if you change your mind.**

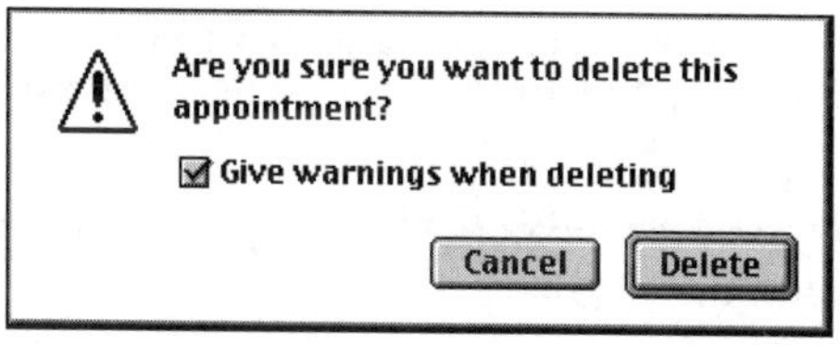

Figure 13-9:
Simply
delete an
undesirable
appointment.

⚠ Are you sure you want to delete this appointment?

☑ Give warnings when deleting

Cancel   Delete

Arranging entries on the Contact List (Address Book)

Being able to keep all your name and address information on your little pocket computer is a wonderful benefit because you can quickly and easily look up what you need to know. What happens, though, if you lose that information? There goes your social life! Luckily for you, you can keep all that info safe and sound on your desktop computer because you're not likely to lose both your desktop computer and your Palm device at the same time.

(For some reason, the Palm Desktop software calls the Address Book the Contact List. Both terms can be used interchangeably.) To bring up the Contact List, just click the View Contact List button on the left side of the toolbar or choose View⇨Contact List (or ⌘+Shift+C) and continue to the following sections. You won't have a problem making sense of the Contact List; when you open it, you see a list of names from which to select on the left side of the screen and full details of the person you select in the columns to the right.

Adding a new Contact List entry

To add a new entry to the Contact List on Palm Desktop, follow these steps:

1. **Click the Create Contact button on the toolbar (or choose Create⇨Contact). You can also press ⌘+Option+C within the Palm Desktop software to add a new contact.**

   Whenever you choose to create a new contact, the window for that contact opens, with boxes for information such as names, phone numbers, and work and home addresses, In addition, you see a screen for entering information; by default, the Name Entry screen appears. When you finish entering info there, click the close box in the upper-left corner of the entry screen. Then, click in one of the boxes in the window (for example, Phones) to display that data-entry screen.

2. **Type the first name of the contact in the First Name text box.**

   The text appears in the First Name text box, as shown in Figure 13-10.

3. **Enter the contact's last name, title, and company name in the appropriate boxes. Click the close box in the upper-left corner of the Name box to close that section.**

4. **Click the Phones box to enter the contact's telephone numbers in the appropriate phone number boxes.**

   Your choices for telephone number are work, home, fax, and other.

5. **Click the check box button to the right of the phone number you want shown on the Contact List.**

   The check box you click now contains a check mark to show that you selected it.

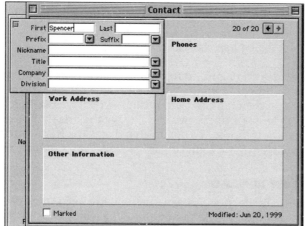

Figure 13-10:
To add a new address, just fill in the form.

6. **Click the Work Address box or the Home Address box to enter the contact's appropriate address. Enter the information you want in the boxes.**

7. **Click the Close box in the upper-left corner of the Contact dialog box when you finish entering information on that contact.**

   You can move to the next or preceding contact by clicking the left and right arrows in the upper-right corner of the dialog box.

You can enter a bunch of information in a Contact List entry, or you can just fill in a few blanks.

Editing an address record

Because more people than ever move around and change their jobs and addresses, you have to plan on making lots of changes to the Contact List. These steps show you how to edit an address in Palm Desktop:

1. **With the Contact List window visible, double-click the name of the person whose record you want to change.**

   The Contact dialog box opens.

2. **Add new information in the same way as you entered it originally.**

   For more information, see the preceding section "Adding a new Contact List entry."

3. **Select any information you want to change and type the new information.**

   The text you enter replaces the information you selected.

4. Click the Close box in the upper-left corner of the window when you finish.

The Contact dialog box closes.

TIP

If you make changes on Palm Desktop rather than on your Palm device, you can save the old address in your archive. Just select the address record, tap Ctrl+C to copy, and then tap Ctrl+V to paste — you have two identical records. If you delete one of the two and change the one that's left, you have the old address safely stored. To dig up an old address from your archive, see the section "Archiving Your Palm Organizer Stuff," later in this chapter.

Attaching a note to an address record

For business or personal reasons, you may want to keep track of what you say and keep a record of whom you say it to. You can store this info in the form of notes on the Contact List.

Follow these steps to attach a note to an address record in Palm Desktop:

1. With the Contact List window visible, double-click the name of the person whose record you want to annotate.

The Contact dialog box opens.

2. Click the paper clip icon in the upper-left corner of the dialog box. A pop-up box displays the message "Attach To." Choose the New Note menu item from the list.

The Note dialog box opens, as shown in Figure 13-11.

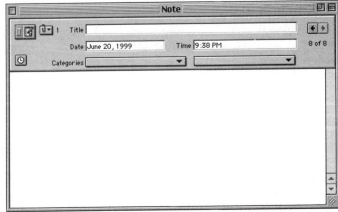

Figure 13-11:
Notes have their own dialog box, in which you can enter your information.

3. Enter the title and text of your note.

The text you type appears in the Note box. You can add the date, time, and category for the note.

4. **Click the Close box of the Note dialog box when you finish entering information.**

The Note dialog box closes. To view your note, just click the folder icon with the paper clip on it next to the person's name on the Contact List (on the far left side of the screen); the note appears in a separate window.

Finding the name you want

To quickly find a person's vital information, tap the Find icon on the toolbar. It's the one with the magnifying glass on it. You can just type the first few letters of the person's name in the text box. When you type a letter or two in the Starts With text box, Palm Desktop highlights the first name on the list that starts with those letters, followed by any others that match. If that's not the exact name you're looking for, the one you're looking for probably isn't far away. You can scroll down the list and click the name you want or keep typing letters until the name you want to find is highlighted. You can open that person's address record by double-clicking his name or by clicking her name and then clicking the Display button.

Deleting a name

Sadly, sometimes you just want to wipe a person's name from your list. To remove the name of someone you just don't have contact with anymore, just click her name on the Contact List and press the Delete key on your keyboard. A warning box is displayed to make sure that you really want to do the deed; if you're sure, click OK. You can also press ⌘+E when the Contact List is open to delete an entry.

If you change your mind, you can always restore any address record you've saved in an archive. See the section "Archiving Your Palm Organizer Stuff," later in this chapter, for details.

Doing stuff with your to-dos

Even though you may know what to do, you have to remember to do it. The Task List lets you add to a Palm device the items you need to do so that the Palm device can remind you to do them.

(The Palm Desktop software refers to the To Do List as the Task List. Both terms can be used interchangeably.) To bring up the Task List, just click the View Task List button on the toolbar or choose View⊳Task List, and continue to the following sections The tasks and their corresponding information are listed in the window.

Creating a to-do item

Nothing could be easier than entering a task on the Task List. If only doing the tasks were so easy!

1. **Click the Create Task button on the toolbar (or choose Create⇨Task). The keyboard shortcut for creating a new task is ⌘+Option+T.**

   The Task dialog box appears, as shown in Figure 13-12.

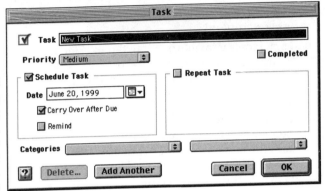

Figure 13-12:
The Task
dialog box,
ready to be
filled in with
your to-dos.

2. **Type what you need to do in the text box to the right of the word *Task*.**

3. **Add information or make any changes you want to the task.**

   In this dialog box, you can change the priority, make the task repeat, schedule the task (create a due date), or set a reminder for the task. You can also assign the task to a category. If you know that you may not complete the task by the due date you have set and you want it to carry over to the next day in your calendar, check the box next to Carry Over After Due. You can add another task from this dialog box after you've created the first one by pressing the Add Another button.

4. **Click the OK button.**

   The name of your task appears on the Task List with the information you specified for it.

Setting the priority for a to-do item

How do you know which of the vital items on the Task List to do first? You have to set priorities. You have enough categories to assign as the priority for each task to make sure that you do the important things first.

Follow these steps to set the priority of a task item:

1. **With the Task List visible, double-click the name of the task for which you want to set a priority.**

2. **Click the pop-up menu next to the word *Priority* on the left side of the window.**

The choices you can assign for the priority are highest, high, medium, low, and lowest.

3. Click the OK button.

The priority you assign appears next to the task item.

You can have more than one to-do with the same priority, and you can even make every task your top priority.

Assigning a category to a to-do item

Because some of your tasks must be done at home and others can be done only at work, you can keep track of which task you need to do next by assigning your tasks to categories. When you're at work, for example, you don't have to remind yourself to visit the water cooler.

To assign a category to a to-do item, follow these steps:

1. With the Task List visible, double-click the name of the task item to which you want to assign a category. This step opens the Task dialog box.

2. Click the pop-up menu next to the word *Categories* on the left side of the window.

The drop-down list of available categories appears, as shown in Figure 13-13.

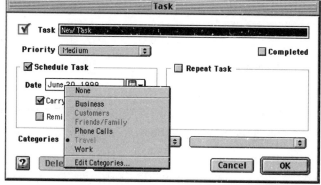

Figure 13-13:
Some tasks
are easily
categorized.

3. Click the category you want to assign to the task.

The category you click appears in the Category text box.

4. Click the OK button.

The category you assign appears next to the task.

Adding categories

You can maintain your collection of categories either on your Palm device or on Palm Desktop. Every time you HotSync your data, the categories you set up on your Palm device are mirrored on Palm Desktop and vice versa. The categories you set up and modify in one area of the software (Task lists, for example) are also modified in all other areas of the software (Notes or Appointments, for example).

Follow these steps to create a new category:

1. **With the Task List visible, double-click a task and choose Edit Categories from the pop-up menu next to the word *Categories* (or choose Edit⇨Categories⇨Edit Categories).**

   The Edit Categories dialog box opens, as shown in Figure 13-14.

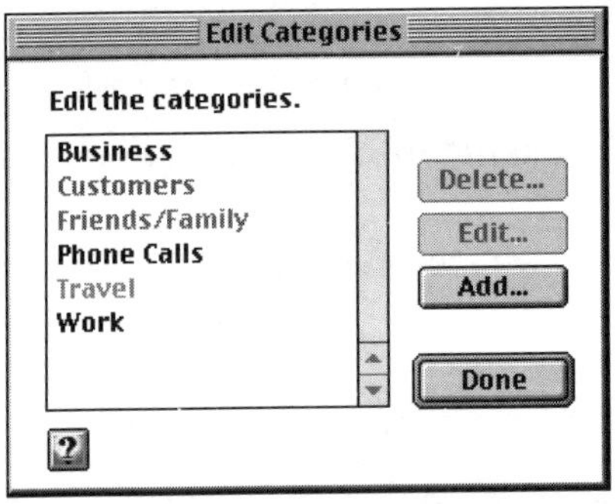

Figure 13-14:
Create new categories or edit or delete existing categories in the Edit Categories dialog box.

```
═════════ Edit Categories ═════════
 Edit the categories.

 ┌─────────────────────┐   ┌──────────┐
 │ Business            │   │ Delete...│
 │ Customers           │   └──────────┘
 │ Friends/Family      │   ┌──────────┐
 │ Phone Calls         │   │ Edit...  │
 │ Travel              │   └──────────┘
 │ Work                │   ┌──────────┐
 │                     │   │ Add...   │
 │                     │   └──────────┘
 │                   ▲ │   ┌──────────┐
 │                   ▼ │   │ Done     │
 └─────────────────────┘   └──────────┘
 ┌───┐
 │ ? │
 └───┘
```

2. **Click the Add button.**

   The Categories dialog box opens.

3. **Enter the name of the category you want to add and assign it a color.**

   The name you enter appears in the New Category dialog box.

4. **Click OK.**

   The new category appears in the Edit Categories dialog box.

5. **Click Done.**

   The Edit Categories dialog box closes.

TIP

You can add, delete, or edit categories at any time within the Palm Desktop software by choosing Edit⇨Categories⇨Edit Categories. Whatever changes you make to the categories are reflected wherever categories are used.

You can have no more than 15 categories on your Palm device or on Palm Desktop. If you try to exceed 15 categories, the program adamantly (but nicely) refuses to add new categories.

Deleting categories

If you temporarily lost your mind and added some categories you now regret, you can just wipe out your excess categories and get back to basics.

Follow these steps to delete a category:

1. **With the Task List visible, double-click a task and choose Edit Categories from the pop-up menu next to the word *Categories* (or choose Edit⇨Categories⇨Edit Categories).**

   The Edit Categories dialog box opens, as shown in Figure 13-14.

2. **Select the name of the category you want to delete.**

   The category you select is highlighted to show that you selected it.

3. **Click the Delete button.**

   A warning box opens, asking whether you want to delete this item.

4. **Click Delete.**

   The Delete Category dialog box closes, and the category is deleted.

5. **Click Done.**

   The Edit Categories dialog box closes.

Unfortunately, when you delete a category used by a task, the category defaults to None on the list rather than allow you to assign the task to another category.

Renaming categories

If you change your mind and want to rename a category, follow these steps:

1. **With the Task List visible, double-click a task and choose Edit Categories from the pop-up menu next to the word *Categories* (or choose Edit⇨Categories⇨Edit Categories).**

   The Edit Categories dialog box opens.

2. **Click the name of the category you want to rename or change the color of.**

   The name of the category is highlighted to show that you selected it.

3. **Click the Edit button.**

   The Categories dialog box opens, as shown in Figure 13-15.

4. **Enter the new name of the category you want to change.**

   The name you type replaces the old name in the Categories dialog box.

5. **Click OK.**

The name you entered replaces the preceding name of the category in the Edit Categories dialog box.

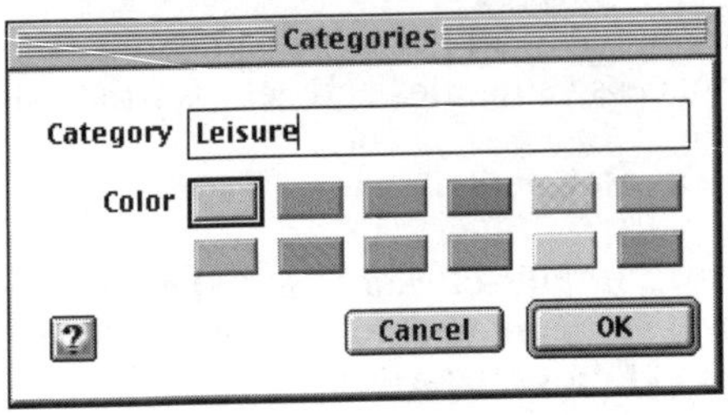

Figure 13-15:
You can
rename your
categories
and change
their color
at any time.

6. **Click Done.**

The Edit Categories dialog box closes.

Changing the due date of a task item

Your Task List can do more than tell you which tasks to do; it also helps you remember when to do them.

When the task was created, it was given the default due date of that date. Follow these steps to change the due date of a task item:

1. **With the Task List visible, double-click the name of the task item for which you want to change the due date. This step opens the Task dialog box.**

   The default date shown is the date when you created the item.

2. **Click in the Date text box in the Schedule Task area of the dialog box, and type the date you want to change it to.**

   You can also use the pop-up menu to the right of the text box to pick a specific date on the little calendar that pops up.

3. **Click in the Carry Over After Due check box if you want tasks you haven't accomplished to stay on the list after the due date. You can also check the Remind check box if you want to be reminded of the task at a specified time interval.**

4. **Click OK.**

   The Task dialog box closes, and the date you chose appears in the Date column of the Task List window.

You can also set a task to repeat itself at any given interval by putting a check in the check box next to words *Repeat Task* in the Task dialog box.

Deleting a task

Sometimes, you get lucky and can mark a task off the list before you even have to do it. Follow these steps to delete a task item on Palm Desktop:

1. **With the Task List visible, click the name of the task you want to delete.**

2. **Press the Delete key or click the Delete icon (the one with the trash can icon) from the toolbar. You can also press ⌘+E on your keyboard.**

   A warning box appears, asking whether you're sure that you want to delete the task.

3. **Click Delete.**

   The task is deleted.

If it turns out that you did complete the task, be sure to mark the task as complete. The little check box next to the name of the task is there for that reason.

Working with memos

Entering memos on Palm Desktop is easier than using Graffiti because memos usually contain lots of text, and you can type them much faster than using Graffiti or typing individual letters on the Palm organizer's on-screen keyboard. You can also copy and paste text to a memo from other desktop programs, such as a word processor.

Palm Desktop for the Macintosh refers to memos as *notes*. They're the same thing. Contacts can have notes attached to them; you enter them in the same way.

To bring up your list of notes, just click the View Note List button on the toolbar or choose View⇨Note List (tap ⌘+Shift+N), and continue to the following sections.

Creating a note

Sometimes, you need certain information that's not exactly an appointment and not exactly a to-do item, but you still need it on your Palm device. The simplest way to keep miscellaneous information on hand is to create a memo, or note. Nothing could be easier.

Follow these steps to create a new note on Palm Desktop:

1. **Click the Create Note button on the toolbar (or choose Create⇨Note).**

   The Note window appears with the cursor in the Title text field.

2. **Type the title of your memo.**

   The text you type appears in the title text box, as shown in Figure 13-16.

3. **Click in the main text window area and type the main text of your memo.**

   You can also assign a category to the note or choose to attach the note to a contact or task, for example, from this window.

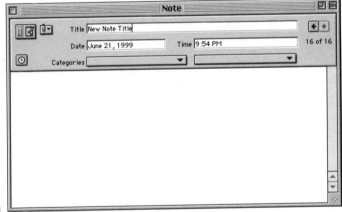

Figure 13-16:
Give your memo whatever title you like.

4. **Close the Note window when you're finished.**

   The title of your note appears on the list of notes in the Note List window.

 If you don't like to type, you can also copy and paste text into a note. Just select text from a word-processing document or even from the World Wide Web, tap ⌘+C to copy the text, start Palm Desktop, create a new note, and then tap ⌘+V to paste the text directly into the note.

 You can easily add the date and time to a note by clicking the small clock icon in the Note window. The current date and time are pasted into the window where the cursor is located.

Reading a note

You don't have to read your memos on Palm Desktop; just send them to your Palm device, and then read them anywhere you want. To read a memo, just double-click one of the notes in the Note List window. The window for that note opens and you can read your memo.

To read through all the memos on your desktop quickly, zip through the entire list by tapping the up or down arrow keys and then tapping the Return key when the one you want to read is highlighted. Another way to get through the list quickly is to tap the left or right arrow keys in the Note window to show you the next or preceding note.

Printing a note

Believe it or not, you can also print things from the desktop. Although some people have clever methods of beaming their Palm organizer data to especially well-equipped printers, the process is still tricky, and most printers aren't up to the job. Because most people have printers hooked up to their desktop computers, printing from the desktop is the quickest way to see Palm computing data on paper.

To print a note from Palm Desktop, follow these steps:

1. **With the Note List window visible, click the title of the memo you want to print.**

2. **Choose File⇨Print (or press ⌘+P).**

   The Print window appears. This window enables you to choose the items you want to print and the layout you want to use. You can then preview the way it will look when it's printed on paper by tapping the Preview button.

3. **Click Print.**

   The Macintosh Print dialog box opens. You can specify printing information, such as the number of copies you want.

4. **Click Print.**

   The memo is printed.

The first time you print something in Palm Desktop, the Paper Planner Interview window opens. You can specify one of the popular brands of organizers and corresponding binder size on the pop-up list. If you don't, just keep the default choice of None.

One cool thing about the Palm Desktop software for the Macintosh is that you can choose to print a list of contacts, notes, tasks, or even your calendar from the Print dialog box. Just click the Print icon on the toolbar (or choose File⇨Print) from anywhere within the Palm Desktop. You can click the icon for the choice you want and see the preview on the right side of the window.

Editing a note

If you use memos frequently, you certainly want to change a few of them now and then. The biggest advantage to keeping memos in electronic form is that the text is so easy to change.

Follow these steps to edit a note on Palm Desktop:

1. **With the Note List window visible, double-click the title of the note you want to edit.**

   The Note window appears.

2. **Make any changes you want to the memo.**

3. **Click the Close button in the upper-left corner of the window.**

   The window closes and your changes are saved as part of your memo.

Replacing a large amount of the text in a memo usually kills off the text you replace. One thing you can do with memos on Palm Desktop that you can't do on a Palm device is copy entire memos and then just change one of them. To duplicate a memo, click the name of the memo to select it, and press ⌘+D (or choose Edit⇨Duplicate Note). You then have two identical memos. Just change one, and you have two different memos.

Categorizing a note

Categories are particularly useful after you've collected more than a few dozen memos. Categorizing not only makes memos easier to find but also lets you see your memo collection more easily on your Palm device because its small screen can show only 11 memos at a time.

Follow these steps to assign a category to a note on Palm Desktop:

1. **With the Note List window visible, double-click the title of the memo you want to categorize.**

   The Note window opens.

2. **Click the category pop-up menu (the downward-pointing triangle) above the memo text and choose the category you want, as shown in Figure 13-17.**

   The category you choose appears above the memo text.

The categories shown on the list are the same for notes, tasks, contacts, and calendar items. When you edit a category, it changes for all the Palm device functions that use them.

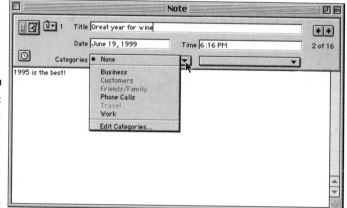

Figure 13-17:
Change the category to one on this list or make up a new one.

Deleting a note

Follow these steps to make your notes go away:

1. **With the Note List window visible, click the title of the memo you want to delete.**

2. **Choose Edit⇨Delete Note. You can also press the Delete key on your keyboard, press ⌘+E, or tap the Delete icon on the toolbar.**

   A warning box opens, as shown in Figure 13-18, asking whether you want to delete this note.

Figure 13-18:
Make sure that you want to delete that note.

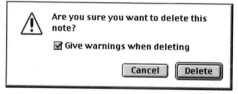

3. **Click Delete.**

   Zap! The memo is gone.

If you're tired of seeing those warning boxes every time you want to delete something, make sure that the check box next to Give Warning While Deleting is unchecked.

Some Macintosh-Only Features of the Desktop Software

The Macintosh version of the Palm Desktop software enables you to do some cool things that the Windows version doesn't.

Customizing the look

You can change the way your Palm Desktop application windows and taskbar look by adding some "spice" to them. You change the "decor" by choosing Edit⇨Preferences. The Preferences window opens, and, by default, the decor icon is chosen. You can scroll through the list to preview the different choices for the new look you want. One favorite is Red Chile Peppers. You can test your new decor by clicking the Apply button. If you have any desktop windows open in the background, they change, and you can see the results. Try as many as you like with the Apply button. After you have decided on a new look, click the OK button. The dialog box closes, and you're all set with your new look.

Look, ma, no hands!

One of the best features about the Macintosh version is the Instant Palm Desktop. The menu icon for it appears to the left of the application menu in the upper-right corner of your Macintosh screen.

The Instant Palm Desktop menu lets you do many essential tasks without having to start the Palm Desktop software. From the menu, you can see your appointments, events, and tasks for the day. You can create appointments, tasks, contacts, notes, and events, you can even quickly start the Palm Desktop software or the HotSync Manager software or switch to it from another application. Believe it or not, you can designate certain contact names and phone numbers to place on the menu for easy access (the menu even dials the numbers for you!).

The most useful feature of this menu is its capability to help you search for contacts whenever you need to without having to start up the desktop software: You just choose Find Contact from the menu and type the first few letters of the contact's last name. A list of all contacts matching the letters you typed is displayed.

You don't have to worry about installing this feature because it's controlled by the Instant Palm Desktop extension, which is automatically copied to the Extensions folder inside your System Folder when you install the Palm Desktop software.

Furnishing Your Palm Device

You can furnish a Palm device as lavishly (or sparingly) as you want. Feel free to fill it up with some games, a spreadsheet, or whatever else you want.

Checking memory

Before you start adding things to your Palm device, make sure that you have room for all of it. A Palm III with 2MB of memory, for example, has less room for programs than a couple of your average floppy disks. A PalmPilot Professional has only 1MB of memory, or half the space of a Palm III. A Palm device protests if you try to put too much stuff on it.

Follow these three steps to see how much space is available on a Palm III:

1. **Tap the Applications soft button.**

   The applications list appears.

2. **Tap the Menu soft button.**

   The menu bar appears.

3. **Choose App⇨Info.**

   The Info screen appears. The line at the top of the Info screen says something like `Free Memory: 849K of 960K`, as shown in Figure 13-19.

Because most Palm organizer applications are somewhat small, as long as you have a few hundred kilobytes of memory (abbreviated *K* by computer folks), you should be okay. Remember, though, that every time you add an item to one of the standard Palm organizer applications, like the Contact List or the Date Book, you use up a little more memory. Leave yourself some breathing room. You can free up some memory by either deleting applications, as I describe later in this chapter, or by deleting lots of items from the standard Palm organizer applications. The easiest way to delete records en masse is to use Palm Desktop, as I describe in earlier sections of this chapter.

If you're still using a PalmPilot Professional or earlier model, the process for checking memory is a little different because earlier Palm devices have a separate Memory application. To check how much memory is available on those models, tap the Applications soft button and tap Memory.

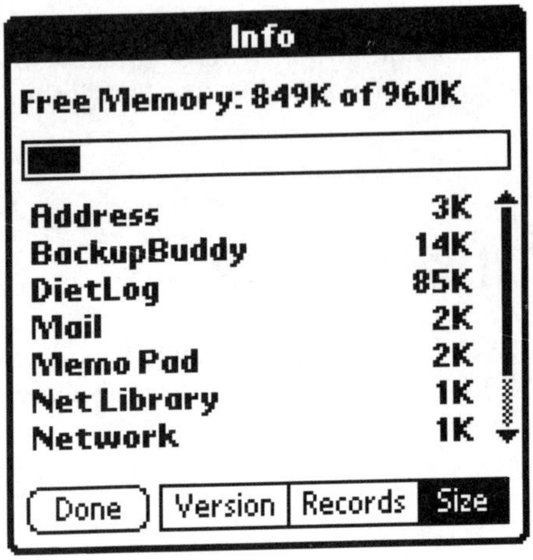

Figure 13-19:
Before you
install a new
program,
check your
memory to
see whether
you have
enough
room.

Info

Free Memory: 849K of 960K

Address	3K
BackupBuddy	14K
DietLog	85K
Mail	2K
Memo Pad	2K
Net Library	1K
Network	1K

[Done] [Version | Records | Size]

Although you can upgrade the memory on a Palm device fairly easily, it costs a few bucks. A company named TRG specializes in selling extra memory for your Palm device. Check out Chapter 16 for more info about upgrading.

Installing applications

Programmers write zillions of programs for Palm devices. You can get many programs over the Internet, and I include a sampling of particularly useful or fun programs on the CD that comes with this book. All you have to do to install an application on a Palm device is copy the application to your desktop computer from the Internet or from the CD and then locate that file with the Install Tool, which is part of the HotSync Manager program.

Remember that the Install Tool doesn't install applications; it *prepares* applications for installation. After picking an application with the Install Tool, you have to perform a HotSync. Just place the Palm device in its cradle and tap the HotSync button. (For more info about HotSyncing, see the section "Setting Up Your Macintosh to HotSync," earlier in this chapter.)

Using HotSync Manager

To install Palm programs by using the HotSync Manager, follow these steps:

1. **Launch HotSync Manager.**

   HotSync Manager is located in the Palm folder with the Palm Desktop application.

2. Choose HotSync⇨Install (or press ⌘+I).

The Install Handheld Files window opens, as shown in Figure 13-20.

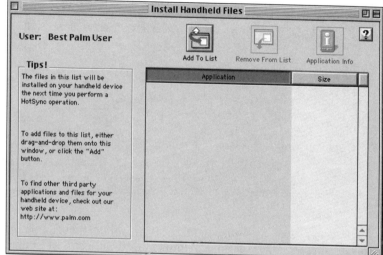

Figure 13-20:
Add new programs from the Install dialog box.

3. Click the Add to List icon.

The Open dialog box opens.

4. Click the name of the file you want to install.

The filename you click is highlighted to show that you selected it. If you downloaded the application from the Internet or are installing applications from the CD, browse until you find the application you want to install.

5. Click Add File.

The Open dialog box closes, and the filename you picked is now listed in the Install Handheld Files dialog box, as shown in Figure 13-21. You can get information about the application you picked by clicking it once to select it and then clicking the Application Info icon.

6. Close the Install Handheld Files window.

7. Tap the HotSync button on the cradle of your Palm device.

The HotSync process begins, and the program is installed on your Palm device.

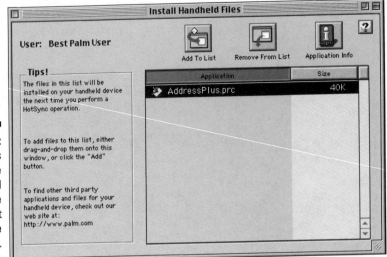

Figure 13-21:
Programs
that will be
installed
during the
next
HotSync are
listed.

You have an even easier way to install Palm applications if you're comfort-able dealing with files on the Macintosh Desktop. Just find a Palm application file (Palm files end with .PRC, .PDB, or .PQA) and drag it to the Install Handheld Files window. The program is installed the next time you HotSync.

Deleting applications on a Palm III or later

The process of deleting applications differs slightly on the Palm III and later models from the way it works on earlier models. Follow these steps to delete a program from a Palm III or later:

1. **Tap the Applications soft button.**

   The applications screen appears.

2. **Tap the Menu button.**

   The menu bar appears.

3. **Choose App⇨Delete.**

   The Delete screen appears, as shown in Figure 13-22.

4. **Tap the name of the application you want to delete.**

   The name you tap is highlighted to show that you selected it.

Delete

Free Memory: 849K of 960K

BackupBuddy	14K
DietLog	85K

(Done) (Delete...)

Figure 13-22:
Clean out
the old by
deleting
unwanted
applications.

5. **Tap Delete.**

   The Delete Application dialog box opens.

6. **Tap Yes if you're sure. If you change your mind, tap No.**

   If you tap Yes, the application is deleted, and its name disappears from the list of applications in the Delete dialog box. If you tap No, the dialog box closes, and the application remains.

7. **Tap Done.**

   The Delete screen closes.

Deleting applications on a PalmPilot Professional or earlier model

Follow these steps to delete a program from a PalmPilot Professional (or earlier model):

1. **Tap the Applications soft button.**

   The applications screen appears.

2. **Tap Memory.**

   The Memory application opens.

3. **Tap Delete Apps.**

   The Delete Applications screen appears.

4. **Tap the name of the application you want to delete.**

   The name you tap is highlighted to show that you selected it.

5. Tap Delete.

The Delete Application dialog box opens, as shown in Figure 13-23.

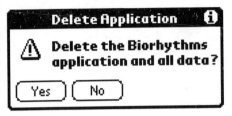

6. Tap Yes if you're sure. If you change your mind, tap No.

If you tap Yes, the Delete Application dialog box closes, and the application is deleted. If you tap No, the dialog box closes, and the application remains.

7. Tap Done.

The Delete Application screen disappears.

You can always reinstall applications you've deleted, by using the same procedure described in the section "Installing applications," earlier in this chapter.

Protecting Your Turf

If the worst happens and you lose your Palm device, you can always buy a new one. What about all your data, though? Luckily for you, Palm Desktop makes it easy to reinstall all your precious data.

Restoring your Palm data

If you upgrade to a new Palm organizer model or have to replace a lost, stolen, or destroyed Palm device, you can restore everything that was on your old Palm device with a simple HotSync:

1. Put the Palm device in its cradle.

2. Tap the HotSync button on the Palm device cradle.

The HotSync Manager on the desktop Macintosh is launched, and the HotSync Progress dialog box opens. The Users dialog box opens on the desktop screen.

3. Click the name of the user whose data you want to install on the Palm device — it's probably your name.

The name you click is highlighted to show that you selected it, as shown in Figure 13-24.

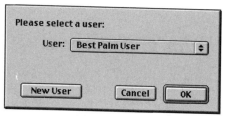

Figure 13-24:
Pick the user whose data should be on this Palm device.

Please select a user:

User: Best Palm User

New User   Cancel   OK

4. Click OK (on the desktop).

The HotSync Manager then transfers all the user information from the desktop to your Palm device. After a few minutes, the dialog box closes, and you're all set.

If you use one desktop computer to synchronize more than one Palm device, don't assign the same username to more than one Palm device. The HotSync program can get confused and send the wrong data to the wrong Palm device, or, worse, make data disappear.

Backing up your data

If you use only the programs that come in the box with your Palm device, you don't have to worry about backing up. If you HotSync regularly to keep your data current, you're covered. Your data from all the standard Palm organizer applications gets saved by Palm Desktop every time you HotSync. Of course, you should regularly back up the data on your desktop machine.

On the other hand, if you installed programs that don't come preinstalled on your Palm device, those programs may not automatically back themselves up like your standard Palm applications do, so you need a backup program to keep those files safe. Check with the developer of the software to see which backup software you have to use, or go to the 3Com Web site, at www.palm.com, to find a Macintosh-compatible utility that can back up your nonstandard programs automatically.

If you've added nothing to your Palm device except for a few games, don't worry about backing up. Backups are a concern only if you've added programs that add data themselves, like spreadsheets, databases, time and billing applications, or similar programs. If your Palm device was issued to you at work, check with your system administrator about whether you have to do anything special with backups.

Archiving your Palm organizer stuff

A Palm device can hold only a fraction of the information a desktop computer can. To save space on your Palm device, clear things out regularly. A Palm device has a Purge function in the Date Book and Task List that automatically gets rid of unneeded items and moves them to an archive file, if you want. For more info about purging Palm organizer items, see Chapter 6.

Viewing archived items

Palm Desktop is the only place where you can open and view archived items. In addition, you can create a backup copy of information by exporting it from an application to an archive file. Exporting information to an archive file does not remove information from the Palm Desktop software or from your Palm device.

You can work with records in the archive file or restore to the current application the records in an archive file. To open the archive file, double-click the file's icon. Most commands you use in the current Palm Desktop applications are available in archive files.

Follow these steps to view archived items in Palm Desktop:

1. **Choose File➪Open.**

   The Open Archive dialog box opens, as shown in Figure 13-25. Whenever you perform a HotSync operation, archived records are added to the file named User Data Archive in the folder with your username in the Users folder. Browse until you find this file.

2. **Click the name of the archive file you want to view.**

3. **Click OK.**

   The Palm Desktop window appears, ready for you to look through and recover archived items.

Figure 13-25:
Find those
old deleted
items by
opening an
archive file.

```
┌─────────────────────────────────────┐
│     [ Shawn ⬍ ]        ▭ Minerva    │
│  ▣ Backups            [   Eject   ]  │
│  ▣ Conduit Settings                  │
│  ▣ Files To Install   [  Desktop  ]  │
│  ▣ User Data                         │
│  ▣ User Data Archive  [  Cancel   ]  │
│                       [   Open    ]  │
└─────────────────────────────────────┘
```

Accommodating Multiple Users

Most people use a Palm device in conjunction with a desktop computer in order to simplify data entry and keep the data on their Palm devices safe. You don't have to limit yourself to one Palm device per computer, though. Palm Desktop enables you to synchronize Palm devices with different users. The first time you HotSync your Palm device, the HotSync Manager asks for your username. The Palm device username you enter (or choose) is added to the list of usernames in Palm Desktop. Each time you put a Palm device in the cradle attached to that desktop computer, the program recognizes which Palm device is in the cradle whenever you tap the HotSync button. That way, after you've set up a computer to HotSync a particular Palm device, the desktop computer always knows which Palm device it's dealing with and synchronizes to that particular person's information.

The Palm Device Name Game

Although all Palm devices look pretty much alike in those little tiny boxes, each one has one important difference: the name of the user. You can find out which name is assigned to the Palm device you're using by tapping the Applications soft button and then tapping HotSync. The HotSync screen displays the name of the user assigned to it. A Palm III shows the username in the upper-right corner of the screen. Older Palm devices say `Welcome, username`. Also, whenever you perform a HotSync, the name of the user whose data is being synchronized appears in the HotSync Progress dialog box. You determine the Palm device username the first time you perform a HotSync. If you try to HotSync a Palm device to a computer that hasn't ever seen a Palm device with that username, the HotSync Manager asks whether you want to set up a new account for that user.

Chapter 14

Palm Seventh Heaven

- -

In This Chapter

▶ What you get with a Palm VII

▶ Caught in the Palm.Net

▶ Wireless e-mail

▶ About signal strength

▶ Special Palm VII applications

▶ Personal Palm VII programs

- -

*N*o doubt you've heard all sorts of hoopla about the new, wireless Palm VII. If you didn't rush out and buy one as soon as it became available, you may be wondering whether you're missing something. Maybe, maybe not. I'm convinced that in the future, everyone will carry a device that does the things a Palm VII can do. At the moment, the Palm VII has some genuine benefits as well as some definite drawbacks, so you may want to think twice about tossing out your old Palm device until you know whether the Palm VII has what you want. In this chapter, I show you how to get the most from your Palm VII if you have one or how to make an earlier-model Palm product give you many of the same features.

"Should I Get a Palm VII?"

The Palm VII puts an unusual collection of features into a single package. The unit is slightly larger than the older Palm III and has an antenna on the right side of the screen. You have to flip the antenna up to use the wireless features. Flipping up the antenna turns the device on and opens the Applications picker to the Palm.Net category, where you find all your Palm.Net applications, the ones that require a wireless connection. The first time you start your Palm VII, the Palm.Net Activation program runs and tells you everything you need to enter to get your Palm.Net account up and running. If you already have an earlier-model Palm device, you may have all you need for the moment. If you have a Palm III or later, you may be able to get yourself an IR-equipped pager or cell phone and end up somewhat better off than if you bought a Palm VII. It depends on what you need.

Palm VII: A perfect business product

Today, nearly everyone is a knowledge worker, and we're all more mobile than ever. The Palm VII is the perfect way to connect knowledge workers to the knowledge they work on.

To most businesses, 600 bucks is a small price to pay to give roaming employees instant access to essential corporate information, sales literature, order status and all sorts of other real-time data. Although the Palm VII can get information from any Web site, it does not allow you to surf anywhere on the Web the way you can on a desktop computer. Most businesses don't want employees fooling around on the Web during business hours, so the limitations of the Palm VII are perfect in a business setting.

Also, because the Palm VII is easy to use and is a no-brainer to get running, businesses don't have to mess around trying to set up their own wireless networks and new kinds of software to keep roaming salespeople connected. Traveling salespeople can even enter orders directly through a Palm VII and satisfy their customers on the spot.

Palm VII: A pretty good consumer product

Although many big businesses will jump to adopt the Palm VII in a heartbeat, individuals and small-business users may consider other options for now. If you already use a pager or if you need to get e-mail on the go and need to be notified when e-mail messages arrive, you may do better to get 2-way pager service, an IR-equipped pager, and a program named Beam Link, from JP Systems, to enable your pager to communicate with your Palm device. Although the Palm VII gives you the convenience of dealing with a single device, it can't notify you when messages arrive, so if you still need to carry the pager, why not have the tools you need? (I explain more about pagers and wireless modems for your Palm organizer in Chapter 19.)

Although the Palm VII is essential for people in certain situations, others may be able to get along nicely with well-chosen accessories and an earlier-model Palm device. The following table shows what I recommend if you're not sure whether to spring for a Palm VII:

If You Need This	Get This
A single, pocket-size unit that can exchange e-mail and view snippets of text from the Internet	A Palm VII
A true pager that can notify you when messages arrive and allow you to respond with your own replies	A Palm III or later, an infrared-equipped 2-way pager, and Beam Link software (from JP systems)
Full-fledged mobile Internet access in a package small enough to fit in a purse or briefcase (but too big for most pockets)	Any Palm device and a Minstrel wireless modem

Your Palm.Net Account

When you flip up the antenna on your Palm VII for the first time, have your credit card ready because the first thing the device wants to do is sign you up for the Palm.Net service that makes those wonderful wireless features possible. And why not; that's why your bought a Palm VII, right? Otherwise, you could have saved money and bought a cheaper Palm organizer.

Web surfing? Web clipping?

Lots of people are excited at the notion of surfing the Web wirelessly from their Palm VII. Unfortunately, that's not really what a Palm VII does. When people say "surf the Web," they expect to fire up a program like Netscape and browse any page anywhere on the World Wide Web. That's not what a Palm VII does. The Palm VII does something called *Web clipping*. Web surfing is to Web clipping as riding the waves at Maui is to dipping your toes in the baby pool. You don't get the full experience of the Internet; you get only selected samples, or *clips*. That's not all bad, though. The Internet is so enormous that some people don't want to see everything — they just want a few, useful things. That's what Web clipping does: It gives you just what you need and no more and lets you get your information while you're on the go.

The other catch to Web clipping is that you can't assume that you'll be able to view any Web site out there. You have to install a special little program, a *Palm Query Application* (or *PQA*), for each site you want to view. If you want weather information, you need to use the weather program. If you want sports scores, you need to look at a sports application, such as the ESPN program. If you want to look at your own Web site, you have to write a PQA to view your own site. It's easy; I show you how to build a PQA later in this chapter, in the section "Creating Your Own Palm Query Applications." If you've purchased a Palm VII so that you can see a goofy new site every day, you're out of luck unless you want to write a goofy new PQA every day.

Palm.Net — you're gonna pay!

If you think that you're going to go slinging data through the air without paying, think again, buddy! The Palm Connected Organizer people have decided to simplify your life by offering only one choice of wireless data service so that you can use the Palm VII wireless features. The service is named Palm.Net. In addition to building Palm.Net access right into the Palm VII, they also charge you an arm and a leg for using Palm.Net. The basic packages run $9.95 a month for an impossibly small amount of wireless service (50K) and $24.95 for a small amount of wireless service (150K). After you run through your allotment of wireless service, you have to pay 30 cents per kilobyte of information you either send or receive. That may not seem like much, but it mounts up fast. I get about 1,000 e-mail messages each week on my regular desktop e-mail service. By my estimate, if I were to pay for that e-mail at Palm.Net rates, I'd run up a bill of about $1,200 each month just to receive e-mail. That's right — you have to pay to receive e-mail on your Palm VII. Think about that before you start handing out your Palm.Net e-mail address — whenever anyone sends you an e-mail, *you pay!* So if you have a cell phone, you know the drill: Give your Palm.Net e-mail address only to people you're willing to pay to hear from. A better idea is to use an e-mail system on your desktop computer that lets you set up rules to forward mail from certain people to your Palm.Net e-mail address and don't give out your Palm.Net address.

You don't need to know anything special to start Palm.Net service, although you should try to remember the username and password you assign yourself when you kick off Palm.Net service, because you need to know those things later if you want to check to see how much you've spent on Palm.Net service or make changes in your account settings. For the most part, you never need to set up Palm.Net service again, so don't worry too much.

Checking your Palm.Net account from a Palm VII

It's easy to run up a bodacious bill on Palm.Net if you don't watch what you're doing. Fortunately, you can keep an eye on the tab by using the Palm.Net program that comes with your Palm VII. If money is no object for you, send me a note and I'll keep track of your Palm VII balance for you. I also have a bridge you can buy.

To check your Palm.Net account from the Palm VII:

1. **Raise the antenna on the Palm VII.**

   The Palm.Net group of applications icons appears.

2. Tap the Palm.Net icon.

The Palm.Net opening screen appears, as shown in Figure 14-1.

Figure 14-1:
See how
much you
owe for
wireless
service
through the
Palm.Net
application.

3. Tap My Account.

The My Account screen appears. An insertion point (blinking bar)
appears on the Username line, as shown in Figure 14-2.

Figure 14-2:
Enter your
username
and
password.

**4. Enter your username in Graffiti or by using the on-screen keyboard
(refer to Chapter 2 for more info about entering text).**

The name you enter appears on the Username line.

5. **Tap Unassigned next to Password.**

   The Password dialog box appears, as shown in Figure 14-3.

Password
Enter a password:
flowers
(OK) (Cancel)

6. **Enter your password in Graffiti or by using the on-screen keyboard (refer to Chapter 2 for more info about entering text).**

   Your password appears in the Password dialog box.

7. **Tap OK.**

   The Password dialog box closes and the My Account dialog box reappears. The word *Assigned* now appears next to the word *Password*.

8. **Tap the Submit button.**

   The Account Summary screen appears, showing how many units you've used and how many remain available on your Palm.Net account.

You can just turn your Palm VII off when you're done checking your account balance. You can also switch to another program by tapping the Application button or any other hard button.

Checking your Palm.Net account on the Web

Checking the status of your Palm.Net account through a regular computer on the Internet is more efficient and economical than checking from the Palm VII itself, although it doesn't inspire as much envy in your peers. So why bother? Because you can get more detailed information from the Palm.Net Web site than you can from the Palm VII. If you care about things like that, follow these steps to check your Palm.Net account from a regular Web browser:

1. **Go to the Palm.Net Web site, at** `www.palm.net`.

   For more info about dealing with the Web, get a copy of *The Internet For Dummies* for the type of computer you're using. It was written by John Levine, Margaret Levine Young, and Carol Baroudi (and published by IDG Books Worldwide, Inc.).

2. Click My Account.

You can see a link on the left side and another in the middle of the page. When you click My Account, the Palm.Net main menu appears.

3. Click Account Summary.

The My Account Customer Login screen appears.

4. Enter your username and password.

Your username is the one you made up when you first subscribed to Palm.Net service. Your Palm.Net username is the part of your Palm.Net e-mail address to the left of the @ sign. For example, if your Palm.Net e-mail address is `efuddheimer@palm.net`, your username is efuddheimer.

5. Click Submit.

Your Account Summary appears, as shown in Figure 14-4, showing how much you've paid, how many kilobytes you've used, and how many kilobytes remain before you start owing extra money for going over your limit.

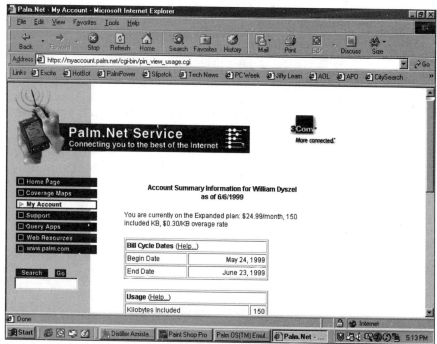

Figure 14-4:
You can also check your wireless charges on the Palm.Net Web site.

Several choices are available on the Palm.Net Web site that don't show up on the Palm.Net application on your Palm VII. The link labeled Account Detail shows you a complete summary of how many units you use each day.

Sending Wireless E-Mail with iMessenger

Strangely enough, two completely separate e-mail programs are included with every Palm VII. The program named Mail grabs messages from your desktop computer every time you HotSync and sends your replies out through your desktop machine when you do your next HotSync.

The iMessenger program, on the other hand, uses the wireless connections of the Palm VII to send and deliver your e-mail messages directly from your Palm VII, even when you're nowhere near your desktop computer. Because the iMessenger program has its own e-mail address, of course, you may need to alert your regular e-mail recipients that there's more than one way to reach you by e-mail. Because you're paying to receive messages on your Palm VII, maybe you want to limit the number of people who know your Palm VII e-mail address.

Creating a message

No magic is involved in creating a message for wireless delivery. It's really just another e-mail message. Still, you probably want to know some details, so follow these steps to create a message:

1. **With the iMessenger program open, tap New.**

   The New Message screen appears, as shown in Figure 14-5. If you know your recipient's e-mail address by heart, enter that address by using Graffiti or the on-screen keyboard. If you do this part of the step, skip ahead to Step 7.

   If you don't know your recipient's address, you can look it up in the Address Book. In that case, continue with Step 2.

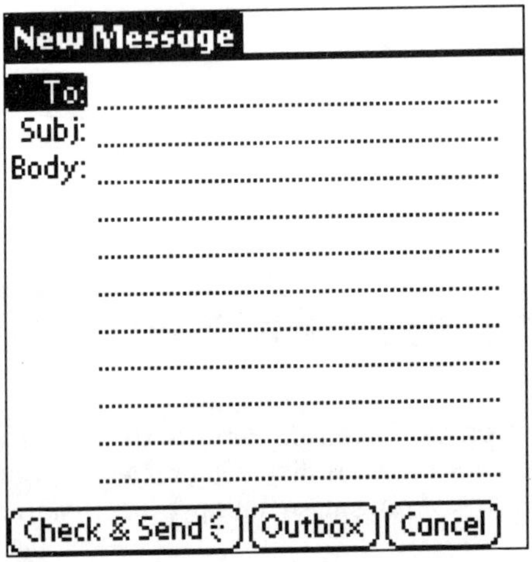

Figure 14-5:
Create a new message in the iMessenger program.

```
┌─────────────────────────────────┐
│ New Message                     │
│ ┌───┐                           │
│ │To:│ ..........................│
│ Subj: ...........................│
│ Body: ...........................│
│       ...........................│
│       ...........................│
│       ...........................│
│       ...........................│
│       ...........................│
│       ...........................│
│       ...........................│
│       ...........................│
│ (Check & Send ≑)(Outbox)(Cancel)│
└─────────────────────────────────┘
```

2. **Tap the word *To*.**

   The To screen appears.

3. **Tap Lookup.**

   The To Lookup screen appears, showing the e-mail addresses of the people you entered on your Address List. It doesn't show everyone in your Address Book, just those who have e-mail addresses. I like that part.

4. **Tap the name of the person to whom you're sending the message.**

   The recipient's name is highlighted, as shown in Figure 14-6.

Figure 14-6: The name of the recipient you choose is highlighted to show that you've selected it.

5. **Tap Add.**

   The address of your recipient appears.

6. **Tap Done.**

   The New Message screen reappears, showing the names of the people you've chosen to send your message to.

7. **Tap the line to the right of Subj.**

   A blinking line, named the *insertion point,* appears, and Subj is highlighted.

8. **Enter the subject of your message by using either the on-screen keyboard or Graffiti (refer to Chapter 2 for more info about entering text).**

   The text you enter appears on the Subject line.

9. **Tap to the right of Body.**

   The insertion point appears, and Body is highlighted.

10. **Enter the text of your message by using either the on-screen keyboard or Graffiti.**

    The text you enter appears on the screen.

11. **Tap Outbox.**

    Your message closes and moves to the Outbox.

Now that you've created a message, you have to tap the Check & Send button on the main iMessenger screen to send the message along to your recipient. If you're outside the Palm.Net coverage area, you may be unable to connect well enough to get the message out. Don't worry: The message stays in the Outbox until you connect to the network successfully.

Sometimes, you don't want to send a message off right away. Sometimes, you and your Palm VII are out in the boondocks where a Palm VII can't communicate, so you have to wait. Tapping the Send Later button moves your message to the Outbox, where it waits until the next time you tap Check & Send. If you're in a big hurry, just tap Check & Send as soon as you've completed your message, and off it goes.

Reading a message

The great thing about the Palm VII iMessenger is that it lets you read messages anywhere. You don't have to rush back to the office or lug a laptop around town; just whip out your Palm VII and see who's been trying to reach you.

To read a message:

1. **Raise the Palm VII antenna.**

    The Palm.Net applications screen appears.

2. **Tap the iMessenger icon.**

    Your list of messages appears.

3. **Tap the message you want to read.**

    The text of the message you tap appears, as shown in Figure 14-7.

4. **After you finish reading the message, tap Done.**

    Your message closes, and the list of messages reappears. A check mark appears next to the message you just read.

Remember that the Palm VII doesn't automatically collect your e-mail messages the way your office computer does. You have to tap Check & Send to see what has come in lately.

Figure 14-7:
Tap the title
of the mes-
sage you
want to
read.

Replying to a message

If you feel anxious to keep up with your e-mail every second of every day, you're probably just as anxious to reply to some of those e-mail messages. Replies are just a simple way of creating a message in direct response to a message someone else sends you. That way, you can tell the sender what you think of a message without needing to look up the sender's e-mail address.

To reply to a message:

1. **With the iMessenger program open, tap the message you want to reply to.**

   The text of the message you tap appears.

2. **Tap Reply.**

   The Reply Options dialog box opens, as shown in Figure 14-8.

Figure 14-8:
Choose
your reply
options,
plain or
deluxe.

3. **Tap Sender.**

   You can choose from two additional options: Include Original Text and Comment Original Text. It's normally a good idea to include some original text when you reply to a message so that the recipient knows what you're replying to. You pay for every single character you send, of course, so do it only sparingly.

4. **Tap OK.**

   The New Message screen appears. Your recipient's e-mail address appears on the To line, and the Subject line shows Re: followed by the subject of the original message. If you chose in Step 3 to include the original message text in your reply, that text appears in the body of your new message.

   You can change any of this text by deleting and adding text as you normally would.

5. **If you want to add new addresses to the To line of the message, enter the new addresses on that line.**

   You can add an address to a message you're replying to in the same way as you do when you create a new message. (See the section "Creating a message," earlier in this chapter, for details.) Normally, you leave this step alone because the address of the person who sent you the original message is already included on the To line when you tap Reply.

6. **If you want to add text to your message, tap to the right of Body.**

   The insertion point appears on a blank line so that you can start writing your reply text.

   If you tap the word *Body* itself, the Body screen appears with the subject of your message at the top. If you enter your text on the Body screen rather than on the New Message screen, just tap Done when you finish entering your text, and continue to Step 8.

7. **Enter the text you want to add by using either the on-screen keyboard or Graffiti (refer to Chapter 2 for more info about entering text).**

   The text you enter appears with the original message's text.

8. **Tap Outbox.**

   Your message closes and moves to the Outbox to await delivery.

Remember that you have to tap Check & Send to get your message out over the airwaves and into the hands of your recipient. If you want to tap Check & Send rather than Outbox, that works, too.

Checking Signal Strength

As the Palm VII becomes popular, you'll be able to take advantage of wireless features nearly everywhere. In the early going, however, you'll be able to use Palm.Net, the Palm VII service, in only selected areas. That means that you'll be fine in most big cities and at airports, although when you're in seclusion deep in the woods, you may be unable to check the headlines on your Palm VII. But that's what seclusion is for, right? The rest of your Palm VII will work fine, but you won't be able to check your e-mail until you return to civilization.

A Palm Query Application can't retrieve information for you unless you're within range of the Palm.Net signal. The Palm.Net signal is available in some locations but not in others, just like your favorite radio program, so you need to check to be sure.

To check Palm.Net signal strength:

1. **Raise the Palm VII antenna.**

   The Palm.Net applications picker appears.

2. **Tap the Diagnostics icon.**

   The Diagnostics program logs on to Palm.Net and shows you how strong your signal is, as shown in Figure 14-9.

Figure 14-9:
The bars in the Diagnostics application show you how strong the Palm.Net signal is where you are.

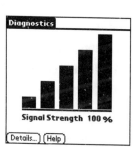

If the signal is weak or absent at your location, you may do better if you move close to a window. If there's just no signal in your area yet, you just have to wait until your area is covered.

Installing Query Applications

The wireless applications you use on a Palm VII get their information from the Internet, but your Palm VII needs to be equipped to view each individual Web site separately with a *Palm Query Application,* or *PQA*. A number of

PQAs are already installed on your Palm VII when you first start it up. The Query Applications that come with your Palm VII include ABC News, for checking headlines; E-Trade, for buying stocks and bonds; MovieFone, for choosing the movie you want to see tonight; and lots of others.

I can't tell you how to use every Palm Query Application any more than I could explain every Web site in existence. Each has its own little quirks, but you can probably figure them out pretty easily.

Palm Query Applications are much like Web pages, in that you can click links to move to a new page or fill in blanks to tell the program what information you want to find. If you're used to surfing the Web, you know that blue, underlined text is a link; clicking a link makes your Web browser display the Web page the link refers to. In a Palm Query Application, links are represented by text followed by the Over the Air icon, which is three little marks that look like a beam of light. Clicking the link shows you new information.

To use a Palm Query Application:

1. **Raise the Palm VII antenna**

   The Palm.Net application picker appears.

2. **Tap the icon for the application you want to use.**

   The main screen of the Palm Query Application you tapped appears.

3. **Enter the information the Palm Query Application requests and tap one of the link buttons.**

   The information you requested appears.

On the day the Palm VII was released, dozens of Palm Query Applications existed. As time goes by, you'll find hundreds of them. You may even create your own. Basically, you just enter information the way you would with any Palm application and tap a link button.

Creating Your Own Palm Query Applications

If you're willing to spend a few extra minutes, you can create your own Palm Query Applications (PQAs) so that your Palm VII can give you a peek at nearly any page on the World Wide Web. Writing Palm Query Applications isn't for everyone, but you don't need to be a super computer geek either. You just need to create a simple HTML page in any current word processor and run it through a free program you can get from the Palm Computing Web site. If you have no interest in writing PQAs, don't feel bad about skipping this section. Just know that PQA writing is pretty simple, although you can get along quite nicely without ever writing one yourself.

The best reason for writing your own Palm Query Application is to give you access to your own web site, if you have one. Bear in mind that because most Web sites were designed to be viewed on a full-size, desktop computer screen in full color, they often look messed up when you try to view them on a Palm VII. In fact, many Web pages are totally unusable from a Palm VII, so don't be surprised. You're the only person likely to write a PQA for your own Web page, so you're on your own. Take heart, though; writing a simple PQA is easier than creating your home page.

The other thing you may consider is that every time you get information from the Internet on your Palm VII through the wireless connection, you pay for what you see. If you write a PQA to link you to a huge, complicated Web site that doesn't work on your Palm VII, you still have to pay for the privilege. If you poke around the Palm Computing Web site, you'll find a Palm VII emulator you can use on your desktop computer to test your PQAs without having to pay for airtime. I don't get into dealing with emulators in this book, but if you spend a great deal of time writing PQAs, you'll want to figure out how to use the emulator to save money.

You have to use a special program, the PQA Builder, for creating Palm Query Applications. You can download it for free from the Palm Computing Web site, at www.palm.com/devzone/palmvii/. There are different versions of the PQA Builder for Windows systems and Macs. Both versions are compressed to take up less space on your desktop computer, so you have to uncompress either one with the compression program for your type of computer. Windows users should use PKZip, from www.pkware.com, or WinZip, from www.winzip.com. Mac users need a program named StuffIt, from www.aladdinsys.com.

After you uncompress the programs, you see a program named *Query Application Builder,* or *QAB.* When you want to run the PQA Builder, you can double-click the program to start it up.

The basic ingredient of a PQA is a simple HTML page. Most word processors, such as Microsoft Word 97, can save any document for you in HTML format, so you don't need to go out and learn how to use another program. Follow these steps to create a simple HTML page in Microsoft Word to link to a Web page:

1. **Start up Microsoft Word.**

   Microsoft Word starts up, displaying a blank page.

2. **Type the name of a Web site, followed by a space.**

   For example, if you type **www.jiffylearn.com** (my Web site), that text appears. When you press the spacebar, the text changes to blue, underlined text to show that Word has created a link to the Internet, as shown in Figure 14-10.

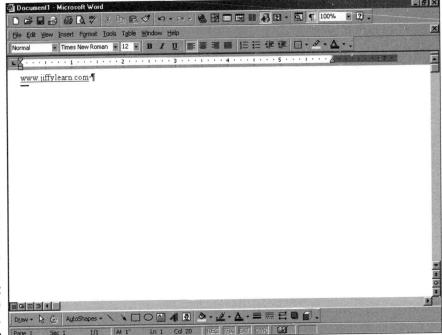

Figure 14-10:
When your text turns blue with an underline, you know that your word processor has turned your text into a Web link.

3. **Choose File⇨Save As.**

   The Save As dialog box appears.

4. **Type a name for your file, such as** My PQA.

   The name you type appears in the File Name text box.

5. **Click the scroll button (triangle) in the Save As Type box.**

   A list of file types appears.

6. **Click Web page (*.htm, *.html) from the Save As Type list.**

   The type you click appears in the Save As Type box.

7. **Click Save.**

   Your file is saved and the Save As dialog box closes.

Now you can go on to convert your new HTML page into a Palm Query Application. Remember where you uncompressed the Query Application Builder files and find the QAB or Query Application Builder program. To convert your HTML page to a Palm Query Application:

1. **Double-click the QAB icon.**

   The Query Application Builder program starts up.

2. **Choose File⇨Open Index.**

   The Open dialog box appears, displaying your list of files.

3. **Double-click the HTML file you created in Word.**

   The Open dialog box disappears and the name of the file you chose appears in the Query Application Builder list, as shown in Figure 14-11.

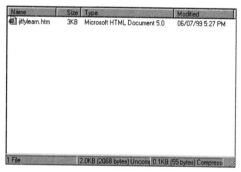

Figure 14-11:
The file you choose appears on the Query Application Builder list.

Don't send dangerous signals

Although most people know what a cell phone does, many don't know what a Palm VII does. The two have much in common, especially the fact that the Palm VII and a cell phone both transmit radio signals. That can be a problem if you're a passenger on an airplane or a visitor to a hospital or a blasting site. Remember that whenever you ask your Palm VII to get information, it has to send out a radio message to tell the Palm.Net system what you want. It's that outgoing radio signal that can cause all those problems. If you're in a situation where people are asked to turn off the power to their cell phones, it's a good idea to avoid raising your Palm VII antenna either. Play it safe.

4. **Choose File⇨Build PQA.**

   The Build PQA dialog box appears.

5. **If you want to assign a new name to your PQA, type the name.**

   The Query Application Builder automatically assigns your PQA the same name as the HTML page you created, such as My PQA, so you don't need to make any changes.

6. **If you want to send your new PQA straight to your Palm VII the next time you HotSync, click the Install to User check box.**

   A check mark appears in the Install to User check box. Make sure that your name is showing in the list box to the right of the words *Install to User,* as shown in Figure 14-12.

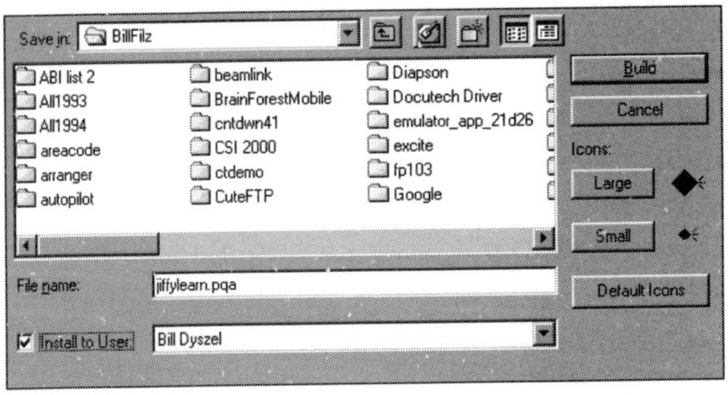

Figure 14-12:
Check this little box, and your application is sent to your Palm VII automatically the next time you HotSync.

Save in:	🗀 BillFilz

🗀 ABI list 2	🗀 beamlink	🗀 Diapson	**Build**
🗀 All 1993	🗀 BrainForestMobile	🗀 Docutech Driver	**Cancel**
🗀 All 1994	🗀 cntdwn41	🗀 emulator_app_21d26	Icons:
🗀 areacode	🗀 CSI 2000	🗀 excite	**Large** ◆
🗀 arranger	🗀 ctdemo	🗀 fp103	
🗀 autopilot	🗀 CuteFTP	🗀 Google	**Small**

File name: jiffylearn.pqa   **Default Icons**

☑ Install to User   Bill Dyszel

7. **Click Build.**

   The Build PQA dialog box closes.

After you've built a PQA, you can install it to your Palm VII just like you would install any Palm application.

Chapter 15

Using the PalmModem

*T*he amount of power you can pack into an itty-bitty Palm device is amazing. But that's not all: Snap on a PalmModem, and look out! Although the modem adds only an inch or so to the length of your Palm device, it extends the little gizmo's reach far enough to explore the entire Internet. The modem also enables you to exchange messages with people all over the world from nearly anywhere. Granted, a modem sets you back by about $129, but that's a small price to pay to put that much power in your pocket. You can also get a $19.95 PalmModem cable that enables you to attach a standard external modem to your Palm device, although you need to be savvy about setting up modems to make that work. I'd stick with the PalmModem.

PalmModem Basics

If you've just purchased a shiny, new, store-bought Palm device and the PalmModem, making them work together is fairly simple. When you see the Palm device and its modem together, you instinctively know how to attach them to one another. Just plug the modem into your Palm organizer the same way you plug the Palm device into its cradle, and plug a phone line into the modem. The two work together seamlessly right from the get-go. After you've used your Palm organizer for a while, however, some settings may get changed or go awry. This section gives you the nitty-gritty details about the PalmModem in case you get in a pinch.

Because the Palm V is so much smaller than any of the other Palm devices, you can't use the regular PalmModem with it; you need the special Palm V modem. It works just like the regular Palm modems — it's just smaller.

Setting up your modem

Your PalmModem doesn't need much attention. You can set it up in a snap. Here's the routine:

1. **Snap your Palm device into the modem.**

   The Palm device makes a slight snapping sound as it fits snugly into the modem.

2. **Plug a phone line into the modem.**

   The phone line snaps into your modem the same way it does when you plug it into your phone.

Just feed your modem a new pair of batteries now and again, and you're fine. The batteries fit behind the little door on the lower-front part of your modem case. Just slide the door downward to open the battery compartment.

The PalmModem's batteries power the modem for only a few hours of continuous operation. You can perform a Modem HotSync or check e-mail about 150 times on a single set of batteries. However, if you want to spend hours surfing the Web (yes, you can surf the Web with your Palm device; more about that in the section "Browsing the Web," near the end of this chapter), your modem runs out of battery power pretty fast. If you plan to run your modem for long periods, buy the optional AC adapter for the modem for $19.95 so that the modem draws power from your wall socket. Remember that the AC adapter powers only the modem, not the Palm device. If you plug your modem into an AC adapter, your Palm device could still run out of juice (although the Palm device runs much longer on a set of batteries than the modem does). So check the Palm device battery level every so often by tapping the Applications soft button and viewing your list of applications. A little battery-shaped icon at the top of the screen indicates the amount of power remaining in your battery.

You need to plug a telephone line into your PalmModem, of course. A jack is located at the bottom of the case — it looks just like the jack on your home telephone. Simply unplug the wire that goes into your telephone, and then plug the wire into your PalmModem.

International incidentals

Just like your hair dryer or your electric razor, the PalmModem is designed to be used in the United States and Canada. If you want to connect your PalmModem to telephone systems outside North America, you may have to buy adapters and make special arrangements because the telephone lines and electrical outlets outside North America sometimes don't work with American electronics. I know of one company, Road Warriors, that specializes in supplying gear to people who travel with computers. Check out the company's Web site, at www.warrior.com, for details about equipment that enables you to hook up a computer in any country on Earth.

Not all phone lines are alike. Your home phone line is the right type of phone line to use with your modem. It's an *analog* line, the old-fashioned kind of phone line. Another type of phone line that offices and hotels often use is a *digital* line. *Do not plug your modem into a digital line!* In some cases, plugging your modem into a digital line can damage the modem. Many hotels now have phones with a special jack on the side labeled *modem* or *data* in which you can safely plug your modem. If you're not sure whether a certain line is analog or digital, just ask. You can feel fairly confident that a phone line in a private home is safe. In an office, a phone line attached to a fax machine is also a good bet.

Setting up your Palm device to use the modem

After you snap your Palm device into the modem and plug in a suitable phone line, you're connected. Just tell your Palm device the type of modem you're attaching, and then enter the settings for the kinds of things you want to do.

To set up your Palm device to work with a PalmModem, all you need to do is plug your Palm device into the modem. The factory settings on a new Palm device enable it to run the PalmModem quite nicely. If your Palm device isn't factory-new, however, the settings may have been changed. To adjust the modem settings for a PalmPilot Pro or Palm III (or to make sure that your current settings are correct), follow these steps:

1. **Tap the Applications soft button.**

   The applications list appears, showing icons for all the programs installed on your Palm device.

2. **Tap the Prefs icon.**

   The Preferences screen appears.

3. **Tap the pull-down menu in the upper-right corner of the screen.**

   The list of preferences categories appears.

4. **Tap Modem.**

   The Modem Preferences screen appears, as shown in Figure 15-1.

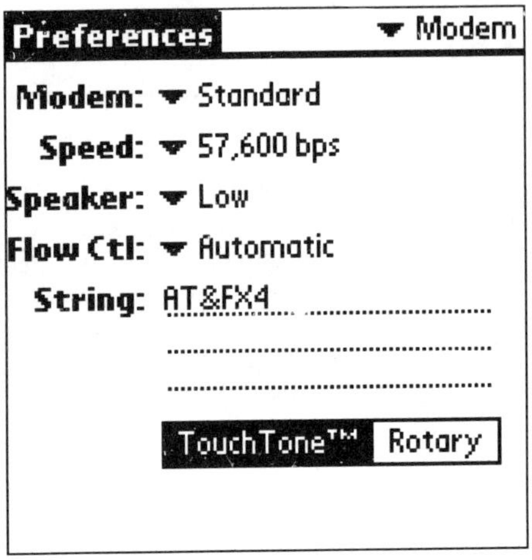

Figure 15-1:
To reconfig-
ure your
modem, go
to the
Modem
Preferences
screen.

```
┌─────────────────────────────────┐
│ Preferences          ▼ Modem │
│ Modem: ▼ Standard               │
│  Speed: ▼ 57,600 bps            │
│ Speaker: ▼ Low                  │
│ Flow Ctl: ▼ Automatic           │
│  String: AT&FX4 ................ │
│          ........................│
│          ........................│
│        [ TouchTone™ │ Rotary ]  │
└─────────────────────────────────┘
```

5. **Tap the triangle next to Modem on the first line of the screen.**

   A list of modems you can use with your Palm device appears.

6. **Choose Palm US/Canada.**

   The words Palm US/Canada appear next to the word *Modem*.

   If you have a modem made by a different manufacturer, choose the appropriate modem.

7. **Tap the triangle next to Speed on the second line of the screen.**

   A list of numbers appears. Each number represents a different modem speed.

8. **Choose 57,600.**

9. **Tap the triangle next to Speaker on the third line of the screen.**

   A choice of speaker volumes appears. Choose either Off, Low, Medium, or High. None of these settings makes the modem speaker obnoxiously loud, but if you absolutely can't stand the shrill sound of a modem making its connection, choose Off.

10. **Choose the modem speaker volume you prefer.**

    The volume you choose appears next to Speaker.

11. **Tap the triangle next to Flow Ctl on the fourth line of the screen.**

    A list appears with the choices Automatic, On, and Off.

12. **Choose Automatic.**

    The word *Automatic* appears next to the words *Flow Ctl.*

13. **Choose the dialing method you use for your telephone by tapping either TouchTone or Rotary at the bottom of the screen.**

    You know best which dialing method applies to your phone line. If you dial your phone with buttons, it's TouchTone. If you still have a dial on your phone, choose Rotary and call the Smithsonian. Your phone is a collector's item.

You can fiddle around with your modem settings a little bit without causing big problems in the way your modem works, but be careful about changing too much. Modems have a way of getting fussy when you can't call someone for help, so after you get things working, leave the settings alone.

One item you should definitely leave alone is the row of crazy characters on the String line, the ones that say something memorable, like AT&FX4. That's a set of instructions that tells your modem how to do its work. If you change this string, you may mess up your modem. If you don't know what a modem setup string is, leave it alone.

Setting Up Your Palm Device for a Modem HotSync

The main purpose of the PalmModem is to enable you to HotSync your Palm device with your desktop computer via a phone line. To successfully HotSync over the telephone, you have to set up your desktop computer as well as your Palm device in advance.

You can't perform a Modem HotSync to a specific desktop computer until you've completed at least one local HotSync with that computer. Doing a local HotSync is important because the HotSync Manager asks you to assign a username to your Palm device, and it creates a set of files and folders dedicated to your Palm device. After you've completed a local HotSync, the HotSync Manager knows which Palm device it's dealing with each time you press the HotSync button, and it knows where to store information about your particular Palm device. If you haven't gone through the local HotSync process at least once, the HotSync Manager doesn't know what to do when it picks up the phone. For more info about how to HotSync and set up your Palm Desktop program, refer to Chapter 11.

If you plan to take your Palm device on your voyage to Mongolia and HotSync from there, you need to run a local HotSync before you go. Also, don't forget your passport and some sensible shoes.

Entering the Modem HotSync phone number

When you perform a Modem HotSync, your Palm device calls your desktop computer on the phone and then runs the HotSync program. The most important information you have to supply is the phone number your desktop computer answers.

To enter the HotSync phone number:

1. **Tap the Applications soft button.**

   The applications list appears, showing icons for all the programs installed on your Palm device.

2. **Tap the HotSync icon.**

   The HotSync screen appears. If you've never entered a HotSync phone number, the box below the Modem Sync icon says `Enter Phone #`; otherwise, the phone number you've already entered appears there.

3. **Tap** `Enter Phone #`.

   The Phone Setup screen appears, as shown in Figure 15-2.

Figure 15-2:
Although HotSync is smart, you still have to tell it what phone number to call by entering the number on the Phone Setup screen.

Phone Setup

Phone #: 555-5685

☐ **Dial prefix:** 9,
☐ **Disable call waiting:** 1170,
☐ **Use calling card:**

(OK) (Cancel)

4. **Enter the phone number to which your desktop computer is connected, by using either the on-screen keyboard or Graffiti (refer to Chapter 2 for more info about entering text).**

   The number you enter appears on the Phone # line.

5. **If your phone system requires you to dial a prefix before making a call, tap the Dial Prefix check box and enter the prefix after Dial Prefix.**

   Some offices and hotels require you to dial an 8 or a 9 before making a call. Enter on the Dial Prefix line the number your system requires.

6. **If you're using a calling card, tap the Use Calling Card check box and enter your calling card on the line below Use Calling Card and after the four commas.**

   The four commas make the modem wait a few seconds before dialing the calling card number, just like you do when you dial the calling card number yourself.

7. **Tap OK.**

Disabling call waiting

I don't understand why call waiting is so popular; I hate when people interrupt my phone conversations. Half the time, the people interrupting my calls are selling products I don't want.

Computers hate being interrupted by call waiting even more than I do. They often do crazy things when the little call-waiting beep sounds, but they never buy things from telemarketers. Fortunately, you can program your Palm device so that it disables call waiting before beginning a HotSync.

Follow these steps just once to tell your Palm device to turn off call waiting:

1. **Tap the Applications soft button.**

   The applications list appears, showing icons for all the programs installed on your Palm device.

2. **Tap the HotSync icon.**

   The HotSync screen appears. The box below the Modem Sync icon displays either `Enter Phone #` or the last phone number you entered.

3. **Tap the box below the Modem Sync icon.**

   The Phone Setup dialog box opens.

4. **Tap the box next to Disable Call Waiting.**

A check mark appears in the box to indicate that you selected it.

To the right of Disable Call Waiting is the number 1170, which is usually the code you dial to turn off call waiting. If the number used to turn it off in your area is different, select the number that appears on-screen and then enter the number that does the trick in your locale.

5. **Tap OK.**

The Phone Setup dialog box closes.

Setting up the Palm Desktop for a Modem HotSync

Doing a HotSync over the telephone has the same result as running a HotSync directly from your desktop computer: It makes the contents of your Palm device identical to the contents of your Palm Desktop. If you have e-mail messages on your desktop computer, copies of those messages are transferred to your Palm device.

When your Palm device performs a Modem HotSync, it dials the phone number of your desktop computer. Your desktop computer then has to answer the phone when the Palm device calls. To be able to answer that call, your desktop computer must

- Have a modem
- Be connected to a phone line
- Be running when you call
- Not be running any other communications program
- Be configured to accept your call

After that, it's easy! Because so many types of computers are out there, I can't tell you how to configure yours to accept your call. Refer to your owner's manual for that. But here's how to configure your computer to wait for your Modem HotSync call:

1. **Start the Palm Desktop.**

The Palm Desktop appears.

2. **Choose HotSync➪Setup.**

The Setup dialog box opens.

3. **Click the Modem tab.**

The modem settings page appears, as shown in Figure 15-3.

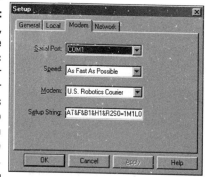

Figure 15-3:
On this tab,
tell the
HotSync
Manager
where your
modem is
installed so
that it can
answer the
phone.

4. **On the Serial Port list, choose the port to which your modem is assigned.**

   You can check which port your modem uses in Windows 95 or Windows 98 by clicking the Start button, choosing Settings⇨Control Panel, and then double-clicking the Modems icon. After the Modems dialog box opens, click the Properties button. The properties page tells you which port your modem uses. The ports are named COM1 through COM4.

5. **In the Speed box, choose As Fast As Possible.**

   I don't know why you'd want to pick anything else. The speed you choose appears in the Speed box.

6. **In the Modem box, choose the type of modem you're using.**

   You can check what type of modem you're using in Windows 95 in the Control Panel, just like you checked the port in Step 4. If in doubt, Hayes Standard should work. The modem you choose appears in the Modem box. The setup string for the modem you pick automatically appears in the Setup String box. The *setup string* is the series of commands your modem uses to configure itself, so don't mess with the string.

7. **Click OK.**

   The Setup dialog box closes.

8. **Right-click the HotSync Manager icon on the taskbar.**

   The HotSync Manager icon is the little circle in the lower-right corner of your screen containing a red arrow and a blue arrow pointing in opposite directions. When you right-click the icon, the HotSync Manager menu appears.

9. **If no check mark appears next to Modem, choose Modem.**

   A check mark appears next to Modem, as shown in Figure 15-4, and then the menu disappears.

Figure 15-4:
Click the
HotSync
icon on the
Windows
taskbar and
then click
Modem.

Now just leave your computer turned on, and go your merry way.

I have both good news and bad news. The good news is that after you set up
the HotSync Manager for a Modem HotSync, you can call up your desktop
computer at any time to update your Palm device. The bad news is that
nobody can receive phone calls on the phone line your computer is connected to because the HotSync Manager answers *all* incoming calls. And you
can't attach an answering machine to that computer. The HotSync Manager
hogs the phone line whether your computer is running Windows or the
Mac OS.

The Modem HotSync trick is best for people who call phone numbers that are
totally dedicated to taking calls from computers, like the phone numbers
many corporations have. If you need to HotSync by modem frequently, you
may want to consider getting an extra phone line.

So why bother doing a Modem HotSync at all? Because doing a HotSync — at
any time, anywhere — backs up your data. After you're completely addicted
to your Palm device (admit it — you're hooked already), you depend on the
collection of information you've amassed. If your Palm device falls from a
gondola or gets rammed by a rhino in the course of your adventures, you can
replace the little critter with a wave of your credit card, but you could lose
months trying to re-create the data.

PalmComputing on the Internet

With the PalmModem, you can connect to the Internet and do two of the
things that make the Internet so popular: exchange e-mail and browse the
Web. I won't pretend that the little Palm device navigates the Internet as
easily or impressively as your mighty desktop computer; the tiny gray screen
shows you only so much. But like someone once said about a talking dog, no
matter how well the trick is done, it's amazing to see it done at all.

Although you need some extra software to be able to exchange e-mail messages or browse Web pages, the foundations are already on your Palm device to enable you to access the Internet and take advantage of what it offers. The Palm III includes *TCP/IP*, the language spoken by all computers connected to the Internet. You never actually see TCP/IP, but if you try to connect a computer to the Internet without it, nothing happens.

Setting up your Internet connection

Before you do anything on the Internet, you have to get connected. You need an *ISP*, or *Internet Service Provider.* An ISP is a company, like Netcom or CompuServe, that gives you a phone number you dial to connect to the Internet. You may be able to use the same ISP you use to connect your desktop computer to the Internet; just enter the same information in the Network Preferences program on your Palm device, and you're on your way. Check with your ISP to see whether you can connect your Palm device to the Internet through your ISP's servers.

When you set up your Internet connection, you also have to set up your modem as I describe in the section "Setting up your Palm device to use the modem," earlier in this chapter.

To set up your Palm device to dial your ISP:

1. **Tap the Applications soft button.**

   The applications list appears, showing icons for all the programs installed on your Palm device.

2. **Tap the Prefs icon.**

   The Preferences screen appears.

3. **Tap the pull-down menu in the upper-right corner of the screen.**

   The list of preferences categories appears.

4. **Tap Network.**

   The Network Preferences screen appears, as shown in Figure 15-5.

5. **Tap the triangle next to Service.**

   A list of the services with which the Palm device is ready to connect appears.

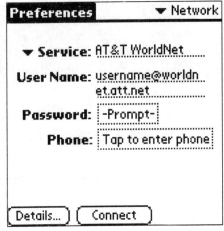

Figure 15-5:
The network
Preferences
screen is
where you
tell your
Palm device
how to con-
nect to the
Internet.

6. **Tap the name of the Internet Service Provider you use.**

   The name of the service you tap appears next to the word *Service*.

   If your ISP doesn't appear, call up your ISP's tech-support area and see what the folks there recommend.

7. **Enter your username on the User Name line by using either the on-screen keyboard or Graffiti (refer to Chapter 2 for more info about entering text).**

   If the User Name line is blank, just tap the line and enter your username. If temporary text appears on the User Name line, select the text and then enter your username.

8. **Tap the box next to Password.**

   The Password dialog box opens, as shown in Figure 15-6.

Figure 15-6:
Enter your
Internet
password
in the
Password
dialog box.

9. **Enter your password.**

   The password you enter appears in the Password dialog box.

10. **Tap OK.**

   The Password dialog box closes.

11. **Tap the box next to Phone.**

   The Phone setup screen appears.

12. **Enter the phone number of your Internet Service Provider by using either the on-screen keyboard or Graffiti (refer to Chapter 2 for more info about entering text).**

   The phone number you enter appears on the Phone # line. You can also set up a dial prefix and a calling card number exactly the same way I describe earlier in this chapter.

13. **Tap OK.**

   The Phone Setup screen closes.

After you set up your network preferences, you probably don't have to mess with them again except to change the ISP phone number when you're traveling. Because many ISPs have toll-free 800 numbers you can use everywhere, you can travel anywhere in North America without changing the phone number.

The Connect button at the bottom of the Network Preferences screen makes the modem dial the phone number you've entered and connects you to the Internet. You don't usually need to tap the Connect button because the e-mail program or the Web browser you normally use starts up your connection automatically. In a pinch, though, you can return to the Network Preferences screen and tap Connect to force your Palm device to connect to the Internet. After you're connected, that same button says Disconnect, so you can tap the Disconnect button to force your Palm device to disconnect from the Internet.

Tapping the Details button displays a screen that shows some of the nitty-gritty details your Palm device needs to know to connect to the Internet. I can't think of any reason you'd change those settings, so leave them alone.

Sending and receiving REAL e-mail

The Palm mail program, which is preinstalled on every PalmPilot Professional and Palm III, synchronizes e-mail with the e-mail program on your desktop computer. Unless a message has successfully arrived on your desktop, you can't synchronize it to your Palm device.

This setup can be a problem if you plan to use your Palm device to get your e-mail while you're on the road, because the HotSync Manager needs to hog your modem 24 hours a day. And if the HotSync Manager ties up your modem all the time while you're traveling, your desktop e-mail program can't dial out to get your messages. For many people, the Modem HotSync feature keeps everything on their Palm device's current *except* for their e-mail.

One solution to this problem is to set up your Palm device to go right to the source and act like a real computer, getting real e-mail from the Internet. If you set up your Palm device to connect to the Internet as I describe in the preceding section, you can use a program like HandMail or MultiMail to go out to the Internet and pick up your messages.

Setting up a Palm Internet e-mail program

You can use several e-mail programs to send and receive e-mail through your Palm device in the same way a conventional desktop e-mail system does. One option is to use MultiMail Pro, a commercial e-mail program. In this section, I show you how to use this particular program, but most e-mail programs require the same sort of setup routine. Although the details differ, the general idea is the same: You have to tell the e-mail program which computer on the Internet holds your e-mail and what username and password enable you to access your mail.

Before you set up an e-mail program to get your messages, you have to install the e-mail program itself. (Refer to Chapter 11 for details about installing programs to your Palm device.) You also have to know how your mail system assigns names to itself and to you. Check with your ISP's technical-support people.

If you were a good little Net surfer, you wrote all that information down, of course, when you set up your desktop e-mail program, so you may not have to call your ISP. If you're like me, though (and who wouldn't want to be like me?), you probably prefer to talk to those friendly people in the middle of nowhere who sit all day and answer phone calls from people like us. Ask 'em whether they have a Palm device, too! Who knows? You could make a new friend and exchange e-mail on your Palm devices. Hoo, boy! There's a big time!

Here's how to set up MultiMail Pro to get e-mail:

1. **After you've installed MultiMail Pro (or the e-mail program of your choice), tap the Applications soft button.**

   The applications list appears, showing icons for all the programs installed on your Palm device.

2. **Tap the MultiMail icon (or the icon for whatever other e-mail program you may be using).**

   The MultiMail screen appears, as shown in Figure 15-7.

Figure 15-7: MultiMail is one of several e-mail programs you can use to send and receive Internet e-mail with your Palm device.

3. **Tap Menu.**

   The menu bar appears.

4. **Choose Options⇨Mail Server.**

   The Mail Server screen appears, as shown in Figure 15-8. Mail servers are the kinds of computers on the Internet that hold mail. Your e-mail program picks up mail from these computers.

Figure 15-8: On the Mail Server screen, you tell your e-mail program where to deliver your mail.

5. **Tap the number of the mailbox you want to set up.**

   You can set up more than one mailbox in many e-mail programs. MultiMail enables you to set up four mailboxes. If you haven't set up any mailboxes yet, tap the number 1.

6. **Enter the name of your mail server on the Server line by using either the on-screen keyboard or Graffiti (refer to Chapter 2 for more info about entering text).**

   You can get this information from the tech-support people at your ISP. And ask those nice people how the weather is wherever they are.

   If you don't want to wait on hold for an hour with your ISP, another way to get this information is to check the settings of your desktop e-mail program. Odds are that you entered the same information there that you have to enter here.

7. **Enter the name of your mailbox on the Mailbox line by using either the on-screen keyboard or Graffiti.**

   Your mailbox name is usually the part of your e-mail address that comes before the @ sign. For example, if your e-mail address is snorkle66@dive.com, your mailbox name is probably snorkle66. Check with your ISP to be sure.

8. **If *Blank* or *Unassigned* appears on the Password line, tap the box in which the word *Unassigned* appears and then enter your password.**

   Again, your tech-support gurus know all this stuff, so be nice to them and ask politely.

9. **Tap OK.**

   If your tech-support people say that that's all you need, you're done. Some systems require other settings.

After you set up a mailbox, you're ready to go.

Sending and receiving Palm Internet e-mail

Your Palm device isn't always connected to your phone line. Otherwise, you'd have to walk all over town with a really, really, really long phone cord dragging around behind you. You can create or read Palm e-mail anywhere, at any time; to actually send the messages, however, you have to make sure that your Palm device is plugged into the modem and that the modem is plugged into a phone line. Then give your e-mail program the command to send and receive messages. HandMail requires you to tap Menu and then choose Mail⇨Send and Retrieve. MultiMail, another popular package, has a Send/Receive button on the main screen.

Palm devices and AOL mail

America Online (AOL) is by far the most popular online service, although it's a screaming pain in the neck when it comes to managing e-mail. Most of the terms I've heard people use to describe the AOL mail system are unfit to be printed here. The folks at AOL have promised to make improvements to their e-mail system, although they haven't followed up on those promises so far.

The people who created HandMail have solved the AOL mail problem: They've developed a version of their program that enables you to send and receive your AOL e-mail via your Palm device. The program costs $49, a bit more than

I wish it would, but it's well worth the money if you exchange lots of mail over AOL.

Not only is reading your e-mail more convenient on a Palm device than on a desktop computer, but a real e-mail program like HandMail also gives you lots of e-mail management tools that aren't available on the AOL desktop program, such as the ability to use rules to send in-coming mail to different mailboxes and look up e-mail addresses from your Palm Address Book. You can visit the makers of HandMail at the company's Web site, at www.smartcode-soft.com

Browsing the Web

So you can't believe that you can surf the Internet on your Palm device? Well, it's true. Granted, most Web sites look poor on that teensy little screen, but you can find a great deal of text on the Internet, too, and text looks fine on an itty-bitty screen.

There's a catch, of course. Before you can surf the Web with your Palm device, you need two things: an Internet connection and a Web browser. In the section "Setting up your Internet connection," earlier in this chapter, I show you how to connect to the Internet. You also have to get a Web browser and install it on your Palm device.

I've tried two Web browsers that I like: HandWeb, from Smartcode Software (www.smartcodesoft.com) — the company that also created HandMail (see the preceding section) — and ProxiWeb. HandWeb is simple and works much like the Web browsers you may use on your desktop computer, such as Netscape Navigator and the one made by that other company (MicroSomething?). The HandWeb program's main shortcoming is that it doesn't do enough to make Web pages look good on that tiny gray screen.

ProxiWeb uses a *proxy server,* which means that it shows you everything on the Web through its computer; its computer interprets the pages you request to make them look better on the Palm screen. Although this process makes the pages look better on your Palm device, the loading time for each page is slow.

ProxiWeb manages to interpret some graphics, but fancy features such as frames and animation that many advanced Web sites use just disappear on a Palm Web browser. The browsers I've mentioned here don't let you bookmark pages the way you do in a desktop Web browser. You can save the URL of a Web page by entering it on a list of favorite pages, but you can't really capture the address easily.

Palm Web browsing is primitive at this point, although I expect rapid progress soon.

Sending a Fax with Your Palm Device

Why would you want to send a fax from a Palm device? Because hundreds of millions of fax machines exist in the world. People who don't have e-mail often have a fax machine.

The best fax program for desktop computers is WinFax, from Symantec (www.symantec.com), so it's not surprising that the same company has developed the best fax program for your Palm device. Named Mobile Winfax for the Palm Computing Platform, the program enables you to send plain-text faxes from your Palm device or to create a fully formatted fax on your desktop computer and send it from your Palm device whenever you want. That last feature is great for people who have standard faxable sales materials they like to send to anyone who asks.

Amazingly, the program also enables you to receive faxes on your Palm device and view them on the spot. Bear in mind that most faxes are tough to view on that tiny Palm screen, although you can scroll up, down, and sideways to see the whole fax a little at a time. When you HotSync, the faxes you received on your Palm device appear on your desktop computer, where they're easier to read and print. My hat's off to the folks at Symantec for putting so much power in such an itty-bitty package.

Part IV
Extending the Life of Your Palm Organizer

The 5th Wave   By Rich Tennant

"OH, WELL SHOOT! MUST BE THAT NEW PAINT PROGRAM ON MY HPC."

In this part . . .

You can't stop Palm Computing progress (not that you would want to). The list of new features and functions for Palm devices is growing, and you'll certainly want to upgrade now and then. This part shows you how to upgrade to the latest model when the time comes.

Chapter 16

Upward Mobility: Upgrading Your Palm Device

I spend most of this book discussing the latest Palm organizer models while scarcely mentioning the hallowed ancestors of these models — the PalmPilot 1000, PalmPilot 5000, PalmPilot Personal, and PalmPilot Professional. What am I, anti-progress? Have I forgotten the sacrifices of the early adopters who bought their Palm devices 18 long months ago? Not at all.

Many Palm devices are upgradeable — especially the early models. Sometimes you just have to install some software, and at other times you swap a tiny memory card, but you can often upgrade to the latest features. Rather than belabor every page of this book with boring distinctions about which model did what, I focus on the Palm III and later models. My suggestion: Anyone with a the PalmPilot 1000, PalmPilot 5000, PalmPilot Personal, or PalmPilot Professional should upgrade to Palm III and stop suffering. Life is short, and upgrades are easy.

The most recent Palm organizer models don't upgrade as easily, and some don't upgrade at all. If you own a Palm V or a Palm VII, you can skip this chapter.

The Wizard of OS

Every computer, even a Palm device, has something called an *operating system* to direct all the activities of the machine. Computer nerds often classify computers by the type of operating system they use. Windows is the best-known operating system; it's the successor to DOS, the system used on the original IBM PC. Although dozens of different companies manufacture Windows computers, you refer to any of them as Windows machines. You used to be able to say the same thing about the Macintosh: Apple allowed several clone makers to manufacture machines similar to the Macintosh that ran the Mac OS. All these clones were also called Macs. Because Apple pulled the plug on the Mac clone makers, however, only Apple makes Macs these days.

Computers that run the same operating system do the same things, more or less, and run the same programs. Every so often, the companies that write operating systems improve their products and issue new versions of their operating systems. Microsoft made a big splash when it released a new version of Windows a few years back, named Windows 95. The company made a smaller splash with the more recent release of Windows 98. Apple also peps up its operating system now and again, offering System 7, followed by System 7.5, and then Mac OS 8.

A Palm device also has its very own operating system, the *Palm OS*. When the Palm people release a new Palm model, they often release a new version of their operating system as well. You can find the latest version of your Palm OS on the Palm Computing Web site, at www.palm.com.

Upgrading Made Easy

You can upgrade three elements of your Palm device:

- Operating system (or Palm OS)
- Memory card
- Desktop program

You need to know these two essential facts about upgrading your Palm device:

- If a Palm device can be upgraded, you would do so by installing a new memory card.
- Any Palm device can work with any version of the Palm Desktop.

That's it. Simple? Of course!

Upgrading Your Palm Device

Before you tackle a Palm OS upgrade, you have to know which version of Palm OS you're using. Here's how:

1. **Press the Date Book hard button (or any of the other hard buttons).**

   The Date Book application appears.

2. **Tap Menu.**

   The menu bar appears.

3. **Choose Options⇨About Date Book.**

   The About Date Book screen appears, as shown in Figure 16-1. The Palm OS version number appears on the left side of the screen.

Figure 16-1:
The
Options⇨
About
command
shows you
which
Palm OS
version
you're
using.

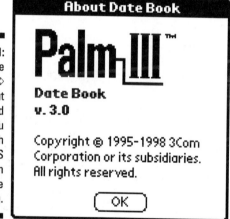

If your Palm OS version number is less than 3.0, you can buy and install the Palm 2MB upgrade card to give your Palm device all the latest features (read more about the upgrade card later in this chapter).

Installing a new version of the Palm OS

The simplest way to upgrade your Palm device is to install the latest version of the Palm OS, the operating system that all the Palm organizer programs rely on. The Palm people offer constant improvements to the Palm OS and post the new improvements, called *patches,* on the Internet. You can check out the Palm Web site, at www.palm.com, for the latest information about Palm OS patches (see Figure 16-2).

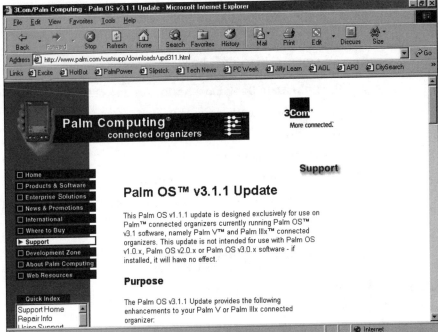

Figure 16-2:
Check the
Palm
Computing
Web site for
the latest
upgrades
to the
Palm OS.

Although you can install a patch to the operating system of many Palm devices, you can use patches only for the operating system made for the level of Palm organizer hardware you're using. For a PalmPilot 1000, you can use only Palm OS 1.0 and the patches that go with it — versions 1.1, 1.2, and so on. For a PalmPilot Personal or PalmPilot Professional, you use Palm OS 2.0 and the patches numbered 2.1, 2.2, and so on. If you want to make your Palm OS jump a whole level, from Palm OS 2.0 to Palm OS 3.0, you have to install a memory card that can handle Palm OS 3.0, which turns your unit into a Palm III.

If you do choose to download a patch to upgrade your Palm OS, you have to install it just like you install any other Palm organizer program: with the Palm Install Tool. Refer to Chapter 11 for more info about installing applications.

Installing a new memory card in a pre-Palm III model

What separated the Professionals from the Personals (in the early PalmPilot world, anyway) was a tiny circuit board called the *memory card*. It's a little smaller than a corn chip (but not as edible, so don't dip it in guacamole). If you take the memory card out of a PalmPilot Personal and install the Palm III card — *voilà* — you have a Palm III! Actually, you have something that thinks like a Palm III in the body of a PalmPilot Personal. It's like a brain transplant: The thinking improves, but the body stays the same (unless you're the Frankenstein monster, in which case you probably have more immediate problems). You can upgrade a PalmPilot Personal so that it becomes a Palm III, but you won't have the handy backlight for reading your screen in the dark; that feature is available on the PalmPilot Professional and later models.

The Palm people still sell the Palm III upgrade card for about $130 at the time this book was written. Be aware, though, that Palm device prices change quickly as new models come out, and upgrade cards may be discontinued by the time you read this chapter.

The first few PalmPilot models were designed so that you could easily upgrade them. They even have doors on the backs of their cases for swapping memory cards with little fuss.

If you're comfortable swapping electronic components, upgrading your Palm device will be a snap. If you're anxious about fiddling with chips, just take your time and follow these steps:

1. **Perform a full HotSync to back up your information.**

   You lose all your data when you change your memory card, so make sure that the copy on your PC is current. (For more information about performing a HotSync, refer to Chapter 11.) Also, if you've installed a number of add-on programs, you lose them, too. You may want to check out a program named Backup Buddy, which I mention in Chapter 12, for help in saving and restoring third-party programs.

2. **Place your Palm device face down on a table or any other smooth, flat surface.**

   The two access doors are located on the back of the unit.

3. **Clear static by touching the metal backplate of your computer.**

   A good jolt of static electricity can damage the tiny memory card.

4. **Remove the battery door.**

5. **Remove the batteries.**

   Would you have a brain transplant with no anesthesia? Of course not.

6. **Remove the large access door at the top of your Palm device.**

   Often, you can simply press on the door and slide it upward and off the case. You can release the door by pressing a straightened paper clip into the hole just below the door (the hole that's *not* marked Reset). The memory card is in a white mounting bracket.

7. **Turn your Palm device so that the memory card faces you.**

   You'll find the card a bit easier to remove that way.

8. **Press outward on the two small metal tabs on each side of the memory card to release the card, and then tilt it from the top.**

   After you slightly tilt the card away from the bracket, it's free and ready to be removed.

9. **Pull the memory card out of your Palm device.**

   Wiggle the card a little to free it up as you remove it.

10. **Store the old memory card in a safe place.**

    If anything goes wrong with the new card, you can put the old one back in.

11. **Insert the new memory card into exactly the same position in which the old card sat.**

    Snap the new card into the brackets. If it's a Palm III memory card, make sure that the two little infrared bulbs point toward the top of the case.

12. **Reinstall the batteries.**

    The battery door should snap tightly shut.

13. **Press the power switch to see whether your Palm device turns on and runs.**

    If you've seated the memory card properly, the unit should run perfectly. If the unit fails to run, gently press the memory card into the bracket to ensure that the card is seated correctly.

14. **Reinstall the memory door (or install the new memory door if you've installed a Palm III memory card).**

    The memory door snaps tightly shut.

After you've replaced the memory card, you have what amounts to a brand-new Palm device with no data. You can perform another HotSync to restore all the information in the standard Palm organizer applications. If third-party applications were installed before you upgraded, you have to reinstall them with the Palm Install Tool. Refer to Chapter 11 for more info about installing applications.

Although your Palm device is pretty hardy, be sure to do an upgrade in a reasonably safe, clean location. Don't change memory cards in a sandstorm or under water. And try to avoid swapping memory cards while riding your motorcycle (especially if you're driving); you could lose the card and be unable to find it. What would the other Hell's Angels think if you couldn't start your Palm device?

Upgrading a Palm III

According to Palm Computing legend, when Jeff Hawkins was inventing the PalmPilot, he cut a little block of wood about the size of one and walked around with it in his pocket to see whether it was the right size to write on. It's not surprising, therefore, that the first few PalmPilot models were all shaped like a little block of wood. By the time the Palm III came out, the company was bigger and had been purchased by the huge 3Com Corporation. I guess that the big outfit had some designers on staff who thought that the homely little-block-of-wood look was not exactly chic, so they applied something called "industrial design" to the little Palm device and came up with a new look: the slightly rounded little-block-of-wood look. Personally, I liked the old look better: The stylus was easier to get to, and the old machine fit cleanly into the PalmPilot cradle and modem.

The Palm III is a very different beast from the Palm IIIx when it comes to upgrades. The following directions are only for a Palm III. At the time I wrote this chapter, the Palm people had not started offering any kind of upgrade card for the Palm IIIx.

Also, the Palm III has no door for the memory card because the new design requires that the memory go in sideways, so the physical process for changing the memory card in a Palm III is different from the process for changing the memory card in any other Palm device. Here's the routine:

1. **Perform a full HotSync to back up your information.**

   You lose all your data when you change your memory card, so make sure that the copy on your PC is current. You also lose any add-on programs you installed. Refer to Chapter 12 for more info about backing up third-party programs.

2. **Place your Palm device face down on a table or any other smooth, flat surface.**

   Four screws are visible on the back of the unit.

3. **Clear static by touching the metal backplate of your computer.**

   A good jolt of static electricity can damage the tiny memory card.

4. **Open the battery door.**

5. **Remove the batteries.**

   I'm told that you can get away with removing only one battery, but why not go all the way?

6. **Remove the four screws on the back of your Palm device and remove the back of the case.**

   The entire back of the case comes off, revealing the memory card inside. The memory card sits sideways inside the case. The card is a little green circuit card, about the size of two postage stamps. That sounds small, but it's the biggest thing you see inside the case.

7. **Turn your Palm device so that the memory card faces you.**

   The card is a bit easier to remove that way.

8. **Press outward on the two small metal tabs on each side of the memory card to release it, and then tilt the card from the top.**

   After you slightly tilt the card away from the bracket, it's free and ready to be removed.

9. **Pull the memory card out of your Palm device.**

   Wiggle the card a little to free it up as you remove it.

10. **Store the old memory card in a safe place.**

    If anything goes wrong with the new card, you can put the old one back in.

11. **Insert the new memory card into exactly the same position in which the old card sat.**

    Snap the new card into the brackets.

12. **Reinstall the back of the case and replace the four screws.**

    The case snaps on tightly.

13. **Reinstall the batteries.**

    The battery door should snap tightly shut.

14. **Press the power switch to see whether the Palm device turns on and runs.**

    If you've seated the memory card properly, the unit should run perfectly. If the unit fails to run, reopen the case and reseat the memory card.

After you complete your upgrade, you have to perform another HotSync to restore your data. You also have to reinstall any programs you added to your Palm device before the upgrade. (Refer to Chapter 11 for more info about HotSyncing and Chapter 12 for more info about installing applications.) Of course, at the time I wrote this book, the Palm people didn't offer an upgrade card for the Palm III or Palm IIIx. A few months is an eternity in Palm Computing time, however, so you may encounter other options by the time you read this book. If I had ESP, I'd tell you what those options will be, but if I *really* had ESP, I wouldn't be writing this book; I'd make zillions winning all the lotteries, and I'd retire to Fiji.

I'm not saying that you can't upgrade a Palm III right now. A company named TRG (www.trgnet.com) offers a variety of upgrade cards for Palm organizers. The company's products can increase the total memory of your Palm device to as much as 8MB. (See Chapter 19 for more info about TRG upgrade boards.)

You may think that 8MB sounds like a great deal of memory, considering that you started out with 2MB or less, but if you have a large address list or if you do ambitious tasks on your Palm device, you can use up space in a jiffy.

Upgrading the Palm Desktop Program

You can upgrade the Palm Desktop for Windows for free by downloading the latest version from the Palm Web site, at www.palm.com. At the time I wrote this book, the Palm Desktop 3.0.1 was the latest version, so if that's what you have, you don't have any reason to upgrade.

To see which version of the Palm Desktop you're using, open your desktop program and choose Help⇨About. If you're using Version 3.0, you see the screen shown in Figure 16-3. If you're using an earlier version of the desktop program and you're using Windows 95, Windows 98, or Windows NT, you're better off upgrading to Version 3.0.1. Remember that you can use any version of the desktop program with any Palm model.

Figure 16-3:
You can upgrade the Palm Desktop for free, so you may as well get the latest version.

Macintosh users have an entirely different desktop program than Windows users. (Refer to Chapter 13 if you're a Mac user.)

Chapter 17

Palm Software By Profession

*N*early anyone who can get out of bed in the morning can find some use for a Palm device. As long as you need to keep track of people, tasks, or ideas, you can take advantage of Palm organizer software. In this chapter, I list specific professions that can benefit from specially designed Palm software. I know some professionals, however, who rely on their Palm devices without any extra software; a rabbi in New Jersey, actors in Hollywood, and farmers in Mississippi all get something special from the little computers in their pockets. I apologize if I leave out your profession, but if I do, you can search for Palm software by checking the list of Web sites and other resources in Appendix A, in the back of this book. Several products mentioned in this chapter require you to install a product named Jfile first. For more info about Jfile, see the manufacturer's Web site, at www.land-j.com. The program costs $19.95 to register. You can also use a competing database named MobileDB, from Mobile Generation Software, at www.mobilegeneration.com. Some of the software listed in this chapter is free. Some titles are offered as shareware, which means that the people who created the program rely on your honor to send in a donation in exchange for the product. Some programs are demos, which work for free for a limited time, and then you have to buy a copy. Quite a few of these programs are real, live, cash-on-the-barrelhead commercial software. Although I list prices and terms wherever possible, you may want to check with the manufacturer to confirm the price and find out how to use the program.

Architect/Building Professional

Putting up a building means putting up with zillions of details. The **Punch List** (www.punchlist.com) program helps you track the details of large projects and make sure that everything is done on time and in order. Designed for professionals in the construction industry (but useful for people in any detail-oriented profession), Punch List synchronizes with your desktop PC and enables you to maintain lists of tasks that need to be done, along with the names of the people who are supposed to do them. By using Punch List on your Palm device, you collect information at the building site; then, when you HotSync to your desktop, the desktop portion of Punch List automatically sends faxes to your subcontractors with task lists and notes about uncompleted tasks. Punch List is commercial software from Strata Systems that costs $199 for each user. You can reach the company by phone at 888-336-3652.

Athletic Coach

When Vince Lombardi said, "Winning isn't everything; it's the only thing," nobody dared to say, "That's meaningless, Coach!" Would you? If you're a coach who wants to give your team meaningful information, get a copy of the **Athlete's Calculator,** from Steven's Creek Software (www.stevenscreek.com). It's free for one-time use, but you have to pay $14.95 for the registered version. This program enables you to rattle off statistics about time, distance, and pace and also perform calculations on the spot. Now you can demand 110 percent from your athletes and scream when you get only 109 percent.

Bartender

Every purveyor of potent potables needs a collection of recipes for popular concoctions. **Drinks,** as shown in Figure 17-1, is a collection of 145 recipes for drinks, ranging from an Alabama Slammer to a Zombie. Because Drinks is a Jfile database, you have to install the Jfile program before taking advantage of your newfound repertoire. If you want to customize the collection, you can add recipes for beverages of your own invention. You can download Drinks from www.palmcentral.com and use it for free.

Figure 17-1:
When your
customers
want more
than a shot
and a beer,
look up
something
more inter-
esting on
the drinks
list.

```
┌─────────────────────────────────┐
│ Database Item            ◀ ▶     │
│ Name:      Oreo Cookie│           │
│ Contents:  2 Oreo cookies, 1     │
│            oz Creme de Cacoa,    │
│            4 oz Vanilla ice      │
│            cream                 │
│ AddOns:    various               │
│ Type:      Blender               │
│ Glass:     various               │
│ Notes:     ...................   │
│                                  │
│ (OK) (Cancel)  (New) (Del)       │
└─────────────────────────────────┘
```

Couch Potato

I won't mention any names, but many people need help in the diet and exercise departments. **DietLog,** from SoftCare Clinical Informatics (www.dietlog.com), is the most popular Palm program for munch-management. Research shows that nothing shocks you into good behavior faster than recalling just how badly you've eaten in the recent past. DietLog helps you track your food intake and set suitable diet goals for your age, sex, height, and weight. You can download a free trial copy of DietLog, which runs for 15 days. If you haven't given up on your diet by then, you can order the full-featured version for $59; just call 800-676-7793. I plan to start using DietLog . . . tomorrow.

Electrical Engineer

EE Toolkit can help electrical engineers perform many of the routine calculations involved in building electronic projects. It can calculate the resistance of resistors and the capacity of capacitors and perform many other useful electronic tasks. You can even draw pictures on a built-in doodle pad. Hey! Even I can handle that! You can download a free, 14-day trial version from the designers' Web site, at ww.mindspring.com/~jgrand/eetoolkit.htm. If you haven't electrocuted yourself after two weeks, contact Pilot Gear HQ at www.pilotgear.com to buy the $20 high-powered version.

Environmentalist

Whenever you're creating a cleaner environment, you have to know exactly how clean you've made it. **ImagiProbe** connects your Palm device to any number of scientific sensors, from oxygen sensors to barometers, and collects precise information on a minute-to-minute basis. The software that comes with the ImagiProbe system also enables you to add sketches or notes to each data-gathering session. You can find out more about the product at the manufacturer's Web site, at www.imagiworks.com.

Help Desk Technician

Remedy Help Desk, from Remedy Corporation, is part of an elaborate system you use to track and manage computer problems in a large organization. If you've ever worked as a computer-help-desk person, you know how much trivial information you need to organize and keep current. You also need to know how many times technicians visit a certain computer and how many things are done to that machine. Remedy Help Desk enables field technicians to enter information about problems and solutions while in the field, and then update the big company database by performing a simple HotSync. For more about Remedy Help Desk, see www.remedy.com.

Lawyer

Perry Mason may have spent all his time orating in courtrooms, but real lawyers have to spend time keeping track of documents and tracking their billable hours. **Amicus Attorney** is part of a practice-management system that's designed to help lawyers run their businesses and track their billings accurately on a desktop computer or office network. The program includes a link to your Palm device so that you can document billable activities as you perform them. Unless you're the kind of lawyer who works for free, Amicus Attorney can help you stay on top of your business. Contact Gavel & Gown Software at www.amicus.ca.

Manager

PalmProject is a simple program that enables you to keep track of tasks that occur in sequence, as shown in Figure 17-2. If you're making a movie, for example, you need to write a script and then hire a director, and then cast actors, and then shoot the film, and so on. PalmProject enables you to enter as many as 99 tasks, each of which can be linked to an earlier task. You can display lists of required resources and milestones and choose either a five-day workweek or a seven-day workweek. If you're a Microsoft Project user, you can also export projects from PalmProject and run them in Microsoft Project, which enables you to create elaborate flowcharts and reports. You can visit www.pda-ware.com for a free trial version of PalmProject or buy the full-featured version for $19.95 at www.pilotgear.com.

Figure 17-2:
Plan before
you act!
Good
planning
can give
you a
competitive
edge.

PalmProject				
No.	Task	Start	Dur.	End	Lnk
1	Buy Maps	7/30	1	7/31	0
2	Rent Elephant	7/30	2	8/3	0
3	Cross Alps	8/3	5	8/10	2
4	Beseige Rome	8/10	3	8/13	3
5	Return elepha	8/13	6	8/21	4

(New) (Details) (Done)

Minister

Yes, your Palm device even has room for the Good Book. You can download a free copy of the King James version from PalmCentral (www.palmcentral.com) — 1.2MB of pure inspiration. If you don't have a Palm III, you probably don't have room for 1.2MB of inspiration, so you need to check out the King James version that's split up into five sections; even a little bit of inspiration goes a long way. You can also find devotional text from a variety of religions at the PalmCentral Web site and around the Palm Web ring.

Meeting Planner

Whenever you organize events, you have to keep lots of information handy wherever you go. Documents to Go, from DataViz, lets you store fully formatted copies of documents you create in Microsoft Office and carry them around on your Palm organizer. You can't edit the documents on your Palm device, although sometimes just having your most important documents in your hip pocket is enormously valuable.

Molecular Biologist

OligoCalc is a tool for molecular biologists. According to Ray's PalmCentral archive, it's a "calculator for molecular biologists who have to deal with oligonucleotide synthesis and purification. You will get the most common physical characteristics of oligonucleotides — extinction coefficient, molecular weight, etc." Yeah, well, whatever that is, OligoCalc does it for free. Download a copy at `www.palmcentral.com`.

Musician

You may be used to the on-screen keyboard that lets you enter text, but **PocketSynth** gives you an on-screen piano keyboard, as shown in Figure 17-3, for composing melodies and then playing them back. You can enter one-part tunes as simple as "Yankee Doodle" or as complex as Beethoven's *Fifth Symphony* by tapping a tiny piano keyboard. If you value your sanity, stick with simple tunes like "Yankee Doodle" because that itty-bitty keyboard will drive you nuts. PocketSynth includes a variable metronome that enables you to play your songs at whatever speed you like. Of course, everything you play on PocketSynth sounds like the squeaky little tones that always come from your Palm device, but if you've ever wanted to hear your Palm device whistling "Dixie," PocketSynth can make it happen. Developer Eric Cheng offers PocketSynth on his Web site, at `www.echeng.com/Pilot/pocketsynth.htm`. The suggested fee is $12.

Figure 17-3:
Compose your first sonata on your Palm device by using PocketSynth.

New York City Taxi Driver

Unlike nice, orderly cities, the New York City system of street addresses is totally nonsensical. I could give you examples, but why bother when you can make sense of it all with **NY CrossTown 1.5** from True North, Inc. (northisup.com). For only $12, you can instantly come up with the nearest cross street from any avenue address or find the nearest avenue to any street address. If you don't need NY CrossTown because you never visit the Big Apple (or you have a chauffeur), count your blessings.

Parent

Are your kids bugging you to buy a new puppy? Or are they just bugging you? Distract the little darlings with a **DigiPet.** DigiPet, as shown in Figure 17-4, is the Palm Computing version of those popular electronic pet keychains. Your little electronic beast has many of the charming qualities of a real pet, including the need to eat, get sick, demand your attention at all hours, and have "accidents." DigiPet is available in English and Japanese versions. The program was developed by Shuji Fukumoto and is available at www.wakuwaku.ne.jp/shuji or from www.palmcentral.com. Best of all, it's free.

Figure 17-4: DigiPet can keep you busy, whether you like it or not. Remember, parents: It's only a game. This DigiPet is friendly, but not the brightest beast.

Physician

More Palm organizer medical programs are available than you can shake a scalpel at. Several companies offer programs that enable doctors to keep track of patient data and update patients' records from the bedside. **Mobile Medical Data,** at www.medcomsys.com, is one of the better-known products for keeping patient records.

Pilot

The fact that Palm devices are so popular with airplane pilots is no surprise. **AirCalc** is one of many Palm applications designed to perform the kinds of calculations that airplane pilots need. You can calculate such things as True Altitude (TALT), True Airspeed (TAS), and Mach Number (MN), as shown in Figure 17-5. Unfortunately, AirCalc can't handle frequent-flyer miles. Another favorite program is **AvCheck,** a simple checklist program that reminds you to complete every step of your preflight preparations so that you don't skip anything essential, such as fuel or parachutes. If you're the type who makes checklists before you go on vacation, you can use AvCheck for that purpose, too, and create your own checklists on your desktop computer by using the AvCheck converter. You also may want to have your little checklist obsession checked out by a shrink. The program is available from the developer's Web site, at www.infoequipt.com. The Personal version costs $29.95, and the Professional version (for flight schools and fleet operators) runs $59.99.

Figure 17-5: AirCalc figures out the more important calculations you need while flying. Try to make the plane go up quickly and down slowly, please.

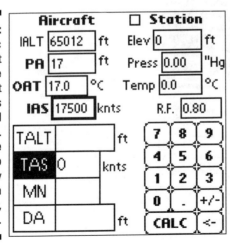

Psychic

Are you a real psychic? If you're really a psychic, you know who you are. Naturally, all psychics who are worth their crystal balls need to play a little Tarot to blow off steam between seances; those cosmic vibrations can get intense. The **Tarot Assistant** deals and interprets pentacles, swords, and cups in a flash and keeps unsavory psychics from dealing wizards from the bottom of the deck. The program is a text-only offering; no pictures — sorry. Because you're psychic (and because you're reading this book), you know that you can find the program at the PalmCentral Web site, at www.palmcentral.com. If you were really a psychic, though, you wouldn't need to read this paragraph because you'd already know.

Salesperson

Salespeople are people people, so the standard Palm organizer programs, especially the Address Book, are a must for anyone in sales. But the standard applications lack the powerful contact management and sales automation features you find in desktop programs like **Goldmine** and **Act!** Fortunately, you can set up both those programs to send their most important information to your Palm device. Most of the best sales-automation programs include a Palm link, so all you need to do is ask the manufacturer how to use your sales program with a Palm device.

Stockbroker/Investor

If you have megabucks tied up in the stock market, you want up-to-the-minute news about what's happening on Wall Street. Years ago, you needed an expensive stock ticker to get the latest from the exchanges, but now you can use a Palm device equipped with **Reuters Market Clip** and the Novatel Minstrel Wireless Modem to give you the very latest stock info, no matter where you are. Trade stocks from roadside, poolside, or fireside. Becoming a Palm investment mogul isn't all that expensive; the whole package, including the wireless modem and the Palm device, runs a few hundred bucks, plus a monthly charge for wireless service. That's small change compared to your enormous capital gains, right? If you're a professional broker or dealer, you have to pay additional exchange fees as well. Contact Reuters at www.marketclip.reuters.com or call 888-9STOCKS.

Teacher

Who says memorization is boring and old-fashioned? Okay, maybe it's old-fashioned, but you can make memorization fun by using one of the flash card programs available for your Palm device. One of the most versatile programs, **Flash!**, imports lists of text from the Memo Pad and converts them into a system you can use to drill students in collections of facts. The program even has a quiz mode that automatically generates a multiple-choice test and keeps track of the number of right and wrong answers you choose, as shown in Figure 17-6. You can download a free demo of Flash! from homunculus.dragonfire.net/flash.html. Jaime Quinn, the author of Flash!, asks you to send him a voluntary donation of $14.95 or have a meal in his favorite restaurant in Mexico. Another popular memorization program is **JTutor**, from Land J Technologies, the same company that offers JFile. The company's Web site is at www.land-j.com.

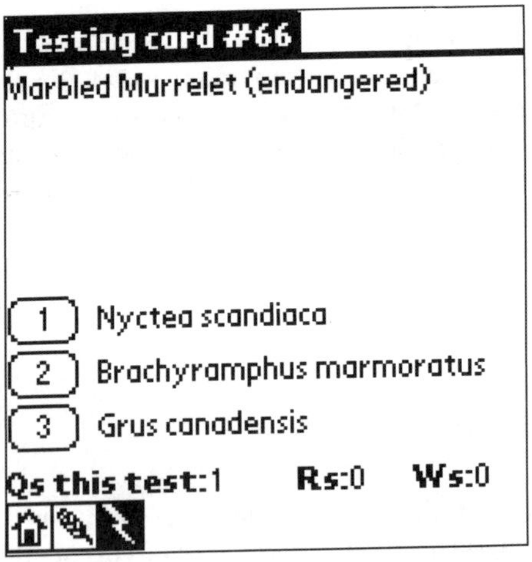

Figure 17-6:
Get ready to win that big TV game show by drilling trivia with Flash! "I'll take birds for $100, Alex."

```
┌──────────────────────────────────┐
│ Testing card #66                 │
├──────────────────────────────────┤
│ Marbled Murrelet (endangered)    │
│                                  │
│                                  │
│                                  │
│  ( 1 )  Nyctea scandiaca         │
│  ( 2 )  Brachyramphus marmoratus │
│  ( 3 )  Grus canadensis          │
│ Qs this test:1    Rs:0    Ws:0   │
│ ⌂ ✎ ▚                            │
└──────────────────────────────────┘
```

Telemarketer

If you make a large number of phone calls, trying to figure out where you're calling by looking at an unfamiliar area code can be tough. The free area codes database at PalmCentral (www.palmcentral.com) can help you figure out where you're calling when your fingers do the walking. The program can't help telemarketers know when to call people in order to catch them during dinner or while they're in the shower, but most telephone sales people already have that trick down to a science. You have to install JFile, the Palm organizer database program, before using the Area Code list.

Travel Agent

You didn't become a travel agent because you like to sit at home; you like to go places; the farther, the better. When you travel to a foreign country, you may need to ask for help to find a hotel room, restaurant, or restroom. **Small Talk** is an electronic phrase book that helps you get what you need when you don't speak another country's language. I even know of some travel agents who lend (or give) their clients a Palm device equipped with the program to keep their customers happy. See Chapter 20 for more about Small Talk, or point your Web browser to www.conceptkitchen.com. The program costs $49.95 for two languages or $79.95 for all five languages. Available languages include English, French, Spanish, German, and Italian.

Writer

A Palm device is a gift for this writer; I always get my best ideas when I'm farthest from a computer. The most useful type of writer's tool is the outliner, a program that automatically organizes a series of thoughts into a numbered list. One of the most popular Palm outliners is **BrainForest Mobile Edition;** it costs $30 to register. BrainForest enables you to quickly pull together an outline of your thoughts lickety-split, as shown in Figure 17-7, and arrange them in several different outlines. After you empty your thoughts into the outliner, you can rearrange the outline by dragging and dropping any item to the location(s) where you want it. BrainForest is only one popular outliner; another popular one is **Thought Mill,** which is $17.95 from Hands High software. Both products are available at www.palmcentral.com.

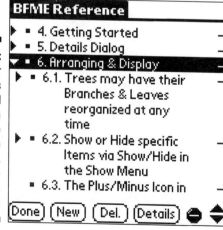

Figure 17-7: Put your thoughts into logical order with a Palm device outliner like BrainForest. Linear thinking! What a concept!

Part V
The Part of Tens

The 5th Wave   By Rich Tennant

"It's a Weber PalmPit Pro handheld barbeque with 24 btu, rechargeable battery pack, and applications for roasting, smoking, and open-flame cooking."

In this part . . .

I've spent an entire book telling you what your Palm
device can do; now, I tell you a few of the things it can't
do — believe me, it's a short list. In this part, I also tell you
about some cool stuf f— both software and hardware —
that you can add to your Palm device to make it even more
productive.

Chapter 18

Ten Things You Can't Do with a Palm Device — Yet

. . . .

In This Chapter

▶ Viewing two programs at the same time (I wish)

▶ Linking items between programs (a pipe dream)

▶ Searching and replacing text (wouldn't it be nice?)

▶ Recording voice notes (not that I would use this feature anyway)

▶ Creating recurring To Do items (please, please, please)

▶ Beaming e-mail (into the wild blue yonder)

▶ Dial the phone (Hello!)

. . . .

*Y*ou can make your Palm device do a surprising number of tasks for you, considering how little the bugger is. But you may expect to be able to do certain things that just aren't on the menu yet. In this chapter, I tell you about ten (or so) things you can't do with a Palm device — yet. You can be sure that thousands of programmers are toiling away in basements and garages to come up with products that expand the Palm device's repertoire, so don't be surprised if many of these gaps are filled in fairly quickly.

View Two Programs at the Same Time

Palm organizer programs have windows and buttons that remind you a little bit of common Windows or Macintosh programs. However, you can look at two different programs at the same time on a Mac or Windows PC; you can't do anything like that with a Palm device. I don't know how you'd make sense of what you'd see on that tiny screen if you tried to display two programs at one time, but sometimes I wouldn't mind seeing my appointments and to-dos at the same time. Right now, it's one at a time, please.

Link Items between Programs

Not only are you limited to seeing one program at a time, but you also can't link items in one Palm organizer program to items in another Palm organizer program. I would find it very handy if I could link an appointment in my Date Book with a person in my Address Book. That way, whenever the reminder for the appointment pops up on my Palm device, I could hop right over to the person's address record to jog my memory about who the person is and why we're meeting.

Search and Replace Text

The Memo Pad is just a convenient place to enter and save text; it's not a word processor. You can use the Palm Find program to look up items that contain a certain word, but you can't do some of the more clever word-processing tricks, like search and replace, that you can with popular word processors, like Microsoft Word.

Record Voice Notes

Some competing handheld computers include a little microphone that enables you to dictate short notes to yourself by simply talking. Later on, you can listen to what you recorded and write down what you said. Personally, I don't want a feature like that, not when I can scribble a quick memo to myself in Graffiti. The Windows CE devices offer it anyway, though. Voice recording is a cute feature, I guess, but voice recordings chew up lots of memory, and they always make you sound like you're underwater. Besides, those Windows CE machines still aren't Palm devices. 'Nuff said.

Create an Appointment That Spans Two or More Dates

Suppose that you work the graveyard shift in an office, factory, or, heaven knows, even a graveyard. (I'm not ready to write *Palm Devices For Vampires* just yet.) If you plan to hold a meeting that starts at 11:30 p.m. and ends at 1 a.m., you're out of luck. Palm appointments can happen only during the span of a single day. You'd have to break up your meeting when the clock strikes midnight and start again. And try to finish your meeting before sunrise, when the werewolves all go home.

Use Superscripts and Subscripts

If you're the mad-professor type who frequently shouts "Eureka!" and then jots down something like $E=mc^2$, you won't be able to enter the superscript number *2* for your formula just yet. You can enter all sorts of foreign accents and special characters, but you can't enter superscript and subscript characters. Most people don't create footnotes or mathematical formulas on a Palm device all that often, but those who do have to wait for a future version of the device. Then you can really shout "Eureka!"

Create Recurring To Do Items

Although you can't create recurring to-do items with your Palm device or the Palm Desktop program, you can synchronize your Palm device with another desktop program that lets you create *recurring tasks,* which are to-do items that repeat at regular intervals. The task of filing your quarterly tax payment is an example of a recurring task. If you enter that kind of task in your Palm device, you can't just enter the task once and then tell your Palm device to make it recurring. Your only choice is to enter the task in January, April, July, and October. Fortunately, if you enter the task in a different desktop program that allows recurring tasks, the Palm device automatically repeats what it sees on the desktop. A program named ToDo Plus, from Hands High software (www.handshigh.com), adds recurring to-do items to your Palm device.

Assign Multiple Categories to One Item

If you have items that could fit into more than one category, you have to pick just one. For example, if you have a Key Customer category and a Business category, you may want a name to appear in both categories. Sorry, no can do.

Categorizing Dates

Do you want to categorize your appointments just like you categorize the Tasks on your To Do List? Sorry! No can do! Some desktop organizers, such as Microsoft Outlook, can do the job for you, but the category information doesn't show up on the Palm device. Palm developers plan to add this feature.

Beam E-mail

You're used to the idea of sending your email flying magically through the air, but if you want to beam e-mail from one Palm unit to another, you're out of luck. Suppose that you have just received a great new tuna fish joke by Palm VII e-mail and you want to beam it to your buddy across the conference room — sorry, Charlie, you have to forward it like any other e-mail. You can copy the contents to a memo, and you can beam the memo, but that's not the same.

Dial the Phone

It would be awfully nice if you could look up a phone number in the Address Book and have the Palm device dial the number for you by squeaking out the telephone tones from the Palm speaker. Unfortunately, those little squeaks aren't strong enough to get a response from the phone system just yet. Several companies are planning to offer a wireless phone with an actual Palm device built-in; although you may find that feature on those units, regular store-bought Palm devices can't make the connection quite yet.

Other Things a Palm Device Can't Do

I can think of quite a few things I wish that a Palm device could help me do, but, sadly, I'm on my own. Here are a few problems nobody even pretends that a Palm device can solve, although I believe that I've heard of other products that are supposed to fit the bill:

- Wash away the gray in just five minutes
- Get the red out
- Help you lose weight while eating all you want
- Give dandruff the brush-off
- Save 50 percent on all your long-distance calls
- Balance your energy
- Discover your Inner Warrior (or your Inner Geek)
- Seize the day
- Purify your blood
- Open the secrets of your Inner Mind

Chapter 19

Ten Nifty Palm Accessories

As citizens of a consumer-based society, we all have an important responsibility: *to buy stuff!* Thank heavens you bought this book. Don't stop there, though; buy another copy, and then check out the list in this chapter to see which Palm device gewgaws you simply can't live without. Remember that your economy depends on you!

GoType Keyboard

I can't hide it: I'm nuts about my GoType keyboard. It's just a little plastic keyboard with a built-in Palm cradle that enables me to use good, old-fashioned touch-typing to enter data to my Palm organizer. Every time I use it, I'm glad that I took that high school typing class. Although my top speed in Graffiti is well under 30 words per minute, I really fly with a GoType keyboard, perhaps 40 words per minute, in my case. (Whew! Look out!) For only $79.95, the GoType keyboard makes your Palm organizer the world's best note-taking device. Check out the manufacturer's Web site, at www.landware.com.

Canon BJC-50 Printer

Canon makes several portable, battery-powered printers with an IR port just like on your Palm III or later. If you use printing software on your Palm device (such as PalmPrint or IR Print) you can print memos, appointments, or any number of things you've created on your Palm organizer. My favorite printer model is the tiny Canon BJC-50, which is smaller than a carton of cigarettes (and much better for your health). You can also connect the Canon BJC-50 to your regular computer with a cable and use it just like any other printer. Sometimes you just need to commit something to paper, so the Canon portable printers fill the bill quite nicely.

PDA Survival Kit

Because your Palm device has virtually no moving parts, it has almost nothing that can wear out except the screen itself. After you've scribbled a few millions words of Graffiti, the plastic screen can take quite a beating. A company named Concept Kitchen offers a collection of accessories, the PDA survival kit, for keeping the screen of your Palm organizer sparkling. The kit includes WriteRights, small layers of plastic you can add to your Palm device screen to reduce wear and tear. Some people stick plain old transparent adhesive tape to the Graffiti area — a perfectly adequate solution, although the tape can be tricky to remove. The kit also includes Brain Wash, a screen-cleaning system for getting the grime off your Palm device screen without using any nasty abrasives or chemicals that could scratch or cloud your screen. Brain Wash consists of two items: a moist towelette and a dry towelette. Karma Cloth, another product cooked up by Concept Kitchen, is perfect for giving your screen a quick buffing; the cloth can even remove minor scratches. Karma Cloth contains some protective substances that make your Palm screen clearer and smoother and, therefore, easier to use. And, of course, a Karma Cloth can bring you good luck if you rub your screen just right.

Extra Styluses

You can find scads of new and improved styluses (or is that styli?) for your Palm device, many of them made by the same folks who make fancy and expensive writing pens. If you want a stylus that displays your taste, class, and distinction, check out the better office-supply stores. I happen to like the snazzy combination stylus-pen made by the Cross pen people, which works wonderfully and makes a splendid gift. (I only mention that so that when the holidays come, you'll know what to send me. Thank you very much!) If you want a plain old stylus that fits in the little stylus well on your Palm organizer, you can get a three-pack of plastic styluses for about five bucks. Check with the merchant who sold you your Palm device. If you own a Palm device that has a lid (such as the Palm III, Palm IIIx, or Palm VII), you can also get chic-colored lids and styluses to match your wardrobe. Ooh la-la!

Card Scanner

Corex Technologies makes two products for entering business card data into your Palm device: CardScan 3.0, which is software for scanning business cards from any scanner, and CardScan Plus 300, a special scanner that's perfectly sized for business card scanning. If you travel to attend trade shows or conferences regularly and need to get business card info entered into your Palm device and desktop contact manager in a hurry, the Corex card scanner can help you. The scanner doesn't attach directly to your Palm device; you attach the scanner to the desktop or laptop computer that you use as the host for your Palm device. Scan your collection of business cards into the host computer first. When all the cards are entered into the host computer, put your Palm device in its cradle and do a HotSync.

UniMount

For those who frequently use a Palm device in the car, Revolv Design Company makes a special device, named the UniMount, to keep your Palm device easy to see and use on the road. I don't recommend using your Palm device while driving, but when you're stopped, you might want to consult it for the address of the person you're going to see or that person's phone number if you plan to call from your car phone. Speaking of telephones, you can also attach your cell phone to the UniMount right next to your Palm device to make a little mobile office for yourself. All you need now is a water cooler.

TRG Memory Boards

You can upgrade certain Palm organizers to hold as much as 11MB of data by using one of the auxiliary memory boards from the Technology Resource Group. That's enough memory to store the names and addresses of more than 100,000 of your closest friends. Of course, the things cost as much as $300, more than you may have paid for your Palm organizer in the first place, but sometimes you just can't get along without lots of memory. If you need only a little bit of extra space, check out FlashPro, a software program from the same company, which I describe in Chapter 20.

DeLorme TripMate GPS Receiver

Loading a map onto your Palm organizer is great, but having your Palm device show your current location on the map is even cooler. For that, you need a receiver that can pinpoint your location by using signals from navigational satellites that are part of the Global Positioning System, or GPS. The Tripmate GPS receiver is a tad smaller than the Palm organizer and has its own battery power. When you connect the Tripmate GPS receiver to a Palm device running DeLorme Street Atlas USA (included with the receiver), your Palm screen can show you exactly where you're located and how to reach your destination. You can even keep track of your speed, time, heading, and elevation. About the only thing it can't tell you is how far you are from the next restroom. I think that requires a different type of satellite.

Minstrel Wireless Modem

Normally, you need only one wire to do everything you have to do with a Palm device: the wire from the cradle of your Palm device to your desktop computer. With the Minstrel wireless modem (from Novatel Wireless), you can cut that number down to no wires, and what a difference it makes! Sit by the pool and read your e-mail, surf the Web while sitting on the beach, check your stock portfolio while waiting for the movie to start — there's no end to what you can do. Of course, you have to pop another $240 or so, plus about $40 bucks a month to use the special type of wireless service (named CDPD) the Minstrel modem uses. Some wireless service providers offer package deals that include both a Minstrel modem and service as a package deal. A Palm III with a Minstrel modem is only a tad larger than the Palm VII, and the cost is fairly comparable. You can't count on being able to use the Minstrel wireless modem everywhere because the CDPD network doesn't cover the entire Earth or even the entire United States, but if you're in an area covered by CDPD, you can go completely cordless. When you do, send me an e-mail; I'll be by the pool.

Cases

It seems that scores of people — from the very classy Coach leather works to inmates at the Funny Farm — are turning out wallets that can store and protect your Palm device. Personally, I use the Co-Pilot, from E&B Cases, because it has room for cash and a few cards, but it's still small enough to keep in my front pocket. You can check out E&B at www.ebcases.com. Another popular case manufacturer is RhinoSkin, at www.rhinoskin.com. The best-known RhinoSkin product is a titanium Palm device case that looks like it was torn off a tank and could probably survive being shot from a cannon. I prefer a softer, gentler Palm device case.

Chapter 20

Ten (Or More) Ultracool Commercial Software Programs for Palm Devices

. . . .

. . . .

*B*ehind the friendly face of a Palm device is a real computer waiting to take on the work you want to do. All you have to add is the right software.

Many of the better Palm organizer programs aren't available as shareware; you have to buy the programs up front. In this chapter, I give you a sampling of the commercial, pay-before-you-play programs I consider worth paying for. You can find many more than the ones in this chapter; software companies release new programs every day, but I put these programs at the top of the class.

I include on the CD that comes with this book a selection of the more popular shareware programs. Check out Appendix C for a list of programs on the CD.

T9

Some folks take to using Graffiti the way a cowboy takes to riding a horse. Others would rather not horse around with Graffiti. That's why a product named T9 (from Tegic Communications) was invented — to offer a familiar telephone-style keypad for entering text, as shown in Figure 20-1, just like entering those famous alphabetic phone numbers, such as 1-800-FLOWERS. The people who invented T9 also sell the program to cellular telephone manufacturers so that people can send e-mail from their cell phones more easily. (Some cell-phone makers are also buying the Palm Computing operating system. Qualcomm, a big cell phone manufacturer, now makes a phone with a built-in Palm device, the PDQ phone.) I find Graffiti faster on the whole because I've had a lots of practice, but if you want to start entering text into your Palm device in a jiffy, you can pick up the use of the T9 keyboard in a flash.

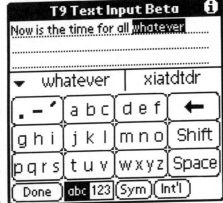

Figure 20-1:
With T9, you can let your fingers do the talking.

QuickSheet

Spreadsheets were the first highly popular programs for desktop personal computers back in the darkest days of DOS. QuickSheet (from Cutting Edge Software) is the first really useable spreadsheet for the Palm device. You can get a shareware spreadsheet named TinySheet that costs only a few bucks, but if you do any serious work with spreadsheets and you want to do any of that work on your Palm device, it's worth spending the money for QuickSheet instead. You can synchronize QuickSheet with an Excel 5.0 or later spreadsheet on your desktop computer to take advantage of the collection of work you've amassed over the years. You don't find the kind of power in QuickSheet that you do in major desktop programs like Excel. QuickSheet doesn't have nearly as many automated functions, and it has no autofill or drag-and-drop copying, but if you ever need to carry around and update a tiny version of your most important spreadsheet, QuickSheet gives you a way to do it for only $49.95.

FlashPro

Gloria Vanderbilt didn't say, "You can never be too thin or too rich or have too much memory on your Palm device," but she could have. At the time I wrote this book, most Palm devices came equipped with as much as 2MB of memory for storing addresses, appointments, programs, or whatever you store. The Palm IIIx is a little roomier, with 4MB. Although that's a reasonable amount of memory at first, you can fill the thing up without much effort, especially with the help of your desktop computer or a good e-mail program.

The engineers at TRG specialize in building things that help expand the capacity of Palm devices. FlashPro ($29.95) takes advantage of the fact that your Palm organizer often has some "hidden" (or *flash*) memory, where the device saves its most important programs, like the standard applications and the operating system. If you buy FlashPro, you can store in flash memory some of the programs you've added to your Palm device, which is like adding 40 percent to your available memory. If you need a little extra memory and want to spend only a little extra money, FlashPro is just the ticket.

FlashPro works only with the Palm III, Palm IIIx, and Palm V. If you upgrade an earlier Palm device with a Palm III upgrade card, from either 3Com or TRG, you can use FlashPro just as though you have a real Palm III. Sad to say, the Palm VII has no flash memory available, so you can't use Flash Pro on your Palm VII.

Forms Programs

The more you do with your Palm device, the more you want to do. If, sooner or later, the standard Palm Computing applications don't do it for you anymore, you may have to resort to a do-it-yourself solution. If you're not ready to turn into a programmer (I'm certainly not), you can use other programs to create simple forms for entering and managing data on your Palm device. Although you have to create your forms on a PC running Windows 95 or later, you can install on the Palm device the forms you create.

Pendragon Forms (from Pendragon Software) is the simplest and least expensive of the forms programs available. You can choose from a limited assortment of predesigned forms (for an example, see Figure 20-2) and link those forms to a file on your PC or to a Microsoft Access database. If you want to make your fortune writing slick programs you can sell to other Palm device users, Pendragon Forms probably isn't for you. If you just need a quick way to catalog your collection of rare tulip bulbs, Pendragon Forms can get you there easily.

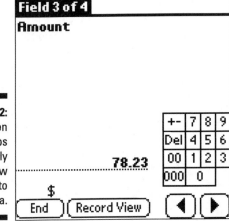

Figure 20-2:
Pendragon
Forms helps
you easily
create new
ways to
enter data.

The other important forms program is Satellite Forms, from Puma Technology. A step up from the price and performance ladder of Pendragon Forms, Satellite Forms enables you to build your own forms from scratch and write real programs (see Figure 20-3) you can install as separate programs that show up as icons on your Palm organizer applications list. Don't expect to master Satellite Forms in a single sitting; the program comes with two thick manuals to tell you how to create applications. Still, if you have ambitious ideas about creating programs for the Palm devices but you're not ambitious enough to become a master programmer, Satellite Forms is for you.

A recent addition to the Palm form-creation toolbox is Palm Factory, written by a fellow named Brad Goodman. He offers Palm Factory for free from his Web site, at www.alcita.com/palmfactory. The program is a much simpler tool for less ambitious projects than you'd take on with other forms programs, but, heaven knows, the price is right.

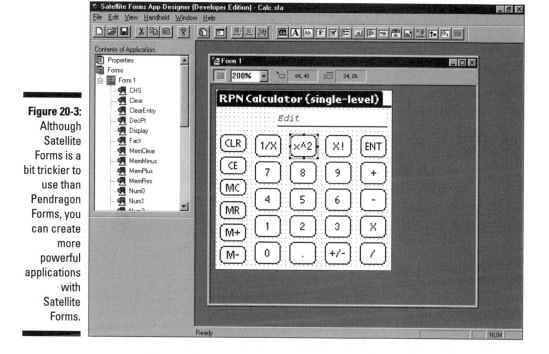

Figure 20-3: Although Satellite Forms is a bit trickier to use than Pendragon Forms, you can create more powerful applications with Satellite Forms.

Actioneer for the Palm Computing Environment

Wouldn't it be nice if you could just use plain English to enter notes about your upcoming tasks and appointments and have your Palm device sort out which application gets the entry? Actioneer does exactly that for you. Just start up Actioneer, and then enter plain text, like **Meet Bob Monday 9 am**, as shown in Figure 20-4. Actioneer automatically creates an event named "Meet Bob Monday 9 am" on your calendar. You can define keywords to help Actioneer automatically send items containing certain words to the application or category you want. You still have to know how to use the standard Palm Computing applications to see the things you've entered, but at least you can rely on plain English when you're adding information. If you're a Microsoft Outlook user, you can get a desktop version of Actioneer that performs the same magic on the information you enter in Outlook.

Figure 20-4:
Actioneer
translates
your plain-
English
entries and
creates
items in the
proper Palm
organizer
program.

DeLorme Street Atlas

Having someone's street address on your Palm device is even more useful when you can find the street on a map. The DeLorme Street Atlas software links up to your Palm device and gives you a copy of a street map and driving directions right on your Palm device, along with your list of names and addresses. The product runs on your desktop computer, which means that you can print the maps and include parts of the map in other documents. If you want to add the DeLorme TripMate GPS Receiver that I mention in Chapter 19, your Palm device can show your current location on a map via a satellite signal. How cool is that?

CardScan

Face the facts: Some people still don't own a Palm organizer. That means that when you go to conferences or trade shows, most people give you conventional business cards rather than beam their cards to your Palm device. Until that unfortunate problem is fixed, you need a quick way to enter business cards in your Palm device. The CardScan software (from Corex Technologies Corporation), which you can buy for $49 or get for free when you buy a CardScan Plus 300 business card scanner, reads the text on all those business cards and creates contact records in your favorite personal information manager. Unfortunately, you have no way to connect the scanner directly to the Palm device and cut out the middleman; however, you can use the Corex software with any scanner you want.

Small Talk

Small Talk (from Concept Kitchen) is an interactive electronic language translator for people who travel frequently. I'd call Small Talk a phrase book rather
than a translator because it translates only a handful of sentences that cover
the most common situations a traveler might encounter, such as checking in to
a hotel, finding transportation, and ordering a meal, as shown in Figure 20-5.
You can't use Small Talk to translate today's Parisian newspapers, although
you can use it to help order *escargots*.

Figure 20-5:
Small Talk
makes your
Palm device
serve as an
electronic
phrase
book.

WinFax Mobile for the Palm Organizer

If you have the PalmModem, you can turn your Palm device into a pocket-size
fax machine with WinFax Mobile, from Symantec (www.symantec.com). Fax
any item from the Memo Pad to any standard fax machine, and include your
own cover page. You don't even have to remember the recipient's fax
number; just look up the number in the Address Book.

Synchronization Programs

The folks who invented the PalmPilot were smart enough to make it work
with the programs you already have on your Windows PC. You may already
have a PIM (personal information manager) you're attached to (or stuck
with) for good reasons. As Palm devices have caught on, more and more companies that make PIMs are offering ways to link those PIMs to the Palm

devices. Other companies are making their fortunes by creating ways to connect your Palm device to programs from companies that don't want to support Palm devices (yes, Microsoft — how did you know?).

The Palm Desktop program that comes with your Palm device talks directly to your Palm device every time you hit the HotSync button (for more info about HotSyncing, see Chapter 11). Because the Palm device was made to talk to the Palm Desktop, you don't need another program to act as a go-between. If you're already using a different program for your PIM, though, such as Microsoft Outlook or ACT!, you need a program to translate and move information between your Windows PC and your Palm device. Several programs, called *conduits* or *synchronizing tools,* can do the job for Windows users.

Unfortunately, at the time I wrote this book, Mac users were pretty much stuck with the Pilot Desktop for all their PIM action. However, hope is on the horizon. The Palm people have made available a conduit developer's kit for their upcoming new version of the desktop program so that the conduit makers can create conduits for the popular (and not-so-popular) Macintosh PIMs. Keep an eye on the 3Com Web site, at www.palm.com, for more information.

Windows users can choose between three well-known conduit programs. Although these programs all do a similar job, each offers a slightly different set of features at a different price:

✔ **PocketMirror for Outlook, from Chapura:** The least expensive synchronization program; in fact, you get a copy of the program for free with the purchase of a Palm III or later. If you buy your own copy of PocketMirror, it runs $39.95. PocketMirror can synchronize your Palm device with only Microsoft Outlook and offers relatively few of the more advanced features that competitors offer, but because many people don't use the more advanced features, PocketMirror is a perfectly good choice.

✔ **Desktop To Go, from DataViz, Inc.:** For about $49, synchronizes a Palm device to only Microsoft Outlook and Schedule+, but enables you to do a couple of fancy things when you synchronize that you can't do with PocketMirror, such as tell Outlook to send information from your Outlook custom fields to certain fields on your Palm device. Because almost nobody uses more than one type of PIM, Desktop To Go does a fine job of synchronizing your Palm device. You can also use Desktop To Go to synchronize a limited date range in the Date Book so that you spend less time waiting for your Palm device to finish synchronizing. For example, if you have 100 appointments in your schedule, spread out over the next year, a HotSync takes longer than if you have only a few appointments scheduled in the next week. You may want to tell the conduit to synchronize only the appointments for the next week to speed up the HotSync process.

✔ **IntelliSync, from Puma Technology:** The most powerful and best-known conduit available for the Palm device also costs the most. At $69.95, IntelliSync enables your Palm device to trade information with just about every major personal information manager out there, including Goldmine, Ecco, and Lotus Organizer. If you're an Outlook user, IntelliSync also lets you synchronize your Palm device to any Outlook folders you choose, and it retains the categories you assign to your items in Outlook when those items turn up on your Palm device. IntelliSync is overkill if you use Outlook in only the simplest way, but if you're an Outlook power user or you use organizers other than Outlook, IntelliSync is indispensable.

For more information about Microsoft Outlook, check out *Microsoft Outlook 2000 For Windows For Dummies,* written by yours truly and published by IDG Books Worldwide, Inc.

✔ You can also find IntelliSync products for synchronizing handheld computers with Web sites, laptop computers with desktop computers, and heaven knows what else. If they made a product that synchronized your VCR with your popcorn popper, I wouldn't be surprised.

Before you rush out and buy a special program to synchronize your Palm device with your PIM, check with the people who make your PIM to see whether you can get a free conduit for the program you use. For example, the people who make ACT! offer a special program to link their product with Palm devices. In fact, ACT! 4.0 includes with the program a Palm link right on the CD. Ecco is another well-known PIM that includes a link for your Palm device.

Unfortunately, I can't cover in this book how to use your other PIM; this book is about Palm Computing, after all. Don't fret, though: If you work with another PIM and want to know more about it, try to find a ...*For Dummies* book on the subject. Odds are, one exists.

The three most popular PIMs have books devoted to them. I wrote a book about Microsoft Outlook, cleverly titled *Microsoft Outlook 2000 For Windows For Dummies,* which, as you might guess, I highly recommend. For ACT! users, Jeffrey J. Mayer has written a great book just for you: *ACT! 4 For Windows For Dummies.* Lotus Organizer, which remains popular after years as one of the top PIMs, is covered in *Lotus SmartSuite Millennium Edition For Dummies,* by Michael Meadhra and Jan Weingarten. (All these books are published by IDG Books Worldwide, Inc.)

More Goodies

Okay, I started with a list of ten programs, but I'm excited about other programs out there, so here are a few more quick mentions:

- ✔ **Docs-to-Go (DataViz)**: The same people who make the DataViz synchronization program I already mentioned also make a program that lets you carry around copies of your Microsoft Office documents on your Palm device and view them at any time. Although you can't edit documents, you can admire your skillful formatting and brilliant analysis. Docs-to-Go also synchronizes the documents on your Palm device with the desktop versions every time you HotSync. That way, you can carry around the latest information.

- ✔ **Pocket Quicken**: It was only a matter of time before someone said, "Gee, I'd sure like to have a copy of Quicken on my Palm device." The nice people from Landware worked with the people who make Quicken to produce Pocket Quicken, a convenient way to keep your most important financial data on a Palm organizer. It synchronizes with Quicken 99 to help you keep track of your current balances and lets you make entries to Quicken 99 from your Palm device while you're roaming around.

- ✔ **Pocket Journal:** Outlook users have a module named the Journal that isn't included on the Palm device. The Outlook Journal is a pretty good place to record phone calls and other daily transactions with other people just for your records. Pocket Journal creates a version of your Outlook Journal on your Palm device and synchronizes itself with your desktop version of Outlook. Pocket Journal also offers check boxes for checking off phone calls you've returned, unlike the desktop Outlook Journal. In many ways, Pocket Journal is more useful than the desktop version.

- ✔ **Franklin Planner (FranklinCovey)**: Steven Covey, the man who wrote *The Seven Habits of Highly Effective People* (1989, Simon & Schuster) teaches courses in time management that involve using a Palm organizer. Using a Palm product is obviously a highly effective thing to do. His company also sells software for your Palm device to make you still more effective. I know that you don't miss a trick, so you'll probably check it out on the Web, at www.franklincovey.com.

Appendix A

Internet Resources for Palm Computing

• •

*T*ime flies quickly in the technology business! Every few weeks, a smashing new program for Palm devices turns up from some emerging software genius. Every few months, the geniuses at Palm release a whole new Palm device. How can you possibly keep up? Your best bet for staying abreast of developments is to turn to the Internet. You can find thousands of sources of Palm Computing information on the Internet; this appendix includes a list of my favorites.

The PalmPilot Web Ring

The PalmPilot Web Ring is the place to start. If I were to give you a list of all the Web sites devoted to Palm devices, the list would number in the hundreds, but it would be out of date by the time you read it. A great place to begin your Internet search for Palm Computing Web sites is the PalmPilot Web Ring, which you can access at the 3Com Web site, at www.palm.com. The PalmPilot Web Ring is a chain of hundreds of Web sites that advise Palm device users on how to get the most from their handheld computers. If you explore the Web ring long enough, you encounter all the other sites I mention in this appendix.

Calvin's PalmPilot FAQ

www.pilotfaq.com

Calvin Parker maintains one of the oldest lists of questions and answers about using Palm devices. Although the site is a bit geeky, it's simple and well organized, and it contains more information about Palm organizers than you may ever want to know.

InSync Online

www.insync-palm.com

The Palm people at 3Com run an Internet mailing list named InSync Online, which sends regular messages describing tips, tricks, and special offers for Palm device users. You can sign up at the InSync Web site.

Jiffylearn.com

www.jiffylearn.com

Okay, JiffyLearn is my Web site. Frankly, it's pretty modest, but, unlike with many other Web sites, you can read it from a Palm VII. My site covers the work I do with people who want to simplify their lives and businesses that want to make better use of technology. My two favorite tools for that job are Microsoft Outlook and Palm organizers. Send me an e-mail at pqa@jiffylearn.com, and I'll be happy to send you a Palm Query Application that connects you to my Web site from anywhere you roam with your Palm VII. (See Chapter 14 for more about Palm Query Applications.)

Palm Central

www.palmcentral.com

Palm Central is my favorite source for the latest, greatest, and strangest software available for Palm devices. At one time called Ray's Pilot Files, Palm Central offers downloadable copies of every kind of Palm organizer software, from scientific calculators to a database of the birthdays of every Beanie Baby.

Palm Computing Newsgroups

comp.sys.palmtops.pilot
alt.comp.sys.palmpilot

Gee, what funny-looking Web site addresses. Well, that's because they aren't Web addresses; they're the addresses for two Palm Computing *newsgroups*. The Internet has thousands of these online discussion forums, in which people post and reply to questions, opinions, and announcements on nearly every conceivable topic. You can read any newsgroup by using a newsreading program, such as Microsoft Outlook Express, or by pointing your browser at www.dejanews.com and searching for the word *PalmPilot*.

PalmOS.com

> www.palmos.com

A useful Web site and software archive, PalmOS.com includes reviews of products and software carefully organized into categories. Best of all, it offers a discussion group where you can put in your two cents.

PalmPower Magazine

> www.palmpower.com

I read *PalmPower* magazine daily. Every morning, it lists as many as a half-dozen stories of interest to Palm device users around the Web. Also, the editors of the site prepare monthly features about Palm organizer technology and reviews of new Palm organizer accessories. If you want to follow what goes on in the Palm Computing universe on a daily basis, PalmPower is an important resource.

PDA Dash

> www.pdadash.com

Some people call a Palm device a PDA, which stands for *personal digital assistant,* not *public display of affection* (you know, the kind you used to get in trouble for in high school — if you were really lucky). Of course, there's nothing wrong with displaying your affection for your Palm device, within reason. Anyway, the PDA Dash Web site is devoted to the latest news about personal digital assistants. PDA Dash discusses the PalmPilot as well as the Psion palmtop computers, Rex personal organizers, Windows CE products, and the late Apple Newton. The site is run by Concept Kitchen, a firm that sells some of the accessories I mention elsewhere in this book.

Pilot Gear H.Q.

www.pilotgear.com

Part newspaper, part online store, Pilot Gear is the most likely place to find information about accessories you can buy for your Palm device. The folks at Pilot Gear gladly take your credit card number over the phone or the Web and sell you anything from a modem cable to a fancy leather jacket with a pocket that's just the right size to hold your Palm device.

Pilot Zone

www.pilotzone.com

Like Palm Central, Pilot Zone is an extensive list of downloadable software for your Palm device. Although the Pilot Zone list isn't as exhaustive as the one at Palm Central, the editors of the site evaluate each listed program and apply their own rating system, awarding from one to five airplanes to each program, depending on how much each product impresses them.

3Com

www.palm.com

Point your browser to the Palm manufacturer's Web site for the official word on Palm products, upgrades, and links. You can find a complete collection of articles, Web site links, and the latest versions of all the software you need in order to keep your Palm device in tip-top condition. The 3Com Web site also features links to the Web sites of other companies that manufacture software and accessories for Palm devices.

Appendix B
Troubleshooting Tips

My Palm organizers have rarely given me problems, except when I've messed something up, like letting the batteries run out. That's not to say that nothing can ever go wrong, although most common Palm problems have simple solutions.

"My Screen Taps Don't Work"

Sometimes when you tap a button on the screen of your Palm device, absolutely nothing happens. That's because the Palm software gets a little out of whack over time and can't determine exactly where you're tapping. To fix this problem, tap the Applications soft button and pick the Prefs application. Choose Digitizer in the upper-right corner of the Prefs application. The Digitizer puts a series of X-shaped targets on your screen and prompts you to tap the center of each target. When you tap each target, your Palm device gets readjusted to the relationship between the figures it displays on the screen and the spots where you tap.

"My Screen Is Blank"

What could be more alarming than to turn on your Palm device only to see — nothing! Although a blank screen may be something serious, it also may be something simple, such as having the contrast set too low. Turn the little contrast wheel on the left side of your Palm device to see whether it makes an image appear on your screen. If you have a Palm V, you don't have a contrast wheel; you have to press the button at the top of the case to change the contrast. That means that it's pretty hard to mess up the contrast by accident on a Palm V. If changing the contrast doesn't fix the problem, try putting in fresh batteries.

"The Menu Button Doesn't Work"

If you tap the Menu soft button and nothing happens, the most likely explanation is that no menus are available for the screen you're viewing. Not all screens have menus. For example, when a dialog box is open, you can't look at a menu until you finish using that dialog box and close it.

"My Palm Device Won't Turn Off"

If you can't make your Palm device switch applications and it won't turn off, chances are that you have a misbehaving program. Although the standard programs (Date Book, Address Book, To Do List, and Memo Pad) almost never misbehave, some programs you find on the Web can be finicky that way. If your Palm program is frozen, your only solution is to perform a soft reset, which has the same effect as turning your Palm device off and turning it back on again. To perform a soft reset, unbend a paper clip and press it into the hole labeled Reset on the back of the case of your Palm device. That action normally closes all programs and restarts your Palm device. A soft reset doesn't lose your data; however, a hard reset erases all the data on the Palm device. See Chapter 1 for more info about resetting before performing either kind of reset. If you have a Palm III or later, you can unscrew the end of your stylus; a reset pin inside the stylus does the job even better than a paper clip.

"The Hard Buttons Stick"

If the hard buttons at the bottom of your Palm device stick, you can get the Palm people to repair or replace your unit. Contact the 3Com technical-support folks, at 847-676-1441, for details on getting your Palm device fixed. If your one-year warranty is still in effect, you can get your unit fixed for free; otherwise, a flat $100 charge applies.

"Graffiti Is Always Wrong"

I've found that Graffiti often fails to understand my entries, although most of the time my handwriting is to blame. Sometimes, however, all I need to do is recalibrate my Palm device rather than go back to the first grade for penmanship classes. To recalibrate your Palm device, tap the Applications soft button, tap the Prefs application, and then choose Digitizer from the pull-down list in the upper-right corner of the screen. Follow the prompts that ask you to tap each X-shaped target as it appears.

If running the digitizer doesn't fix your Graffiti problems, make sure that you make each character as large as possible and keep your lines as straight as possible. Of course, there's always that penmanship class. You'll see me there — I'm the one in the corner with the dunce cap.

"My Screen Is Too Dark"

The Palm device screen is often tricky to read when there's too much light (or too little). If you find the screen hard to read, adjust the contrast by turning the contrast wheel on the left side of the case. If you have a Palm V, you have to press the button at the top of the case and adjust the contrast by using the controls that appear on the screen. If adjusting the contrast doesn't do the trick and you're using the device in a fairly dim environment, turn on the backlight by holding down the power button for two seconds.

"My Palm Device Won't Start"

If you drop an early-model Palm organizer (Palm III and earlier) and it doesn't start afterward, the memory card may have shaken loose. The memory card is the heart, soul, and brains of the early-model Palm devices. If the brains of your Palm device get shaken loose, it can have problems, just as any of us would. To reseat the memory card, open the memory door (or remove the back of the case, if you have a Palm III), and then press very gently on the memory card to make it sit more snugly in its fitting. The Palm IIIx and later models don't have a memory card to shake loose, so if they don't start, the problem is most likely dead batteries.

"Beaming Fails"

Remember that beaming works only between a pair of Palm devices that are equipped with an IR port, switched on, pointed at one another, and within about 3 feet of each other. You also have to make sure that the beaming feature is enabled on both units. To check whether beaming is activated, tap the Applications soft button, tap the Prefs application, choose the General option, and make sure that the last line on the General Preferences screen says Beam Receive On. If beaming is turned off, tap the triangle next to Receive and pick On from the drop-down list.

"I Got a 'Fatal Exception' Error"

If you like to try out lots of free software, as I do, now and again you get a program that misbehaves. The result of a misbehaving program is sometimes an error message that says `Fatal exception`. Don't worry — you'll live. You should be able to press the power switch to turn off your Palm device, and then turn it right back on. If hitting the power switch doesn't work, unbend a paper clip and press it into the hole marked Reset on the back of your Palm device.

Appendix C

About the CD

● ●

*S*o, just what is that shiny, round thing stuck to the inside back cover of this book? A coaster? A mini-Frisbee? The newest Pearl Jam CD? No, not quite. It's even better. I've included a selection of my favorite Palm Computing software, plus some software to help you get on the Internet (if you're not already on it).

System Requirements

To use the CD, make sure that your computer meets the following minimum system requirements (if your computer doesn't match up to most of these requirements, you may have problems using the contents of the CD):

- ✔ A PC with a 486 or faster processor or a Mac OS computer with a 68030 or faster processor.

- ✔ Microsoft Windows 3.1 or later or Mac OS system software 7.5 or later.

- ✔ At least 8MB of total RAM installed on your computer. For best performance, Windows 95/98–equipped PCs and Mac OS computers with PowerPC processors should have at least 16MB of RAM installed.

- ✔ At least 120MB (Windows) or 55MB (Mac) of hard drive space available if you install all the software from this CD. (You need less if you don't.)

- ✔ A CD-ROM drive — double-speed (2x) or faster.

- ✔ Recommended: A sound card for PCs. (Mac OS computers have built-in sound support.)

- ✔ Recommended: A monitor capable of displaying at least 256 colors or grayscale.

- ✔ Recommended: A modem with a speed of at least 14,400 bps.

If you need more information about the basics, check out *PCs For Dummies*, 6th Edition, by Dan Gookin; *Macs For Dummies*, 6th Edition, by David Pogue; *Windows 95 For Dummies*, 2nd Edition, and *Windows 98 For Dummies*, by Andy Rathbone; or *Windows 3.11 For Dummies*, 4th Edition, by Andy Rathbone (all published by IDG Books Worldwide, Inc.).

Using the CD

1. **Double-click the file named License.txt.**

   This file contains the end-user license you agree to by using the CD. When you're done reading the license, close the program (most likely, NotePad) that displayed the file.

2. **Double-click the file named Readme.txt.**

   This file contains instructions about installing the software from the CD. It may be helpful to leave this text file open while you use the CD.

3. **Double-click the folder for the software you're interested in.**

   Be sure to read the descriptions of the programs in the following section of this appendix. (Much of this information also shows up in the Readme file.) These descriptions give you more precise information about the programs' folder names and about finding and running the installer program.

4. **Find the file named Setup.exe or Install.exe or something similar, and double-click that file.**

   The program's installer walks you through the process of setting up your new software.

How to Use the CD Using the Mac OS

To install the items from the CD to your hard drive, follow these steps:

1. **Insert the CD into your computer's CD-ROM drive.**

   In a moment, an icon representing the CD you just inserted appears on your Mac desktop. The icon looks like a CD-ROM.

2. **Double-click the CD icon to show the CD's contents.**

3. **Double-click the Read Me First icon.**

   The text file contains information about the CD's programs and any last-minute instructions you need to know about installing the programs on the CD that we don't cover in this appendix.

4. **Open your browser.**

   If you don't have a browser, the CD includes for your convenience the two most popular ones: Microsoft Internet Explorer and Netscape Communicator.

5. **With your browser open, choose File⇨Open and select the CD labeled *Palm Computing For Dummies*.**

6. **Some programs come with installer programs — with those, you simply open the program's folder on the CD and double-click the icon with the words *Install* or *Installer*. Others have a .PRC file you have to install with the InstallApp tool. See Chapter 12 for more info about installing applications.**

After you've installed the programs you want, you can eject the CD. Carefully place it back in the plastic jacket of this book for safekeeping.

What You'll Find

Here's a summary of the cool programs you can find on this CD. Most of them are shareware, which means that the software authors want you to try out the program and, hopefully, like it enough to send them money to keep using it. Many programs work for only a certain amount of time or have other limitations. For more detailed information about the software, such as version numbers or limitations on trials, be sure to read the Readme.txt or Read Me First file on the CD. Most of the software listed here runs on any Palm device, but a few don't run with Palm OS 1.0. If you haven't upgraded and you want to take full advantage of this CD, see Chapter 16 for more info about upgrading. I've noted when certain programs don't run with Palm OS 1.0.

Financial tools

FCPlus Professional

FCPlus is an advanced financial calculator for working out loans, leases, annuities, depreciation, and other big money matters. Doesn't work with Palm OS 1.0.

Pocket Quicken

The dream of every penny-pincher and bean counter is to have up-to-the-minute spending information on hand at all times. Pocket Quicken can make that dream come true by creating a synchronized Palm version of the information you keep in your desktop version of Quicken 99.

Qmate

Quicken users will be happy to know that they can enter their financial data on a Palm device and then HotSync and import the data to Quicken. I think that Qmate could be much easier to use, but if your Quicken data is really important to you, Qmate can help you enter data from the field.

Time Expense Auto Keeper (TEAK)

Gas, oil, repairs, and mileage all go into TEAK so that you know the overall cost of operating your auto. The program simplifies the process of tracking your time, expenses, and automobile mileage on your 3Com-connected organizer as well as on your PC. With the click of a button, you can easily generate comprehensive time, expense, and mileage reports.

Fun and games

Blackjack

A Palm Computing version of the casino favorite, BlackJack deals the cards and takes your bets as you try to beat the house. Legal in all 50 states.

Eliza, Pilot Psychologist

Eliza is a computerized shrink who answers the questions you answer with more questions, just like some real shrinks. Eliza is purely for entertainment; anyone who considers Eliza the equivalent of real psychotherapy needs to have his head examined.

Jpack

The people at J-Land have wrapped up a collection of their most popular programs in Jpack. The collection includes

- **Jfile:** The leading database program for Palm devices. You can find ready-made Jfile databases covering everything from drink recipes to chemical elements.
- **Jshopper:** A shopping list organizer. Arrange your list by store at as many as ten different stores. Keep up with coupons, too.
- **Jtutor:** A flash card program for memorizing information and drilling you to improve your recall.
- **Jookerie:** A game derived from the classic dictionary game in which people make up definitions of words to try to fool their opponents.
- **Jstones:** Described as "an addictive board game," it demands that you earn points by placing markers, or "stones," on a playing board according to an elaborate set of rules.

Klondike

A solitaire game for those moments when a database just won't do.

Language Dictionary

A multilingual dictionary that translates between a variety of foreign languages. Doesn't work with Palm OS 1.0.

Words Per Minute

When you get so good at Graffiti that you think, "Hey! I'm good!" find out how good you really are. WPM checks how fast you enter Graffiti in test sentences. I'm sorry to say that WPM does reduce your score for mistakes. Rats!

Internet tools

Microsoft Internet Explorer

Internet Explorer is one of the two big cheeses in Web browsers. To check out the newest updates, please visit the Microsoft Web site, at www.microsoft.com/ie.

Important note: If you run this software under Windows NT 4.0, it requires Service Pack 3. If you don't have it, please visit the Microsoft Web site. If you do have it, or after you install it, continue the installation and follow the prompts on your screen to install the NT version of Internet Explorer.

MindSpring Internet Access

In case you don't have a connection to the information superhighway, the CD includes sign-on software for MindSpring Internet Access, an Internet Service Provider. If you already have an (ISP), please note that MindSpring Internet Access software makes changes to your computer's current Internet configuration and may replace your current settings. These changes may stop you from being able to access the Internet through your current provider.

To install MindSpring Internet Access, you must run Setup.exe from the Setup subfolder. Setup.exe in the Msprg95 folder does not install the software! After you're signed on, one of the first places you can check out is the MindSpring Web site, at www.mindspring.com. You need a credit card to sign up with the service.

Netscape Communicator

Netscape Communicator is a suite of programs that includes the other big cheese in Web browsers, Netscape Navigator. To check for the newest updates of Communicator, please visit the Netscape Web site, at www.netscape.com.

Palmeta Mail

If you have an older Palm device that doesn't include the Mail program, Palmeta Mail compensates by pulling messages from your desktop e-mail program and turning each into a memo on your Palm device. Palmeta Mail requires Windows 95, Windows 98, or Windows NT 4.0.

Multimedia

AportisDoc

The best known of the document-reader programs, AportisDoc enables you to store and read whole books and short stories on your Palm device. You can also bookmark whatever you're reading so that you can pick up reading wherever you left off.

Documents to Go 2.001

You probably have three or four documents you've created in Microsoft Office that you want to view on your Palm device so that they're on hand wherever you go. That's what Docs-to-Go lets you do. Although you can't edit your documents in this program, you can view them in all their fully formatted glory. When you install this program, you're asked for your registration number. Look for the little check box labeled Install Evaluation Version, and click it to continue the installation.

Image Viewer

You can display photographs on your Palm device with the help of Image Viewer. Although most photos look pretty rough on the Palm device screen, you may still have your reasons for wanting to see pictures on your Palm device. I know of a Palm-device-toting couple who keep their wedding pictures on their Palm devices. Isn't that romantic?

TealPaint

The premiere drawing program for Palm devices, TealPaint enables you to create your own artistic masterpieces, capture screens from other Palm programs, and send them all to your Window 95 desktop computer to be used in conventional graphics programs, like Corel or Adobe Illustrator.

Organizational tools

Action Names

Action Names enhances the Palm Date Book, Address Book, and To Do programs by letting you link the names of people to the activities that involve them. Doesn't work with Palm OS 1.0, and you need a license number to use the program. Visit the Web site, at `www.iambic.com/pilot/actionnames/download.htm`, to register for your 30-day trial license.

Actioneer

You don't need to switch between the Palm Computing applications to enter your appointments and to-dos if you have Actioneer. You can enter plain-

English statements like "Call Bob tomorrow at 2 p.m." into Actioneer and let the program create the appointment or to-do as necessary. Actioneer also offers a similar program for Microsoft Outlook users.

AreaCoder

It seems like the phone company changes everybody's area code every couple of weeks, which makes for a great deal of work when you're maintaining a list of contacts. AreaCoder searches for and replaces changed area codes in your Address Book.

BrainForest

You can find several outliner programs for Palm devices; BrainForest is one of the best known. Organize your thoughts into "trees" with "branches" and "leaves" that you can move, copy, sort, and delete. Doesn't work with Palm OS 1.0.

BugMe!

Whenever you want to be reminded to get back to something in an hour, enter a quick note, and the note sets off an alarm to remind you about it.

IntelliSync

Trade information with just about every major personal information manager with the powerful IntelliSync program. You can synchronize your Palm device to any Microsoft Outlook folders you choose (if you use that program), and IntelliSync retains the categories you assign to your items in Outlook when those items end up on your Palm device. Look for a different program if you use Outlook for minor tasks, but grab hold of this one if you're an Outlook power user or you use organizers other than Outlook.

Mobile DB

This slick little database program keeps track of details like your favorite movies, sports schedules, medical information, or whatever else you want.

PhoneLog

PhoneLog helps you keep track of phone calls you've made and received according to length, time, and category. Doesn't work with Palm OS 1.0.

Punch List

See Chapter 17 for more info about this advanced project manager.

TealDoc

You can read all kinds of Palm text files with a reader like TealDoc. Palm-compatible e-texts are available that cover everything from *The Iliad* and *The Odyssey* to comic book characters you can read on your Palm organizer.

TealGlance

For a quick summary of your next appointments and to-dos as well as the current time and battery level every time you start your Palm device, install TealGlance. Doesn't work with Palm OS 1.0. To make this program work, you must install HackMaster, which you can find on the Internet at Palm Central or other Palm shareware sites.

TealLock

If you're worried that someone may sneak a peek at the confidential information on your Palm organizer, TealLock offers a sophisticated system for keeping your data safe from prying eyes.

TealMeal

What do you want for dinner? Pizza, Chinese, or burgers (again)? TealMeal can help you pick a restaurant that has what you want. You can either enter a list of your own favorite restaurants in TealMeal or download TealMeal databases for cities around the world, from Milwaukee to Kuala Lampur.

TealPhone

If the standard Palm Address Book isn't muscular enough for you, TealPhone bulks it up with powerful search features, a better display, and a quick-seek index bar.

ThoughtMill

Another outliner, ThoughtMill automatically turns the text you enter into a structured outline that you can expand, collapse, or export to the Memo Pad. Doesn't work with Palm OS 1.0.

TimeReporter

TimeReporter is a tool for people who earn a living through hourly billings. Record the time you spend on all your various clients and projects on the job by using TimeReporter.

Synchronization tools

Desktop to Go

Desktop To Go is one of the three major synchronization programs that connect your Palm device to Microsoft Outlook. Desktop To Go is quick and simple and lets you use either Microsoft Outlook or Microsoft Schedule+ in lieu of your Palm Desktop program.

PROFS-AutoPilot

If you *really* like to accessorize, you can get an IBM mainframe to go with your Palm device and use PROFS-AutoPilot to synchronize with the PROFS personal organizer on the mainframe. For the Palm device owner who has everything.

UnDupe

Once in a blue moon, the HotSync process messes up and creates two of everything on your Palm device. UnDupe automatically converts your double vision back to normal.

Utilities

FlashBuilder III for the Palm III

Many Palm devices have a secret area of memory, named *flash memory,* that programs can't use without the help of FlashBuilder. Under the right circumstances, you can get as much as 40 percent more space to use on your Palm. Not all Palm programs take well to being loaded into flash memory, but if the programs you use agree with FlashBuilder, you're in business. Unfortunately, the Palm VII can't handle FlashBuilder; sorry about that.

MakeDoc

Doc files are special compressed text files you can store and read on your Palm device. You can store lengthy documents, even whole books (short ones) in .Doc format and read them with the help of a reader like AportisDoc (also on this CD). The Windows program MakeDoc enables you to create your own .Doc files from files on your PC.

PalmPrint

Like its name suggests, PalmPrint is designed to give your Palm device the capability to send text to a printer. Early versions of PalmPrint could send a print job to a printer with the help of a wire and a special converter. The people who dreamed up PalmPrint have a new version that lets you beam print jobs from a Palm III to an IR-based printer. Pretty slick.

Satellite Forms

You don't need to be a programmer to create your own applications for your Palm device if you use Satellite Forms. For more about Satellite Forms and other forms programs, see Chapter 20.

TealEcho

Whenever the task of learning Graffiti eludes you, TealEcho can help by tracing out in the Graffiti drawing area the image of whatever you draw so that you can see what you've done. Many Graffiti gurus recommend TealEcho. You must install HackMaster for this program to work. You must install HackMaster, which you can find on the Internet at PalmCentral or other Palm shareware sites, for this program to work.

If You Have Problems (Of the CD Kind)

The Palm Computing programs included on the CD in the back of this book run on any Palm device running Palm OS 2.0 or later, and most run with Palm OS 1.0, as long as you can get them installed from your desktop computer. What happens on the desktop computer could be another story.

When it comes to running the CD, the two likeliest problems you may encounter are that you don't have enough memory (RAM) for the programs you want to use or you have other programs running that are affecting the installation or running of a program. If you get error messages like Not enough memory or Setup cannot continue, try one or more of these remedies and then try using the software again:

- ✔ Turn off any antivirus software you have on your computer. Installers sometimes mimic virus activity and may make your computer incorrectly believe that it's being infected by a virus.

- ✔ Close all running programs. The more programs you run, the less memory is available to other programs. Installers also typically update files and programs, so if you keep other programs running, installation may not work properly. This may include closing the CD interface and running a product's installation program from Windows Explorer.

- ✔ Have someone at your local computer store add more RAM to your computer. This step is, admittedly, drastic and somewhat expensive. However, if you have a Windows 95 or Windows 98 PC or a Mac OS computer with a PowerPC or G3 chip, adding more memory can help the speed of your computer and allow more programs to run at the same time.

- ✔ If push comes to shove, just run the Palm Install Tool from Windows (or InstallApp from a Mac), and double-click the name of the program you want to install. If you can't get the CD to run, you may still be able to install Palm organizer programs directly.

If you still have trouble installing the items from the CD, please call the IDG Books Worldwide Customer Service phone number: 800-762-2974 (outside the United States: 317-596-5430).

Index

• *D* •

• V •

IDG Books Worldwide, Inc., End-User License Agreement

READ THIS. You should carefully read these terms and conditions before opening the software packet(s) included with this book ("Book"). This is a license agreement ("Agreement") between you and IDG Books Worldwide, Inc. ("IDGB"). By opening the accompanying software packet(s), you acknowledge that you have read and accept the following terms and conditions. If you do not agree and do not want to be bound by such terms and conditions, promptly return the Book and the unopened software packet(s) to the place you obtained them for a full refund.

1. **License Grant.** IDGB grants to you (either an individual or entity) a nonexclusive license to use one copy of the enclosed software program(s) (collectively, the "Software") solely for your own personal or business purposes on a single computer (whether a standard computer or a workstation component of a multiuser network). The Software is in use on a computer when it is loaded into temporary memory (RAM) or installed into permanent memory (hard disk, CD-ROM, or other storage device). IDGB reserves all rights not expressly granted herein.

2. **Ownership.** IDGB is the owner of all right, title, and interest, including copyright, in and to the compilation of the Software recorded on the disk(s) or CD-ROM ("Software Media"). Copyright to the individual programs recorded on the Software Media is owned by the author or other authorized copyright owner of each program. Ownership of the Software and all proprietary rights relating thereto remain with IDGB and its licensers.

3. **Restrictions on Use and Transfer.**

   (a) You may only (i) make one copy of the Software for backup or archival purposes, or (ii) transfer the Software to a single hard disk, provided that you keep the original for backup or archival purposes. You may not (i) rent or lease the Software, (ii) copy or reproduce the Software through a LAN or other network system or through any computer subscriber system or bulletin-board system, or (iii) modify, adapt, or create derivative works based on the Software.

   (b) You may not reverse engineer, decompile, or disassemble the Software. You may transfer the Software and user documentation on a permanent basis, provided that the transferee agrees to accept the terms and conditions of this Agreement and you retain no copies. If the Software is an update or has been updated, any transfer must include the most recent update and all prior versions.

4. **Restrictions on Use of Individual Programs.** You must follow the individual requirements and restrictions detailed for each individual program in the "About the CD" section of this Book. These limitations are also contained in the individual license agreements recorded on the Software Media. These limitations may include a requirement that after using the program for a specified period of time, the user must pay a registration fee or discontinue use. By opening the Software packet(s), you will be agreeing to abide by the licenses and restrictions for these individual programs that are detailed in the "About the CD" section and on the Software Media. None of the material on this Software Media or listed in this Book may ever be redistributed, in original or modified form, for commercial purposes.

5. **Limited Warranty.**

   (a) IDGB warrants that the Software and Software Media are free from defects in materials and workmanship under normal use for a period of sixty (60) days from the date of purchase of this Book. If IDGB receives notification within the warranty period of defects in materials or workmanship, IDGB will replace the defective Software Media.

   (b) **IDGB AND THE AUTHOR OF THE BOOK DISCLAIM ALL OTHER WARRANTIES, EXPRESS OR IMPLIED, INCLUDING WITHOUT LIMITATION IMPLIED WARRANTIES OF MERCHANTABILITY AND FITNESS FOR A PARTICULAR PURPOSE, WITH RESPECT TO THE SOFTWARE, THE PROGRAMS, THE SOURCE CODE CONTAINED THEREIN, AND/OR THE TECHNIQUES DESCRIBED IN THIS BOOK. IDGB DOES NOT WARRANT THAT THE FUNCTIONS CONTAINED IN THE SOFTWARE WILL MEET YOUR REQUIRE-MENTS OR THAT THE OPERATION OF THE SOFTWARE WILL BE ERROR FREE.**

   (c) This limited warranty gives you specific legal rights, and you may have other rights that vary from jurisdiction to jurisdiction.

6. **Remedies.**

   (a) IDGB's entire liability and your exclusive remedy for defects in materials and workmanship shall be limited to replacement of the Software Media, which may be returned to IDGB with a copy of your receipt at the following address: Software Media Fulfillment Department, Attn.: *Palm Computing For Dummies,* IDG Books Worldwide, Inc., 7260 Shadeland Station, Ste. 100, Indianapolis, IN 46256, or call 800-762-2974. Please allow three to four weeks for delivery. This Limited Warranty is void if failure of the Software Media has resulted from accident, abuse, or misapplication. Any replacement Software Media will be warranted for the remainder of the original warranty period or thirty (30) days, whichever is longer.

   (b) In no event shall IDGB or the author be liable for any damages whatsoever (including without limitation damages for loss of business profits, business interruption, loss of business information, or any other pecuniary loss) arising from the use of or inability to use the Book or the Software, even if IDGB has been advised of the possibility of such damages.

   (c) Because some jurisdictions do not allow the exclusion or limitation of liability for consequential or incidental damages, the above limitation or exclusion may not apply to you.

7. **U.S. Government Restricted Rights.** Use, duplication, or disclosure of the Software by the U.S. Government is subject to restrictions stated in paragraph (c)(1)(ii) of the Rights in Technical Data and Computer Software clause of DFARS 252.227-7013, and in subparagraphs (a) through (d) of the Commercial Computer–Restricted Rights clause at FAR 52.227-19, and in similar clauses in the NASA FAR supplement, when applicable.

8. **General.** This Agreement constitutes the entire understanding of the parties and revokes and supersedes all prior agreements, oral or written, between them and may not be modified or amended except in a writing signed by both parties hereto that specifically refers to this Agreement. This Agreement shall take precedence over any other documents that may be in conflict herewith. If any one or more provisions contained in this Agreement are held by any court or tribunal to be invalid, illegal, or otherwise unenforceable, each and every other provision shall remain in full force and effect.

Installation Instructions

The *Palm Computing For Dummies* CD offers valuable Palm computing software you won't want to miss. To use the CD, follow these steps:

Windows

1. **Double-click the file named License.txt.**

2. **Double-click the file named Readme.txt.**

3. **Double-click the folder for the software you're interested in.**

4. **Find the file named Setup.exe or Install.exe or something similar, and double-click that file.**

The program's installation program walks you through the process of setting up your new software. See Chapter 11 for more info about installing Windows applications.

Mac OS

1. **Insert the CD into your computer's CD-ROM drive.**

2. **Double-click the CD icon to show the CD's contents.**

3. **Double-click the Read Me First icon.**

4. **Open your browser.**

5. **With your browser open, choose File⇨Open and select the CD labeled *Palm Computing For Dummies*.**

6. **Some programs come with installer programs — with those, you simply open the program's folder on the CD and double-click the icon with the word *Install* or *Installer*. Other programs have a .PRC file you have to install with the InstallApp tool.**

See Chapter 13 for more info about installing Mac applications.

For more information about using this CD, see Appendix C.

IDG BOOKS WORLDWIDE
BOOK REGISTRATION

Register
This Book
and Win!

We want to hear from you!

Visit **http://my2cents.dummies.com** to register this book and tell us how you liked it!

- ✔ Get entered in our monthly prize giveaway.

- ✔ Give us feedback about this book — tell us what you like best, what you like least, or maybe what you'd like to ask the author and us to change!

- ✔ Let us know any other *...For Dummies*® topics that interest you.

Your feedback helps us determine what books to publish, tells us what coverage to add as we revise our books, and lets us know whether we're meeting your needs as a *...For Dummies* reader. You're our most valuable resource, and what you have to say is important to us!

Not on the Web yet? It's easy to get started with *Dummies 101*®: *The Internet For Windows*® *98* or *The Internet For Dummies*®, 6th Edition, at local retailers everywhere.

Or let us know what you think by sending us a letter at the following address:

...For Dummies Book Registration
Dummies Press
7260 Shadeland Station, Suite 100
Indianapolis, IN 46256-3945
Fax 317-596-5498

™

BESTSELLING
BOOK SERIES
FROM IDG